Revised and Enlarged Edition

weekendLearning Series

Islamic Studies

Level 8

Mansur Ahmad and Husain A. Nuri

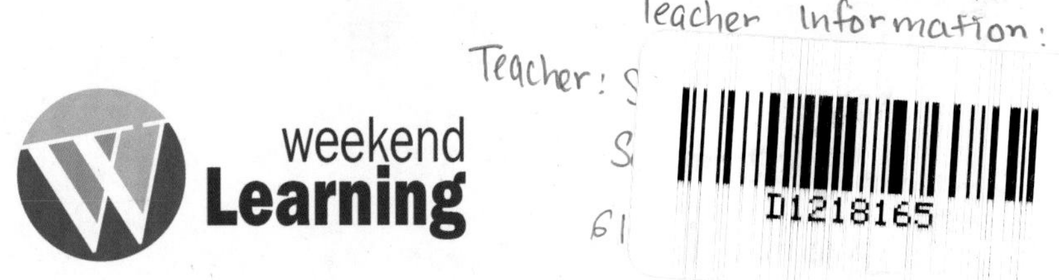

ISBN: 978-1-936569-64-9

First edition: 2008
Second edition: 2009
Third edition: 2012
Reprint: 2013
Revised and enlarged edition: 2018
Reprint: 2018

Cover Design and Photography: Mansur Ahmad
Illustrations: Abira Das, Mansur Ahmad, and Husain A. Nuri,

Weekend Learning Publishers
5584 Boulder Crest St.
Columbus, OH 43235
www.weekendlearning.com

Printed in China

Preface

The concept of a series of Islamic Studies books was conceived in 2002 when both of us were teachers or principals of two weekend schools in two different states. We used several excellent textbooks and reference books in these schools. However, we soon realized there was no single textbook available that could meet our classroom needs. Some of the available books had too many or too few lessons for an academic year. Some lessons were too long for a class hour, and some were too short. Some lessons were too difficult for the ages involved or too basic for higher-level classes. Some books were not written with a 12 year curriculum in mind. The lessons in higher grades, therefore, did not develop from the knowledge base of prior years. Sometimes, extra emphasis was placed on one topic at the cost of other important topics. Thus, we thought a balanced knowledge base was lost.

We always felt there was a better way. We began writing the lessons ourselves to meet the needs of our schools. We involved other teachers in this process. For the next two years, we conducted classes based on the lessons we had prepared. In the meantime, both of us met with other principals and teachers across the country. We wanted to find out how they taught Islamic Studies and what their major concerns were. Most of the principals and teachers we talked to expressed their inability to find or develop a good curriculum. If they had a curriculum, they could not find lessons to complement the curriculum.

This survey prompted us to develop a functional, comprehensive curriculum for weekend schools in the West. We wanted to create a curriculum that would include everything that Muslim students growing up in the West would ideally need to know. We wanted to include topics based on the life experiences of students growing up in the West. Muslim children growing up in the U.S., Europe, and Australia are facing diverse challenges and conflicting pressures at schools and in social circles. They are constantly influenced by the mainstream youth culture. We wanted lessons to address their issues from their perspectives.

The curriculum alone would not be of any use unless there were lessons based on the curriculum. The lessons had to be age-appropriate and suitable for the typical class duration of most schools. As we continued to write and edit lessons over the next two years, we discovered ways to make the curriculum increasingly meaningful.

In 2007, we published coil-bound versions of these books. More than 30 schools in the U.S. and UK used the books. We also received a large number of inquiries from many other schools. Based on the suggestions, comments, and reviews received from many of these schools, we have edited the series of books and made other changes as appropriate.

We are thankful to Allāh ﷻ for giving us the ability to write these books. We pray to Allāh ﷻ to accept our labor and make us successful in communicating the message of Islam. We hope Islamic schools and home schools in the U.S. and other countries will find these books useful. Any errors in the books are our responsibility. We appreciate receiving meaningful comments and suggestions to improve the series.

"Our Rabb! Accept from us, you indeed are the all-Hearing, all-Knowing." (2:127)

January 30, 2008

Mansur Ahmad
Husain A. Nuri

Preface to to the Revised and Enlarged Edition

All praise is due to Allāh ﷻ alone. We are indebted to Him for giving us time, energy, and resources to publish this book and other books in this series. The first edition of the book was published in 2008. Over the next 10 years, we made small editorial changes in some of the lessons. During this time, our books became one of the most-sought-after series all over the world for teaching Islam in weekend schools. Thousands of schools on all the continents adopted our series, and we are indebted to the teachers, students, and above all, to almighty God.

We do not want to remain idle with the success of the series. We have been constantly striving to improve the books to meet the changing and growing needs of the weekend schools. Many schools wrote to us requesting additional materials in some of the lessons. In view of their requests, we have revised and enlarged all the lessons, adding more information and resources. Our utmost focus all along has been to remain extremely loyal and true to the teachings of the Qur'ān and authentic sunnah of the Messenger ﷺ. With the enlarged lessons, teachers are now equipped with many more materials, but the teaching time in class remains the same. Therefore, the challenge will be to maximize the time available in a class by getting the most out of the lessons. This will be possible only when teachers review the lessons before coming to class and prepare themselves to do their best.

We are grateful to Brenda Rusch for editing and proofreading the book. She has not only eliminated some grammatical, punctuation, and spelling errors, but has also improved content flow, transitions, and overall organization. Lihan Yousuf provided help with typesetting. We thank them for their service. May Allāh ﷻ accept our small effort.

August 15, 2018

Husain A. Nuri
Mansur Ahmad

Table of Contents

How to use this book effectively
Instructions for teachers and parents

The lessons in the Level Eight book expand and elaborate understanding of Islamic history, morals, and principles for students growing up in the West. The purpose is to help students understand the connection between the *deen* and the *dunya.* Sensitive issues are addressed, such as dating, friendship, duties towards parents, dietary laws, challenges in middle school and moral-building lessons like trials and hope. Many aspects of early Islamic history are covered in greater detail. Nonetheless, the length of each lesson is kept within a reasonable limit, so teachers can cover the material within a class hour.

We strongly recommend teachers read the lesson before class. Think about how to deliver the content of the lesson. If needed, create index cards with highlighted ideas or the sequence of the discussion in outline form. Most lessons will require the teacher to explain the content of each paragraph rather than reading the lesson aloud. Use a dry-erase board to write the discussion points of the lesson. Help students understand the time line or map if provided in the lesson. Ask questions frequently to reinforce learning and make frequent eye contact with students. Keep track of time so that the material is covered within the allotted class time.

For maximum benefit, each lesson should be completed within one class hour. We recommend that a test be conducted after every fifth or sixth lesson. Weekend Learning Publisher has designed an Excel-based, user-friendly program to record homework and exam scores. This will be useful when report cards are prepared. Teachers can obtain an annotated Teacher's Edition of this book. The book comes with a CD-ROM containing question bank, ready to print exam, PowerPoint slides and homework questions.

Homework:

Teachers are requested to regularly assign and grade homework. The time commitment for homework is about 10–15 minutes per lesson. Parents are strongly encouraged to supervise the student during the homework assignment. Regular supervision of homework by a parent indicates that education is valued.

Teaching Respect:

From an early age, students should be taught to show respect to Allāh ﷻ, His angels, and His messengers. In order to encourage respect, teachers and parents are requested to mention the following:

Whenever the word Allāh ﷻ appears in the book, please add the glorification "*Subhāna-hu wa-Ta'ālā.*" Whenever the word Muhammad, or other words indicating Muhammad (for example Rasūlullāh, the Prophet, or Nabi) appear, please add the prayer "*Salla-llāhu 'alaihi wa Sallam.*" Whenever a student reads the name of a nabi or an angel, please add the prayer "*Alai-hi-s Salām.*" Students should be taught to add the prayer "*Radi-allāhu 'an-hu*" for a khalīfah or a male companion of Rasūlullāh ﷺ. For a female companion, the prayer "*Radi-allāhu 'an-hā*" should be used. These are noted by (R) or (ra).

Suggestions:

Please provide any suggestions, corrections, ideas, and so forth to improve this book by sending an e-mail to the publisher at info@weekendlearning.com. It is a combined effort of the publisher, authors, teachers, and parents to prepare our future ummah. May Allāh ﷻ guide us all! Amin.

A Guide to Features

Interesting Facts

- The paper-making process first began in ancient China in the second century C.E.
- At least two centuries before Jesus, the earliest forms of paper were in use.
- Technology and the use of paper spread from China to Middle East in the 13th century.
- The availability of paper in 13th century Iraq resulted in sudden bursts of knowledge as people began to translate Greek literature into Arabic.
- In the world today, there are about 20,000 different uses for paper.
- The U.S. and Canada are the world's largest producers of paper and paper products.
- The U.S. uses about 68 million trees each year to produce paper and paper products.

Interesting Facts

Interesting Facts are provided in most chapters. These notes are intended to provide additional information pertaining to a theme. The idea is to increase awareness of the subject and to enhance students' knowledge base. These facts will develop curiosity in the minds of students to explore wider areas of learning that might otherwise remain unnoticed.

Points to Remember

The word Qur'ān literally means "The Reading."

A total of 86 suwar (plural of surah) were revealed in Makkah, while 28 were revealed in Madīnah.

The longest sūrah is Al-Baqarah.

The Qur'ān has a total of 6,236 verses.

All sūrah except surah Taubah (#9) start with Bismillah—this sūrah does not have Bismillah in the beginning,

Points to Remember

Points to Remember are provided in most chapters. These key points are closely related to the theme of the chapter and should be remembered to broaden students' knowledge base. Students should be quizzed on these points.

Definition

Blood money: Money paid in compensation to the family of someone who has been killed. In return for the receipt of blood money, the family of the deceased would forgive the killer.

Definitions

Definitions of unfamiliar and novel terms are explained in a sidebar for quick learning.

Time to Review

1. Why should everything in the universe submit to or follow Allāh's rule?
2. Can Allāh be in multiple places at the same time?
3. What are some unique things about Allāh's knowledge?

Points to Ponder

No one other than Allāh created anything in the universe, therefore, no one else is worthy of being a deity. So why do so many people invent deities and idols and worship these objects?

Time to Review and Points to Ponder

Throughout the chapters these features like ask students to stop, reflect on, and review the content learned in the chapter. This enables them to raise intelligent questions from their perspective and reinforce learning.

Unit 1: Knowing the Creator

Knowing the Creator is one of the biggest challenges for human beings. People in the past and present often look for their Creator in unauthorized sources and objects, leading to worshipping the wrong objects and creating false deities. This unit attempts to introduce the Creator, first by identifying Him through the process of classifying His beautiful names. Another way to know Him is to understand His modes of action, and more precisely, His laws. Next, the unit focuses on the objectives of the Qur'ān in order to explain why the Creator sent the Qur'ān. The final three chapters extensively analyze a few selected āyāt from the Qur'ān. Lessons from Sūrah Hujurat describe the ideas of the Creator as He defined ideal social behaviors for mankind. The chapter on True Piety provides an understanding of the deeper meaning of piety, linking it to belief, practice, and conduct. The lesson on Ayātul Qudsi offers another view of the Creator.

Lesson 1: **Divine Names**

Lesson 2: **Sunan of Allāh**

Lesson 3: **Objectives of the Qur'ān**

Lesson 4: **Lessons from Sūrah Hujurāt**

Lesson 5: **True Piety:** *A Synthesis of Belief, Practice, and Conduct*

Lesson 6: **Ayātul Qudsi:** *The Throne Verse*

Unit 1: Knowing the Creator

Divine Names

The Qur'ān says the most beautiful names belong to Allāh. These names tell us much more than the obvious meanings. To understand the deeper meanings, we can classify these names into different categories. This lesson discusses some of these categories and helps us understand the deeper meanings of Allāh's beautiful names.

Sunan of Allāh

In order to consistently and uniformly manage the universe, Allāh has created certain laws of operation. Many of these laws are applicable to Himself. Failure to understand the significance and implications of these laws might result in misunderstanding divinity. In turn, this might give rise to irrational notions about who God is and what God is not. This might prevent one from properly understanding the true teachings of the Qur'ān. This lesson discusses some of the laws of Allah—commonly known as the Sunan of Allāh.

Objectives of the Qur'ān

The main objective of the Qur'ān is to provide guidance. In addition to this, there are many other objectives. Each one of these objectives is also one of the names for the Qur'ān. This lesson discusses the objectives of the Qur'ān and their relative importance in our lives.

Lessons from Sūrah Hujurāt

Islam gives tremendous importance to having a strong, harmonious, and cohesive society. However, improper and miscalculated judgments, along with prejudice and wickedness of the soul, often gives rise to social diseases that might destabilize the fabric of a good society. Sūrah Hujurāt presents a few social circumstances that describe when people might behave in a manner that is morally and ethically wrong. The sūrah also provides solutions to these social diseases. This lesson discusses some of these circumstances and their solutions.

True Piety: *A Synthesis of Belief, Practice, and Conduct*

The Qur'ān contains a beautiful ayāh in sūrah Baqarah that summarizes the meaning of piety, or righteousness. The ayāh points out that piety is not about certain mechanical, ritual functions that believers are accustomed to—it is so much more. The Qur'ān explains that piety has two major components—belief and right practice. This lesson discusses the Qur'ānic interpretation of true piety.

Ayātul Qudsi: *The Throne Verse*

The Throne Verse is one of the greatest verses in the Qur'ān. It describes God's action, knowledge, majesty, power, and dominion. Many consider this ayāh the equivalent of one-third of the Qur'ān because monotheism is the main theme of the ayāh. This lesson discusses the meaning of the ayāh in detail.

Divine Names

Objective of the Lesson:

The Qur'ān says the most beautiful names belong to Allāh ﷻ. These names tell us much more than the obvious meanings. To understand the deeper meanings, we can classify these names into different categories. This lesson discusses some of these categories and helps us understand the deeper meanings of Allāh's ﷻ beautiful names.

The Qur'ān is the word of Allāh ﷻ. Everything in it expresses Allāh ﷻ. Just as everything you say and how you say it reflects you, everything Allāh ﷻ says reflects Him. Therefore, if we want to know more about Allāh ﷻ, we have to read the Qur'ān and find out what He says about Himself. In 6th grade, we studied the "Attributes of Allāh." In this lesson, we will take a deeper look at His attributes.

First, let us learn how the concept of a deity named "Allāh" originated in Arabia, particularly before the advent of Islam. Did Messenger Muhammad ﷺ introduce the term, or did he use an existing term to denote the one and only deity? These questions offer a new approach to understanding "Allāh." To a Muslim student, the concept of Allāh ﷻ as the One and Only Deity is not new. A Muslim child grows up with the knowledge of and belief in Allāh ﷻ. However, the question remains: When we talk about "God" in English, does it mean Allāh ﷻ or some other god? Many Islamic scholars argue about whether the word "Allāh" can be appropriately translated into the English word "God." In other words, does God, as understood in English, aptly represent Allāh ﷻ—the One Deity all Muslims worship?

To a Muslim, it does not matter whether He is called Allāhﷻ or God—He is the One and Only Deity. The Qur'ān allows us to call upon God by any beautiful names, and urges us to call Him by other qualifying names as well. Whatever name we use to call upon Allāhﷻ, He is the center of Islamic monotheism.

In the Qur'ān, Allāhﷻ says the most beautiful names belong to Him.[7:180; 17:110] In Arabic, these beautiful names are called **al-Asmā al-husnā**.

وَلِلَّهِ ٱلْأَسْمَآءُ ٱلْحُسْنَىٰ فَٱدْعُوهُ بِهَا ۖ وَذَرُوا۟ ٱلَّذِينَ يُلْحِدُونَ فِىٓ أَسْمَٰٓئِهِۦ

And to Allāh belong all the finest Names, so call upon Him by these, and leave alone those who violate the sanctity of His Names... (7:180)

قُلِ ٱدْعُوا۟ ٱللَّهَ أَوِ ٱدْعُوا۟ ٱلرَّحْمَٰنَ ۖ أَيًّا مَّا تَدْعُوا۟ فَلَهُ ٱلْأَسْمَآءُ ٱلْحُسْنَىٰ

Say: "Call upon as Allāh or call upon as Rahman. By whatever you call, His are then the most beautiful names." (17:110)

If we study the names, we learn much more about Allāhﷻ. Each of these beautiful names illustrates one of His significant attributes. A famous hadīth narrated by Abū Hurraira mentions that Rasūlullāhﷺ said there are 99 attributes of Allāhﷻ. All these attributes and a few more are mentioned in the Qur'ān.

In order to truly know Allāhﷻ, we should know and memorize His names. All these names focus on a particular quality of Allāhﷻ, so we should try to imitate these beautiful qualities in our behavior.

Most beautiful names

When the Qur'ān says that Allāh'sﷻ names are "most beautiful," it is an indication that Allāhﷻ is Good and Beautiful. This is because the names express His Magnificence. His beauty and magnificence indicate His goodness. The hadīth mentiones that Allāhﷻ has 99 names, but the list of names that people have compiled have small variations. The most important thing to remember is that Allāhﷻ uses these names to describe Himself.

Names confirm tawhīd

Each name for Allāhﷻ not only represents a quality or a characteristic, but also these names confirm **tawhīd**. Tawhīd means Allāhﷻ is the only One. It is the doctrine of the oneness of God. The doctrine of Tawhīd conveys two things: (1) Allāhﷻ is *wāhid*, that is, One, and (2) Allāhﷻ is *ahad*, that is, unique.

Let us see how the beautiful names of Allāhﷻ declare tawhīd.

Allāhﷻ is most-Merciful, which means no one is more merciful than Him. The name the Merciful One indicates the One and Only

Definition

Tawhīd: The most important doctrine in Islam that stands for unity and the uniqueness of God. This doctrine not only points to God as the sole creator, sustainer, provider, and regulator, but also prohibits venerating saints, graves, avatar, and so forth as if they are divine. It also condemns human attempts to reduce God to mere images, idols, or incarnations.

most-Merciful Allāh ﷻ. Similarly, Allāh ﷻ is the Strong, which means there is no one stronger than Him. Once again, the name declares tawhīd—the one and only. Allāh ﷻ is the Creator. It means no one creates except the Creator. Allāh ﷻ is the Permanent—there is nothing permanent but the Permanent One. Everything perishes but Him.[28:88] Allāh ﷻ is the Owner. This means that Allāh ﷻ is the ultimate Owner of everything. If we continue with the list of names, we see that all these names affirm tawhīd, or the oneness of Allāh ﷻ.

The doctrine of tawhīd rejects the possibility of God reincarnated in human or animal form, because these are created beings, therefore, they cannot be God. For the same reason, the doctrine rejects the possibility of one or multiple subordinate gods managing one or multiple areas of God's dominion.

No derogatory names

You will never find bad names on the list of Allāh's ﷻ beautiful names. You will never find the name most-Rude, most-Cruel, most-Jealous, and so forth. You will also never find any mention of Allāh ﷻ as "Father" such as Christians use. Only the most beautiful names belong to Allāh ﷻ.

Classification of the names

All beautiful names of Allāh ﷻ can be classified under three broad categories. These are:

1. Names that describe what Allāh ﷻ is
2. Names that describe what Allāh ﷻ is not
3. Names that describe how Allāh ﷻ interacts with everything—the action names

In the first category are the names that describe Allāh ﷻ. However, we cannot measure all the qualities of Allāh ﷻ that He reveals. Allāh ﷻ is **most-Merciful**, but, we cannot measure all the mercy that He shows. We can only see some of His mercy.

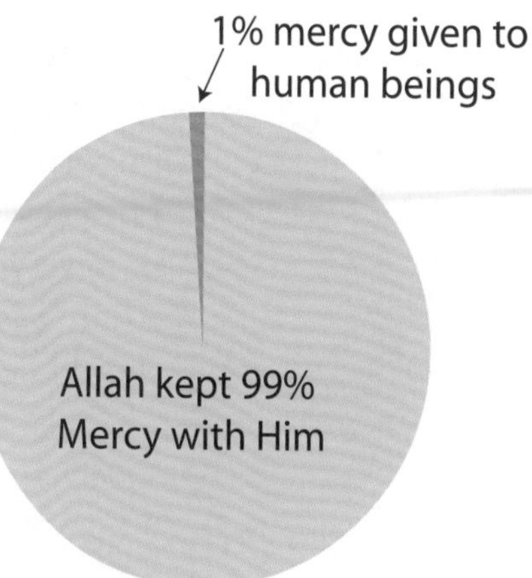

In the second category, we find names that tell us what Allāh ﷻ is not. For example, **As-Salam** (Peace) is Allāh's ﷻ name. This means He is not war, chaos, or disharmony. Another name is **Al-Ghani** (Independent). This means He is not dependent upon anything or anyone. Another name is **al-Quddus** (Holy). This means He is not unholy, imperfect, or tainted.

To provide an example, in a hadīth, Abū Hurairah reported that Rasūlullāh ﷺ said, "Allāh has divided Mercy into one hundred parts, and He kept ninety-nine parts with Him and sent down one part to the earth, and because of that one single part, His creatures are merciful to each other."

Imagine how this one percent of mercy works in human life. We see the mercy of parents towards their children; we see the mercy of people towards others; we see the mercy of leaders towards their citizens, and so on. Human mercy makes it possible for the earth to be a nice place to live. Now think about the 99 percent of mercy that

Allāh ﷻ did not distribute but kept with Him. Now imagine how much more this 99 percent of mercy could do for us and the world!

Similarly, Allāh ﷻ is the **most-Knowledgeable.** Our knowledge is limited to what we study and what we learn. In spite of knowing so much, we still do not know what is under the sea, what is in the universe, what is in the galaxy, what is on the planets, or what will happen two years from now or even two days from now. But Allāh's ﷻ knowledge is such that He knows everything.

In the third category are the names that describe Allāh's ﷻ actions. These actions are Allāh's ﷻ names, and the opposite of these actions are also His names. For example, Allāh ﷻ is *Al-Muhyī*, the Giver or Life, and *Al-Mumīt*, the Taker of Life. Allāh ﷻ is *Al-Mu'izz*, the Bestower of Honor, and *Al-Mudhill*, the Humiliator. He exalts someone with dignity (*Ar-Rāfi'e*) and He abases someone with humiliation (*Al-Khāfid*). He forgives (*Al-Ghaffār*) and He punishes (*Al-Qahhār*). All these actions apply only to Allāh's ﷻ creations, not to Him. For example, Allāh ﷻ can give life to His creation, but not to Himself, because He is already alive. Similarly, Allāh ﷻ can punish someone, but He, Himself, is beyond punishment.

Another method of classification

Regarding the action names of Allāh ﷻ, we noted that some names could be paired with their opposites. This is another way of classifying His names.

One group of names describes the attractive and gentle attributes of Allāh ﷻ. Some examples are names such as Merciful, Compassionate, Loving, Kind, Forgiving, and Beautiful. Another group of names describes the opposite of the previous group. Some examples are names such as Subduer, Constrictor, Humiliator, Delayer, Avenger, and Majestic.

Limitless qualities of Allāh ﷻ

We cannot completely measure the qualities, attributes, or essence of Allāh ﷻ. We also cannot fully describe His qualities.[6:103] There is nothing that is similar to Him.[42:11] The important question is: How can we know Him through His names? We can know Him by learning and implementing these qualities, to the best of our best ability in our everyday activities. Allāh ﷻ is Merciful. Therefore, we should show mercy to others. Allāh ﷻ is Forgiving. Therefore, we should forgive others. Allāh ﷻ is Just. Therefore, we should be just and fair to others.

99 Beautiful Names of Allāh ﷻ

Allāh	Allāh
Ar-Rahman	The most-Kind
Ar-Rahīm	The most-Rewarding
Al-Malik	The Absolute Ruler
Al-Quddūs	The Pure One
As-Salām	The Source of Peace
Al-Mu'min	The Inspirer of Faith
Al-Muhaymin	The Guardian
Al-'Azīz	The Victorious
Al-Jabbār	The Compeller
Al-Mutakabbīr	The Greatest
Al-Khāliq	The Creator
Al-Bārī'	The Maker of Order
Al-Musawwir	The Shaper of Beauty
Al-Ghaffār	The Forgiving
Al-Qahhār	The Subduer
Al-Wahhāb	The Giver of All
Ar-Razzāq	The Sustainer
Al-Fattāh	The Opener
Al-'Alīm	The Knower of All
Al-Qābid	The Constrictor
Al-Bāsit	The Reliever
Al-Khāfid	The Abaser
Ar-Rāfi'e	The Exalter
Al-Mu'izz	The Bestower of Honors
Al-Mudhill	The Humiliator
As-Sami'i	The Hearer of All
Al-Basīr	The Seer of All
Al-Hakam	The Judge
Al-'Adl	The Just
Al-Latīf	The Subtle One
Al-Khabīr	The All-Aware
Al-Halīm	The Forbearing
Al-'Azīm	The Magnificent
Al-Ghafūr	The Forgiver
Ash-Shakūr	The Appreciative
Al-'Ali	The Highest
Al-Kabīr	The Greatest
Al-Hafīz	The Preserver
Al-Muqīt	The Nourisher
Al-Hasīb	The Accounter
Al-Jalīl	The Mighty
Al-Karīm	The Generous
Ar-Raqīb	The Watchful One
Al-Mujīb	The Responder to Prayer
Al-Wāsī'i	The All-Comprehending
Al-Hakīm	The Perfectly Wise
Al-Wadūd	The Loving One
Al-Majīd	The Majestic One
Al-Bā'ith	The Resurrector
Ash-Shahīd	The Witness
Al-Haqq	The Truth
Al-Wakīl	The Trustee
Al-Qawi'	The Possessor of All Strength
Al-Matīn	The Forceful One
Al-Wali	The Governor
Al-Hamīd	The Praised One
Al-Muhsī	The Appraiser
Al-Mubdī'	The Originator
Al-Mu'īd	The Restorer
Al-Muhyī	The Giver of Life
Al-Mumīt	The Taker of Life
Al-Hayy	The Ever-Living One
Al-Qayyum	The Self-Existing One
Al-Wājid	The Finder
Al-Mājid	The Glorious
Al-Wāhid	The Only One
Al-Ahad	The One
As-Samad	The Satisfier of All Needs
Al-Qādir	The All-Powerful
Al-Muqtadir	The Creator of All Power
Al-Muqaddim	The Expediter
Al-Mu'akhkhir	The Delayer
Al-Awwal	The First
Al-Akhir	The Last

Az-Zāhir	The Manifest One
Al-Bātin	The Hidden One
Al-Wālī	The Protecting Friend
Al-Muta'āli	The Supreme One
Al-Barr	The Doer of Good
At-Tawwāb	The Guide to Repentance
Al-Muntaqim	The Avenger
Al-'Afūw	The Forgiver
Ar-Ra'uf	The Clement
Mālik al-Mulk	The Owner of All
Dhul-Jalāli Wal-Ikrām	The Lord of Majesty
Al-Muqsīt	The Equitable One
Al-Jāmi	The Gatherer
Al-Ghanī	The Rich One
Al-Mughnī	The Enricher
Al-Māni'i	The Preventer of Harm
Ad-Dārr	The Creator of The Harmful
An-Nāfi'i	The Creator of Good
An-Nūr	The Light
Al-Hādi	The Guide
Al-Badī'	The Originator
Al-Bāqī	The Everlasting One
Al-Wārith	The Inheritor of All
Ar-Rashīd	The Righteous Teacher
As-Sabūr	The Patient One

WEEKEND 1

Homework

1. According to the lesson, which of the following statements is correct?

A. All the names are beautiful.
B. All the names declare tawhīd.
C. All the names declare the mercy of Allāh.
D. Only (a) and (b) are correct.
E. Only (b) and (c) are correct.

2. Each name for Allāh tell us something about Him. Which of the following statements about the names is correct?

A. The names describe what Allāh is.
B. The names describe what Allāh is not.
C. The names describe how Allāh interacts with everything.
D. Some names can be paired with their opposites.
E. All of the above.

3. One of the divine names of Allāh is Ar-Rāfi'e. Find the meaning of the name from the list of names given in the lesson. Then select which name would be the opposite of Ar-Rāfi'e.

A. Al-Khāfid
B. Al-Bāsit
C. Al-Qābid
D. Al-'Alīm
E. Al-Basīr

4. One of the divine names of Allāh is Al-Muhyī. Find the meaning of the name from the list of names given in the lesson. Then select which name would be the opposite of Al-Muhyī.

A. Al-Hayy
B. Al-Mumīt
C. Al-Qayyum
D. Al-Wājid
E. As-Samad

5. What is the Islamic meaning of the term tawhīd?

6. Some of the names of Allāh ﷻ describe what He is not. One of Allāh's ﷻ beautiful names is Al-Basir. Based on the meaning of this name, which of the following choices describes what He is not?

A. He is not clutter.
B. He is not dependent.
C. He is not blind to anything.
D. He is not a forgiver.
E. He is not biased.

7. Many of the beautiful names describe Allāh's ﷻ "actions." All the following choices about the actions of Allāh ﷻ are correct except one. Which choice is incorrect?

A. All the actions apply only to the creations of Allāh ﷻ.
B. Some action names have opposite action names.
C. The action mentioned in the "action names" apply to Allāh ﷻ.
D. The "action names" are some of the beautiful names of Allāh ﷻ.
E. Only (a) and (b).

8. Read ayāt 23 and 24 from sūrah al-Hashr. In total, 13 names of Allāh ﷻ are mentioned in these ayāt. Write all the Arabic names and their meanings below.

	ArabicNames	**English Meaning**
1.	________________	____________________
2.	________________	____________________
3.	________________	____________________
4.	________________	____________________
5.	________________	____________________
6.	________________	____________________
7.	________________	____________________
8.	________________	____________________
9.	________________	____________________
10.	________________	____________________
11.	________________	____________________
12.	________________	____________________
13.	________________	____________________

Sunan of Allāh ﷻ

Objective of the Lesson:

In order to consistently and uniformly manage the universe, Allāh ﷻ has created certain laws of operation. Many of these laws are applicable to Himself. Failure to understand the significance and implications of these laws might result in misunderstanding divinity. In turn, this might give rise to irrational notions about who God is and what God is not. This might prevent one from properly understanding the true teachings of the Qur'ān. This lesson discusses some of the laws of Allah ﷻ—commonly known as the Sunan of Allāh ﷻ.

Many countries have a legal system that includes two broad areas of law. The purpose of the legal system is to punish or deter wrongdoing and provide justice to victims. These two broad areas are criminal law and civil law. Criminal law deals with behavior that is considered a crime against society or the state. For example, murder, assault, robbery, and burglary. Civil law deals with dispute resolution, particularly resolving issues resulting from an injury to an individual or a private party. For example, defamation, breach of contract, property damage. Both criminal laws and civil laws vary according to the jurisdiction, state, and country.

In Islam, you often hear about **Sharī'ah Law**. This law broadly regulates both the public life and private life of a person regardless of where he or she lives. Sharī'ah law is different from the laws of a country or a state because such laws are applicable to the people who live in that country. Sharī'ah law reaches beyond the boundaries of any city, county, state, or country because it regulates a Muslim's public life and private life. We will learn about sharī'ah law in the next year.

There is another type of law that applies to Allāh ﷻ. He has created this law for Himself. It is sometimes known as the **Sunan Allāh** or the Laws of Allāh ﷻ. However, the word "Sunan" (sing. sunnah) does not mean law; it means "actions" or "sayings." Broadly speaking, sunan means "a path," "a way of life" or "tradition and practices." For example, the tradition or practices of the Messengerﷺ is called sunnah. The famous collection of hadīth by Abū Dawūd is known as "Sunan Dawūd" because this collection is a compilation of some of the Messenger'sﷺ sayings.

Sunan of Allāhﷻ

Based on the various meanings of the word sunan, the term "Sunan of Allāh" is best understood as the "practices" or "actions" of Allāhﷻ. These practices or actions are consistent and uniform over time and space, therefore, they can be considered the "laws" of Allāh.

Why has Allāhﷻ created laws for Himself? He creates laws for Himself in order to give us the comfort and assurance that God does not do anything whimsically, in playful manner, or with a biased approach toward someone or some community. This assurance is important because it allows us to trust our Creator. Despite having all the power, He does not violate His practices. This is clearly stated in the Qur'ān in the following manner:

وَلَا تَجِدُ لِسُنَّتِنَا تَحْوِيلًا ﴿٧٧﴾

...and you will not find any change in Our course. (17:77)

سُنَّةَ ٱللَّهِ ٱلَّتِي قَدْ خَلَتْ مِن قَبْلُ ۖ وَلَن تَجِدَ لِسُنَّةِ ٱللَّهِ تَبْدِيلًا ﴿٢٣﴾

The course of Allāh which was in operation from before; and you will never find any change in the course of Allāh. (48:23)

There is another reason Allāhﷻ creates His laws or practices for Himself. As the Creator, Sustainer, Maintainer, and Regulator of the universe, He does not do anything that would disrupt the orderliness of the universe. One uniform law across the billions of galaxies in the universe is a testimony to one Supreme Commander in the universe.

Interesting Facts

Our solar system is located in the center of the Milky Way galaxy. The size of this galaxy is 100,000 to 180,000 light-years. Our galaxy has an estimated 100 billion planets.

How large are some of the planets in our solar system? We could fit 1,000 Earths inside Jupiter. And we could fit 1,000 Jupiters inside the sun.

The observable, or visible, universe has an estimated two trillion galaxies. It is also estimated that there are more stars in the universe than grains of sand on earth!

Types of sunan

There are many sunan of Allāhﷻ. For ease of understanding, these practices can be classified in the following categories:

1. Sunan pertaining to management of the universe.
2. Sunan pertaining to cause and effect.
3. Sunan pertaining to life on earth.
4. Sunan pertaining to guidance and misguidance.
5. Sunan pertaining to reward and punishment.
6. Sunan pertaining to trials and tribulations.

7. Sunan pertaining to sins and sinners.
8. Sunan pertaining to divine justice.
9. Sunan pertaining to victory and defeat.

Now let us see how some of the Sunan of Allāhﷻ work in our lives. These sunan are mentioned throughout the pages of the Qur'ān. The more we understand these sunan, the more we will appreciate the majesty of our Creator and, in turn, submit to Him with full devotion.

Management of the universe

There is a large number of sunan in the Qur'ān about the management of the universe. We will discuss a few of them here.

> *It is not for the sun that it will be possible for it to overtake the moon, nor can the night outstrip the day. And all swim along in an orbit. (36:40)*

> *And it is He Who has made the night and the day, and the sun and the moon; all are floating in an orbit. (21:33)*

> *Don't you see that Allāh causes the night to enter into the day, and He causes the day to enter into the night; and He subjugates the sun and the moon—each pursuing until an appointed term; and that Allāh is Aware of what you do? (31:29)*

These are not casual statements about astronomy, they carry profound wisdom. The purpose of stating these facts and many others is to demonstrate **tawhīd**—the oneness of Allāhﷻ. There is one God in the universe, and this God controls and regulates everything in the universe with a uniform law. There is no chaos or discrepany in the law. We might ask, if Allāhﷻ made the law, would He or could He break the law at His will? After all, He is all-Powerful. The sunan of Allāhﷻ teaches us that Allāhﷻ never violates or breaks His law.

Cause and effect: changing condition

Another sunan realates to changing our condition. This sunan is important because it allows us to understand that unless we take proactive steps to change our circumstances, Allāhﷻ will not change them. This point is beautifully illustrated in the following ayāh:

بِأَنَّ ٱللَّهَ لَمْ يَكُ مُغَيِّرًا نِّعْمَةً أَنْعَمَهَا عَلَىٰ قَوْمٍ حَتَّىٰ يُغَيِّرُوا۟ مَا بِأَنفُسِهِمْ

> *...Allāh would not change a favor which He has conferred upon any people, until they change what is in themselves... (8:53)*

إِنَّ ٱللَّهَ لَا يُغَيِّرُ مَا بِقَوْمٍ حَتَّىٰ يُغَيِّرُوا۟ مَا بِأَنفُسِهِمْ ۗ

> *...Surely Allāh does not change whatever is with a people until they change it by themselves... (13:11)*

This sunan applies to all aspects of our lives—whether we are discussing an individual, a family, a community or a nation. If we experience financial difficulty, a family crisis, or simply a nice and simple life, our situation will not change unless we take action to change it. People who prosper and become successful in life are the ones who define their own destiny. Allāh's ﷻ help arrives when people exert their own effort. His assistance is in direct proportion to the level of efforts we give.

When Rasūlullāh ﷺ experienced extreme challenges in Makkah, he did not remain idle, hoping for Allāh ﷻ would solve his problems. He took specific steps to change the circumstances. He went to Ta'if hoping a change of location would alleviate the situation. When this failed, he did not give up. He contacted some pilgrims from Yathrib and entered into detailed negotiations about possible relocation. When the time of relocation arrived, he took all steps humanly possible to ensure safety as he secretly left Makkah. All the battles he fought in Madīnah are also examples of him taking the initiative to change the situation.

Poor Muslims in many parts of the world today prefer to have large family. They think Allāh ﷻ gave them children and Allāh ﷻ will feed them. Little do they realize that unless they take charge of their lives, strive their best to earn a living, educate their children, and look after the welfare of the family, Allāh ﷻ will not provide them prosperity on a silver platter.

Life on earth: burden of a soul

Another important sunan of Allāh ﷻ relates to how each person must carry certain obligations or responsibilities. Some people seem to have a rather easy, uneventful, and serene life and others seem to have many challenges. This apparent disproportionate distribution of responsibilities among different people sometimes makes us wonder: Why does Allāh ﷻ subject some to ease and some to difficulty. The Qur'ān says:

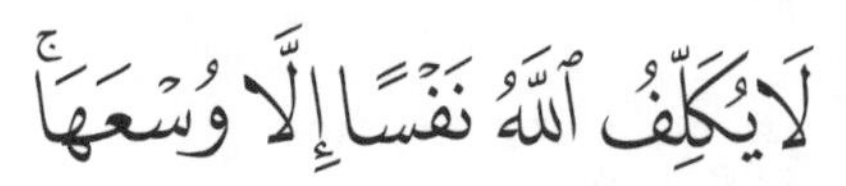

Allāh does not burden any soul but to its capacity... (2:286)

Allāh ﷻ created each individual. He has the wisdom to know the capacity of each person. It is His discretion to allow some individuals to undergo easy of life and other individuals to undergo a more challenging life. Both conditions are tests for us. The burden some of us are made to withstand is within the limits Allāh ﷻ has set for all of us. Nobody is made to withstand a burden beyond human capacity.

Guidance and misguidance

It is estimated that the world practices about 4,200 religions. A few religions are transcultural, meaning people from different cultures and countries follow the religion. Most are purely indigenous faiths, meaning they are localized religions. Based on the number of faiths, some people are clearly guided and many are misguided. Allāh ﷻ says that if He wanted, He could have guided all mankind to have a uniform faith. This means the world would practice one religion. The diversity of religions means Allāh ﷻ

allowed all these faiths to survive and spread. It also means Allāh does not force anyone to accept or reject a faith. If someone wants to be guided, Allāh facilitates the path to guidance. However, if someone wants to reject guidance, Allāh leaves the person alone, but He never misguides him or her. The sunan of Allāh opposes forcing someone to accept guidance or misguidance.

...Do not those who believe know that if Allāh had so pleased He could surely have guided mankind in a body?... (13:31)

...And had He wished, He could surely have guided you all together. (16:9)

Guidance and misguidance: Allāh does not love nonbelievers

To believe or not to believe is a matter of choice. Allāh will not interfere with this choice. However, Allāh makes sure we understand who is dear to Him and who is not. In several āyāt, He says He does not love the aggressors,[2:190] the nonbelievers,[3:32; 16:107; 30:45] the wrongdoers,[3:57] the sinful, treacherous,[4:107; 8:58] and the transgressors.[7:55] He loves those who are good,[2:195; 3:134; 5:93] and the pious.[3:76; 9:7] His actions are in agreement with the sunan He created for Himself. The believers will always earn His mercy, protection, guidance, help and favor.

Guidance and misguidance: Allāh does not command indecency

Indecency refers to an act that is improper of offensive. Any immoral, obscene, vulgar actions are considered indecent. Just as Allāh does not misguide people, He also does not command indecency. People who commit various forms of indecency try to justify their conduct by saying they have divine approval. But Allāh says:

And when they commit an indecency, they say: "We found our forefathers on this, and Allāh has commanded us to this." You say: "Surely Allāh does not command towards indecency. Do you allege against Allāh what you do not know?" (7:28)

Guidance and misguidance: Allāh will never forgive some

Allāh is most-Forgiving and most-Rewarding. He is ever-willing to forgive people. However, His forgiveness is not provided out without qualifications. One has to ask for forgiveness, avoid the sins for which forgiveness is being sought, and amend one's conduct. Only then will Allāh forgive a person's sins. This is His sunan.

Say: "O my bondsmen! those who have committed excesses against their souls, do not despair of the mercy of Allāh. Surely Allāh forgives the sins altogether. He, surely He, is the most Forgiving, most Rewarding."

However, Allāh's sunan also teaches us that He will not forgive some sins. Allāh will not forgive those who do not believe, and die as nonbelievers.

Surely those who disbelieve and keep back from the way of Allāh, and then die while they are nonbelievers, then Allāh will never forgive them. (47:34)

One of the worst types of enemies for the Muslims are hypocrites. However, it is difficult to know who is a hypocrite, because outwardly the person looks like a believer. Keeping this in mind, Allāh did not forbidden Nabi Muhammad or any other person from seeking forgiveness for a hypocrites. However, Allāh will not forgive a sinner just because someone prayed for him or her. The sinner must make amends and seek forgiveness.

It is alike to them whether you ask forgiveness for them, or you do not ask forgiveness for them;—Allāh will never forgive them. Surely Allāh does not guide the evil-doing people. (63:6)

Reward and punishment: What we will receive?

As the most-Merciful and most-Rewarding, Allāh created a sunan about rewarding or punishing people. He does not punish us immediately after we commit a sin. He allows us enough time to realize our mistake, to correct our conduct and to seek forgiveness. He says that if He held people accountable for their actions, not a single person would escape His punishment. But He provides respite until the appointed time.[35:45]

Another sunan of Allāh states that He recompenses good deeds with multiple rewards, but He recompenses bad actions with punishment that is no greater in quantity or intensity than the evil deed (6:160; 27:90; 28:84; 37:39; 40:40; 42:40; 53:31; 66:7; 78:26).

Reward and punishment: Allāh always rewards believers

One of the assuring aspect of Allāh's reward system is that He does not allow any good deeds of believers to go to waste. His rewards never run out. He never forgets any good deeds and never ignores any righteous person regardless of the person's status, wealth, appearance, or nationality. Believers can rest assured that they will receive their rewards and the rewards will always be greater in number than the actual deeds.

And you do persevere, for Allah certainly does not waste the reward of the doers of good. (11:115)

Surely as to those who believe and do good, We shall certainly not waste the reward of him who does a good deed. (18:30)

Reward and punishment: Allāh does not do injustice

As human beings, we are prone to commit injustice against our fellow human beings, animals, and the environment. Love for our family members sometimes prevents us from practicing justice even though we are required to be just.[4:135] In contrast to our biases, Allāh is always just with everybody. Allāh is just not only with human beings, but He is also just with all of creation. He enjoins justice,[7:29] and He is not at all unjust to His servants.[3:182]

Truly Allāh does not do injustice to the weight of an atom; and if it be a good [deed] He multiplies it, and He gives from His presence a great reward. (4:40)

Certainly Allāh does not do injustice to mankind in any way, but men do injustice to themselves. (10:44)

Reward and punishment: Evil plots recoil on evildoers

Another sunan of Allāhﷻ relates to the evil plots of people and how the plots affect righteous people. We should always remember this sunan and never become disheartened. Allāhﷻ says evil people contrive plots to harm others, and Allāhﷻ also plans. He is the most-Excellent of the planners.[3:54] Sometimes evil plots appear monumental, but these come to nothing when Allāhﷻ cancels their plots.[14:46] In another ayāh in the Qur'ān, Allāhﷻ says:

And the evil plots do not recoil on anyone except the authors of it. (35:43)

Trials and tribulations

One of Allāh'sﷻ sunan relates to trials and tribulations. He will test everyone regardless of their faith. Just as a believer cannot escape being tested, a nonbeliever also cannot avoid a test. Allāhﷻ says:

Do men think that they will be left alone on saying: "We believe," and that they will not be tested? (29:2)

In another ayāh, Allāhﷻ says He will certainly test us with various forms of afflictions, and those who persevere will receive blessings and mercy from their Rabb.

And We certainly test you with something of fear, and hunger, and loss of property and lives, and of fruits. And give glad tidings to the perseverers. (2:155)

The reason for these tests is to allow us to realize our sincerity to Allāhﷻ and to distinguish the believers from the false ones. Allāhﷻ encourages us to pray to Him to not subject us to a test that we cannot withstand.

WEEKEND 2

Homework

1. What is the reason that Allāhﷻ has created some laws for Himself?

   A. To prevent accidental misuse of the law.
   B. To distinguish right from wrong.
   C. To punish the guilty.
   D. To prevent Himself from showing anger or mercy.
   E. To assure us of His uniform and unbiased approach in all matters.

2. What is one important message the sunan of Allāhﷻ conveys about the universe?

   A. The universe is vast.
   B. The universe has many paths and orbits.
   C. The universe has many mysteries that human beings will never know.
   D. The principle of tawhīd.
   E. The Day of Judgment is real.

3. Read āyah 8:53 in the Qur'ān. Which sunan is mentioned in the āyah?

   A. Allāhﷻ will confer mercy to those who ask for it.
   B. Allāhﷻ will return evil for evil and good for good.
   C. Allāhﷻ will not change the condition of people until they change it themselves.
   D. Allāhﷻ will not waste the rewards for those who deserve them.
   E. Allāhﷻ will change the condition of others so that they become better.

4. One of the sunan of Allāhﷻ relates to the burden on a soul. Which of the following statements about this sunan is correct?

   A. Allāhﷻ burdens a soul until its capacity is exceeded.
   B. Allāhﷻ burdens a soul lightly, such that it does not break.
   C. Allāhﷻ burdens a soul based on its righteousness.
   D. Allāhﷻ burdens a soul based on its age and sex.
   E. Allāhﷻ burdens a soul only to its capacity.

5. Write one sentence that best describes Allāh'sﷻ principle about guidance and misguidance.

____

6. One of the sunan of Allāh ﷻ relates to how He forgives. Which of the following statements correctly states the sunan about forgiveness?

A. Allāh ﷻ will forgive all sins of Muslims and some sins of non-Muslims.
B. Allāh ﷻ will forgive all sins after the sinner faces punishment.
C. Allāh ﷻ will forgive a sin if the sinner does not realize a sin was committed.
D. Allāh ﷻ will not forgive a person if the person did not treat his or her parents well.
E. Allāh ﷻ will not forgive those who do not believe and die as nonbeliever.

7. Another sunan of Allāh ﷻ relates to how He rewards and punishes people. Which of the following statements about this sunan is correct?

A. Allāh's ﷻ rewards and punishments are commensurate with one's deeds.
B. Allāh's ﷻ rewards and punishments are provided exclusively in the Hereafter.
C. Allāh's ﷻ rewards and punishments are based on one's faith.
D. Allāh ﷻ rewards multiple times for a good deed but punishes equal to the degree of bad deeds.
E. Allāh'sh ﷻ reward system takes into account the wealth and status of a person.

8. One sunan of Allāh ﷻ relates to trials and tribulations. Which of the following statements about this sunan is correct?

A. Those who persevere will escape trials in life.
B. Allāh ﷻ subjects a person to trials because of his or her past misdeeds.
C. Allāh ﷻ will subject a Muslim to a greater trial than a non-Muslim.
D. Allāh ﷻ will not test a sick person because he or she is already suffering.
E. Every soul will face trials regardless of one's faith.

Objectives of the Qur'ān

Objective of the Lesson:

The main objective of the Qur'ān is to provide guidance. In addition to this, there are many other objectives. Each one of these objectives is also one of the names for the Qur'ān. This lesson discusses the objectives of the Qur'ān and their relative importance in our lives.

The first sūrah in the Qur'ān is a small sūrah entitled al-Fātihah. This sūrah is a prayer—essentially we are asking Allāh ﷻ to guide us to the straight path, *the path of those upon whom Allāh has bestowed His favor.* We are also asking Allāh ﷻ not to guide us to the paths of those who have earned anger and who have gone astray.

Guide us on the Right Path. (1:6)

The path of those upon whom You have bestowed favors... (1:7)

By reciting sūrah al-Fātihah, we are asking for guidance, but we may wonder: How do I find guidance? Hoping to find the answer somewhere in the Qur'ān, we then proceed to the next chapter of the Qur'ān—sūrah al-Baqarah.

In the very beginning of sūrah al-Baqarah, the Qur'ān talks about itself. In the second āyah, the Qur'ān says three things about itself:

ذَٰلِكَ ٱلْكِتَٰبُ لَا رَيْبَ ۛ فِيهِ ۛ هُدًى لِّلْمُتَّقِينَ ﴿٢﴾

This Book, no doubt in it, is a guidance for the reverent. (2:2)

1. This is the Book.
2. There is no doubt in it.
3. It is guidance for God-fearing people.

The āyah answers the question we have in mind—how do I find guidance? The answer is: We will find guidance in this book that has no doubt in it.

Almost from the very beginning of the Qur'ān, we learn the objective of the Qur'ān is to guide people who are God-fearing.

What is guidance?

Now that we know the objective of the Qur'ān is to provide guidance, we may wonder what is meant by guidance. In basic terms, guidance is something that provides direction or advice for a course of action. Guidance can also be understood as getting help to make the right choices. Guidance can also mean receiving instructions from a qualified person about ways to deal with difficult or complex issues or to resolve a problem, especially from someone in authority.

Sometimes we can compare guidance to a map or blueprint. A map is a diagram that shows a location. A blueprint is a drawing or design of a structure, usually for a building or an engineering plan. Sometimes a blueprint is used to refer to any detailed plan that can be followed.

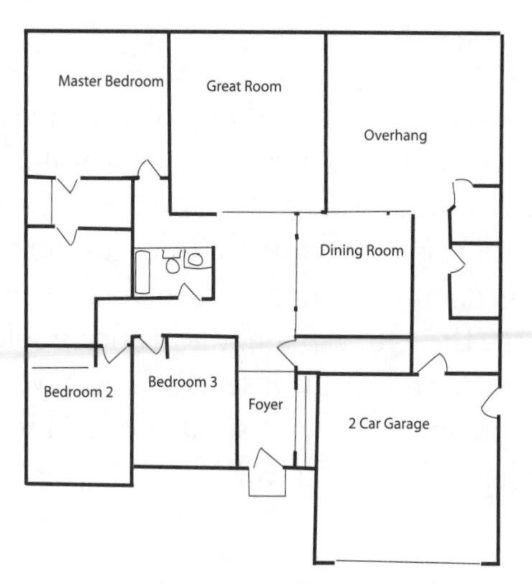

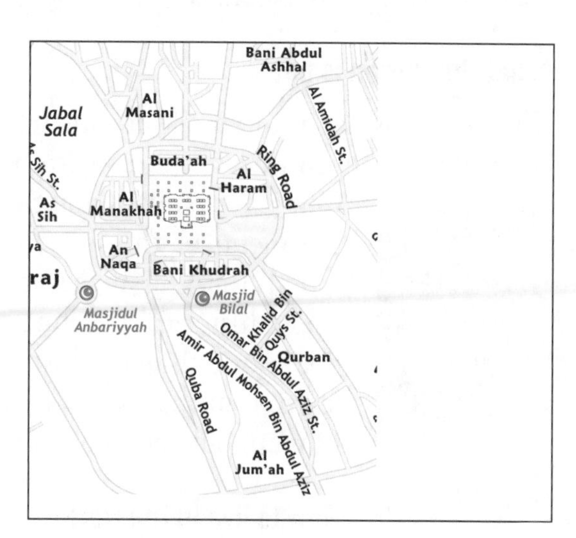

A blueprint of a house and a road map of Makkah

If you are lost while driving, a map or GPS system may help you reach your destination. A map shows the road directions, but it does not tell you what steps you should take and not take. A GPS system may advise you to avoid a toll road, to watch for a construction zone, to take a detour if there are traffic congestion but nothing more.

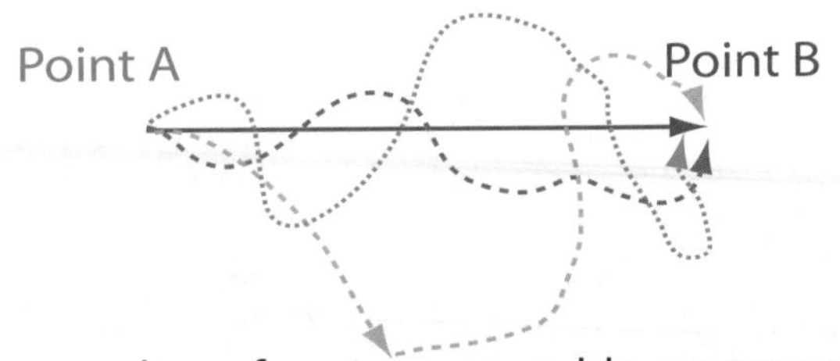

Any number of routes can guide a person from Point A to Point B.

A map or GPS system does not tell you anything about rewards or suffering. A map does not explain how it is to be used. A map has several destinations, and the decision to choose a road is entirely up to you. Also, if you have to reach Point B on the map, you could take a number of routes to arrive there.

We can compare the Qur'ān to a map, but we must remember that it is much more. Some religions advocate that you follow any path because all paths lead to God. This philosophy does not apply to Islam. In the Qur'ān, the way from Point A to Point B is one straight path. You will not find several ways to reach Point B.

Similarly, we cannot equate the Qur'ān to a blueprint of an engineer. To some extent, there are similarities in the plan of action, but the Qur'ān is much more. These differences will become clear once we read the rest of the lesson.

The Qur'ān is guidance

We want to be safe and successful, and Allāh ﷻ wants the same for us. Therefore, Allāh ﷻ has sent us the Qur'ān as Guidance to lead our lives. Without the Qur'ān, we will be lost in our lives, and we will do things we should not do. The Qur'ān is guidance for all of mankind.

The Qur'ān tells us what is Truth and what is falsehood. It reminds us of the rewards that we will receive if we follow its directions. The Qur'ān often gives us good news. It also warns us if we go off track. It repeats some ayāt several times because it is important that we clearly understand the teachings.

What the Qur'ān is not

The Qur'ān is not a storybook. It sometimes tells a parable, or a short story, to remind us what will happen when we do something right or when we do something wrong. The Qur'ān often does not give the details of a story because it emphasizes the moral of the story, not unnecessary details. While describing a moral, the Qur'ān never uses geographical names of places. It never uses a historical timeline, either. The Qur'ān is not a history book. It does not tell us the history of nabi and rasul; it tells us what we can learn from their lives. There are many nabi and rasul mentioned in the Qur'ān, but very few non-prophets are mentioned.

وَمَآ أَمۡرُنَآ إِلَّا وَٰحِدَةٞ كَلَمۡحِۭ بِٱلۡبَصَرِ ٥٠ وَلَقَدۡ أَهۡلَكۡنَآ
أَشۡيَاعَكُمۡ فَهَلۡ مِن مُّدَّكِرٖ ٥١ وَكُلُّ شَيۡءٖ فَعَلُوهُ
فِي ٱلزُّبُرِ ٥٢ وَكُلُّ صَغِيرٖ وَكَبِيرٖ مُّسۡتَطَرٌ ٥٣ إِنَّ ٱلۡمُتَّقِينَ
فِي جَنَّٰتٖ وَنَهَرٖ ٥٤ فِي مَقۡعَدِ صِدۡقٍ عِندَ مَلِيكٖ مُّقۡتَدِرِۭ ٥٥

سُورَةُ الرَّحۡمَٰن

بِسۡمِ ٱللَّهِ ٱلرَّحۡمَٰنِ ٱلرَّحِيمِ
ٱلرَّحۡمَٰنُ ١ عَلَّمَ ٱلۡقُرۡءَانَ ٢ خَلَقَ ٱلۡإِنسَٰنَ ٣
عَلَّمَهُ ٱلۡبَيَانَ ٤ ٱلشَّمۡسُ وَٱلۡقَمَرُ بِحُسۡبَانٖ ٥ وَٱلنَّجۡمُ
وَٱلشَّجَرُ يَسۡجُدَانِ ٦ وَٱلسَّمَآءَ رَفَعَهَا وَوَضَعَ ٱلۡمِيزَانَ
٧ أَلَّا تَطۡغَوۡاْ فِي ٱلۡمِيزَانِ ٨ وَأَقِيمُواْ ٱلۡوَزۡنَ بِٱلۡقِسۡطِ
وَلَا تُخۡسِرُواْ ٱلۡمِيزَانَ ٩ وَٱلۡأَرۡضَ وَضَعَهَا لِلۡأَنَامِ ١٠
فِيهَا فَٰكِهَةٞ وَٱلنَّخۡلُ ذَاتُ ٱلۡأَكۡمَامِ ١١ وَٱلۡحَبُّ ذُو ٱلۡعَصۡفِ
وَٱلرَّيۡحَانُ ١٢ فَبِأَيِّ ءَالَآءِ رَبِّكُمَا تُكَذِّبَانِ ١٣ خَلَقَ
ٱلۡإِنسَٰنَ مِن صَلۡصَٰلٖ كَٱلۡفَخَّارِ ١٤ وَخَلَقَ ٱلۡجَآنَّ
ءَالَآءِ رَبِّكُمَا تُكَذِّبَانِ ١٦

How to live in the world

Allāh ﷻ wants us to live a good life in the world. In order to live a good life, we need to interact with people. The Qur'ān tells us how to behave with other people, how to share with others, and why we should not hurt people. It tells us to stand up against bad things that may harm our society. It tells us why we should work as a team in society. It does not want us to divide ourselves into small groups.

The Qur'ān gives us hope

The Qur'ān also gives us hope. This hope is guaranteed by Allāh. The Qur'ān tells us that even if we have a difficult life, we can ultimately be successful by remaining on the right path.

Qualitative names of the Qur'ān

The Qur'ān is widely known by many qualitative names. Each name tells us one main objective of the Qur'ān. A short summary of these names and their significance is listed below.

1. **Al-Kitāb** means "The Scripture" or "the Book." We already noted that in In Sūrah Al-Baqarah, āyah 2, Allāh calls the Qur'ān al-Kitab.

2. One of the objectives of the Qur'ān is to grant favor to mankind. If the Qur'ān did not exist, mankind would not have found the right guidance. Therefore, Allāh calls the Qur'ān **al-Ni'mat.**

3. Another objective of the Qur'ān is to clearly convey its message. Thus, one of its names is **al-Burhān.** It means the Qur'ān has a clear argument and it has clear proof of truth.

4. The Qur'ān is intended to serve as a Guardian of the previous revelations. It is a guardian of truth. It also prevents corruption from entering the Book. Therefore, another name is **al-Muhaimin**, "the Guardian."

5. The Qur'ān is meant to show us the Right Path in the midst of darkness and ignorance. Therefore, one of its names is **al-Hudā**, which means "the Guidance." The message of the Qur'ān guides us to the Right Path. We also know the Qur'ān as **al-Nūr,** "the Light." This is because the message of the Qur'ān brings us out of darkness and ignorance.

6. The Light shows us the path, but it also shows us the Truth. Therefore, the Qur'ān is also **al-Haqq**, "the Truth." Nothing in the Qur'ān is false.

7. Allāh has made a contract, or agreement, with us. This contract tells us what Allāh does for us and what we should do in return. The contract is the Covenant of Allāh, and since the Qur'ān tells us about the contract, it is **Habl-Allāh**, the "Covenant of Allāh."

8. The Qur'ān is the direct Word of Allāh. Thus, one of its names is **al-Kalām**, "the Word." The words of the Qur'ān are noble words.

Some of the names of the Qur'ān explain how it functions. For example:

9. The Qur'ān distinguishes between right and wrong. Therefore, it is "the Discriminator," or **al-Furqān**.

10. As the Ultimate Guide, the Qur'ān often reminds us of the results of doing good deeds or bad actions. This quality gives it the name **al-Dhikr**, "the Reminder."

Some names for the Qur'ān

Al-'Adl	The Justice	Al-Mu'izah	The Sermon
Al-'Ali	The Lofty	Al-Mubārak	The Blessed
Al-'Arabi	The Arabic	Al-Mubīn	The Clear, the Manifest
Al-'Aziz	The Mighty	Al-Muhaimin	The Preserver
Al-'Urwatu'l Wusqā	The Firm Handle	Al-Mukarramah	The Excellent
Al-Amr	The Order	Al-Musaddiq	The Establisher of Truth
Al-Balāgh	The Message	Al-Mutāharah	The Purified
Al-Basā'ir	The Enlightenment	Al-Mutashābih	The Uniform
Al-Bashīr	The Glad Tiding	Al-Qaiyim	The Strong
Al-Bayān	The Explanation	Al-Qasas	The Narrative
Al-Burhān	The Manifest Proof	Al-Qawlul Fasl	The Distinguishing Speech
Al-Bushrā	The Glad Tiding	Al-Qur'ān	The Reading
Al-Furqān	The Discriminator	Al-Wahy	The Inspiration
Al-Habl	The Rope	An-Naba'ul 'Azīm	The Exalted News
Al-Hakīm	The Judge	An-Nadhīr	The Warner
Al-Hasnu'l Hadīth	The Good Saying	An-Nūr	The Light
Al-Hikmah	The Wisdom	Ar-Rahmah	The Mercy
Al-Hudā	The Guidance	Ar-Rūh	The Spirit
Al-Kalām	The Word	As-Shifā'	The Health
Al-Karim	The Good	As-Shuhuf	The Pamphlets
Al-Kitāb	The Book	As-Sidq	The Righteous
Al-Majīd	The Exalted	As-Sirātul Mustaqīm	The Straight Path
Al-Manādi	The Preacher	At-Tanzīl	The Revelation
Al-Marfū'ah	The Exalted	Az-Zikr	The Reminder
Al-Mathāni	The Repetition	Az-Zubūr	The Psalms

11. When we are confused, the Qur'ān clarifies how we should lead our lives. Therefore, Allāh ﷻ named the Book **al-Mubīn**, "the one that makes clear."

12. If a society follows the teachings of the Qur'ān, all of its social diseases will be cured. Based on the teachings of the Qur'ān, Muslims progressed from a tribal community to a large empire within a few decades. This is the power of the Qur'ān, **al-Shifā'**, "the one that heals."

The list above provides several other names that illustrate the objectives of the Qur'ān. Let us take some time to analyze and appreciate the significance of some of these names.

Homework

1. Which of the following is an objective of the Qur'ān?

A. To provide guidance.
B. To distinguish truth from falsehood.
C. To give us hope.
D. To heal spiritual disease.
E. All of the above.

2. One of the objectives of the Qur'ān is to provide guidance. The lesson uses the example of getting from Point A to Point B. How many ways can a person reach Point B if he or she starts from point A and uses the guidance of the Qur'ān?

A. One way.
B. Two ways.
C. Three ways.
D. Seven ways.
E. Many ways.

3. In sūrah al-Baqarah, āyah 2, the Qur'ān says it is guidance for a certain type of people. What type of people are mentioned in the āyah?

A. The sinners.
B. The hypocrites.
C. The Christians.
D. The God-fearing people.
E. The Arabs.

4. In order to receive guidance from the Qur'ān, we are required to do something. What are we required to do?

A. Apply our intelligence.
B. Read the Qur'ān.
C. Follow the message.
D. Pray for guidance.
E. All of the above.

5. The Qur'ān provides guidance to people who do something. Read āyah 31:3. What should people do to receive guidance from the Qur'ān?

____

6. In order to receive and absorb divine guidance, people are required to use many different senses. Read āyah 7:198. Which two senses are mentioned in the āyah?

1. ______________________________

2. ______________________________

7. Read the last āyah of sūrah Yūsuf. Which four things are mentioned in the āyah as objectives of the Qur'ān?

1. ____________________

2. ____________________

3. ____________________

4. ____________________

8. Ayāh 2:170 mentions that when people are asked to follow the guidance, they reply that they would rather follow something else. What do they want to follow?

____

Lessons from Sūrah al-Hujurāt

Objective of the Lesson:

Islam gives tremendous importance to having a strong, harmonious, and cohesive society. However, improper and miscalculated judgments, along with prejudice and wickedness of the soul, often gives rise to social diseases that might destabilize the fabric of a good society. Sūrah Hujurāt presents a few social circumstances that describe when people might behave in a manner that is morally and ethically wrong. The Sūrah also provides solutions to these social diseases. This lesson discusses some of these circumstances and their solutions.

In a previous chapter we studied the Sunan of of Allāh ﷻ—the laws of Allāh ﷻ. In addition to making the laws of operation and management of the universe, Allāh ﷻ has also made rules and regulations about financial, political, religious, social, and other spheres of human life. In addition to these rules and regulations, Allāh ﷻ has also created a large number of guidelines about proper behaviors to follow in certain situations. Sometimes Allāh ﷻ presents a familiar scenario and then provides guidelines to handle the scenario in a manner that is morally and ethically right for human beings. For example, in sūrah Humazah, Allāh ﷻ presents the case of a selfish slanderer and defamer who is concerned with nothing but money. Then He explains what would happen to such a person in the Hereafter. In sūrah Mā'un, Allāh ﷻ condemns those who perform salāt only as a show of their outward piety, but who do not care to feed the poor and are unwilling to offer the smallest form of kindness to others. There are no laws or rules stated in these sūrahs, but clearly, certain type of conduct are strongly discouraged. Such examples are abundantly available in the Qur'ān.

In this chapter, we will discuss certain situations and the proper guidelines to follow when we face these situations. These situations are presented in sūrah Hujurāt, sūrah number 49. The situations mentioned in the sūrah are as common today as they were in the past, when the Qur'ān was being revealed.

Ascertain truth of a report before acting on it

يَٰٓأَيُّهَا ٱلَّذِينَ ءَامَنُوٓاْ إِن جَآءَكُمۡ فَاسِقُۢ بِنَبَإٖ فَتَبَيَّنُوٓاْ أَن تُصِيبُواْ قَوۡمَۢا بِجَهَٰلَةٖ فَتُصۡبِحُواْ عَلَىٰ مَا فَعَلۡتُمۡ نَٰدِمِينَ ٦

O you who believe! if a corrupt person brings you any news, then ascertain fully, lest you should trouble a people in ignorance, then you become repentant for what you did. (49:6)

One of the teachings of sūrah Hujurāt in ayāh 6 is how to act when one receives a critical message. Most people have a tendency to act hastily upon hearing a report that has not been verified. Whether or not the report has serious implications, people tend to reach a conclusion, form an opinion, and sometimes take action. If the person holds some authority—for example, parents, a teacher, an Imām, a leader—hasty action without verifying the report might create a situation for which they will be sorry later.

A believer is required to exercise caution when any news is brought to him or her, particularly when emergency necessitates taking prompt action. This is particularly important if the emergency involves a war or similar crisis. The Qur'ān teaches us to fully ascertain the truth of the news before carrying out the exigencies of war.

When the situation does not involve war, one must verify a report or rumor before relying on it to reach a decision. Hasty action might cause regret for the one taking the action, or it might hurt the person against whom the action is taken. The Messenger ﷺ, as well as every righteous leader of the community, is morally bound to protect the reputation and dignity of every member of the community by carefully investigating the authenticity of news. The person who spreads false news is typified as corrupt (*fāsiq*, lit. a transgressor, one who is wicked) because carrying and spreading false news is equal to spiritual wrongdoing.

Ayāh 6 was revealed shortly after the Muslims defeated the Banū Mustaliq tribe in 627 C.E. After their defeat, the tribe accepted Islam and agreed to pay zakāh. Later, when the Messenger ﷺ sent Walīd ibn 'Uqbah to collect the zakāh, a misunderstanding occurred. Walīd had diskliked Banū Mustaliq since the period of Jāhiliyyah. When Banū Mustaliq heard Walīd was coming to collect zakāh, they came out to greet him. But Walīd became scared of them, thinking they were actually coming to kill him. He turned around and went back to Madīnah. He reported to the Messenger ﷺ that Banū Mustaliq refused to pay zakāh and wanted to kill him. The Messenger ﷺ was angry about it and decided to send an armed delegation. In the meantime, upon seeing Walīd's strange behavior, Banū Mustaliq sent an envoy to the Messenger ﷺ explaining him had happened. They wanted to greet Walīd, but he had turned around and left. After Messenger ﷺ heard the report of both sides, the tension was pacified. Then ayāh 6 was revealed as a lesson for the Messenger ﷺ and the believers.

Interesting Facts

- Banu Mustaliq was an Arab tribe that lived near the Red Sea border of Arabian peninsula.
- Banu Mustaliq were the allies of the Quraish. Muslims defeated Banu Mustaliq in 627 C.E.
- Among the captives was Juwayriya—the daughter of the Mustaliq chief. Later, Rasūlullāh ﷺ married her, as a result of which entire tribe became Muslim.

Take precautions against three vices

وَاعْلَمُوا أَنَّ فِيكُمْ رَسُولَ اللَّهِ ۚ لَوْ يُطِيعُكُمْ فِي كَثِيرٍ مِّنَ الْأَمْرِ لَعَنِتُّمْ وَلَٰكِنَّ اللَّهَ حَبَّبَ إِلَيْكُمُ الْإِيمَانَ
وَزَيَّنَهُ فِي قُلُوبِكُمْ وَكَرَّهَ إِلَيْكُمُ الْكُفْرَ وَالْفُسُوقَ وَالْعِصْيَانَ ۚ أُولَٰئِكَ هُمُ الرَّاشِدُونَ ٧

And you know that there is with you the Rasūl of Allāh. Were he to obey you in most of the affairs, you would surely suffer; but Allāh has endeared the Faith to you, and made it pleasing to your hearts, and He has made hateful to you unbelief and wickedness and disobedience. These are themselves the rightly guided— (49:7)

In general, human beings have many immoral tendencies. In ayāh 7 of sūrah Hujurāt, the Qur'ān mentions three vices—unbelief, wickedness, and disobedience—that lead people to their ruin.

Using the example mentioned in ayāh 6, ayāh 7 explains how the Messenger ﷺ upheld the cohesiveness of the Muslim community. On many issues, the Messenger ﷺ encouraged collective decision-making by his companions, while at other times he exercised his independent judgment, particularly during wars. Numerous wars and war-like situations in which the Messenger ﷺ lived most of his later life was fertile ground for rumors to originate. If he believed and acted upon such rumors or false reports, particularly during war, people would have been lost for such costly mistakes.

Keeping this message in mind, we should remember that non-belief, wickedness, and disobedience are three vices that lead people to their ruin. The Qur'ān disapproves of these vices, and urges believers to make faith the most endearing element of their hearts.

Help the transgressed, not the transgressor

وَإِن طَائِفَتَانِ مِنَ الْمُؤْمِنِينَ اقْتَتَلُوا فَأَصْلِحُوا بَيْنَهُمَا ۖ فَإِن بَغَتْ إِحْدَاهُمَا عَلَى الْأُخْرَىٰ
فَقَاتِلُوا الَّتِي تَبْغِي حَتَّىٰ تَفِيءَ إِلَىٰ أَمْرِ اللَّهِ ۚ فَإِن فَاءَتْ فَأَصْلِحُوا بَيْنَهُمَا بِالْعَدْلِ وَأَقْسِطُوا ۖ إِنَّ
اللَّهَ يُحِبُّ الْمُقْسِطِينَ ٩

And if two parties of the believers fight, then make peace between them. But if one of them transgresses against the other, then you fight that which transgressed, till they return to the command of Allāh. But when they do return, then make peace between them with justice, and act equitably. Allāh certainly loves the equitable ones. (49:9)

The occasion of the revelation of ayāh 9 is said to be a scuffle between the 'Aws and Khazraj tribes, the chief tribes of Madīnah. The ayāh provides general guidelines for believers in all period of times, so the word fight (*qitāl*) is used to mean not only war, but also any dissension, conflict or controversy regarding an opinion, viewpoint or action.

Human beings live in diverse societies where it is entirely possible for disagreements to arise in everyday matters—large or small. Ayāh 9 begins by pointing out: *And if two parties of the believers fight*—thus, the Qur'ān recognizes that even the believers can have misunderstandings and fight. Under such circumstances, the first thing we need to do is make the utmost effort to establish peace between the two parties.

Peace can be established in many different ways—for example, through arbitration, conflict resolutions and diplomatic efforts. In any of these process, four useful steps can be followed: (1) communicate, (2) actively listen to both parties by being objective in the process, (3) review all options, looking for solutions that will benefit both parties, and (4) offer a win-win solution where both parties feel they are the winner.

Often this process of establishing peace is easier said than done. If peace efforts fail, the ayāh states the next step would be to take the side of the transgressed. We may think that the weaker person is the transgressed party and the more powerful person is the transgressor, but this is not always the case. A weak person can also transgress by taking advantage of loopholes in the law. Our stand should be to support the one who is transgressed. The objective of taking a stand is to *make peace between them*, a command repeated in the ayāh, but this time with an added emphasis that it must be done with justice and in an equitable manner.

The Qur'ān reminds us again and again that we must act equitably (4:105; 5:8; 7:29; 11:85; 16:90; 38:26; 55:9) and establish justice, even if we have to oppose our own family.

> *O you who believe! be upholders of justice, bearers of witness for Allāh, even though it be against your own selves, or parents, and relations; if he be rich, or poor, then Allāh is nearer to both of them; therefore do not follow low desires so that you may act equitably. And if you distort, or keep away, then surely Allāh is ever well-Aware of what you do. (4:135).*

All believers are brothers

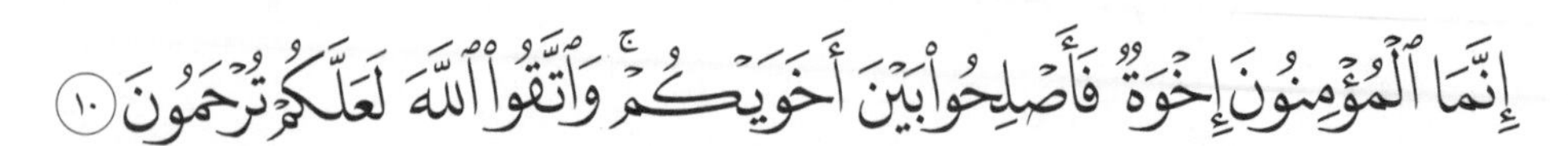

> *The Believers are indeed brothers; therefore make peace between your two brethren, and revere Allāh, that you may be shown mercy. (49:10)*

Use of the word "brother" brings to mind the type of relationship that exists through a blood connection. The blood connection between brothers ties them together in good and bad times. Even if there are minor or major misunderstandings between them, they support and defend one another. Most importantly, they preserve and honor the ties of kinship between them.

In this ayāt, the believers are described as "brothers" of one another. This statement is made with the particle of emphasis *innamā*, giving added weight to the statement. Just as blood-brothers have ties of kinship between them, and strive to support and protect each other, the believers, as brothers, are required to honor similar ties of kinship between them. All believers are part of one Islamic brotherhood, in spite of their differences in language, nationality, and race.

Pay close attention to the wording of the ayāh. It says, *make peace between your two brethren, and revere Allāh.* This implies that when two brothers are in conflict, you have the obligation to intervene. If you do not intervene when you could and should, then you are not obeying Allāh ﷻ.

We should remember that the occurrence of conflicts in society is not an indication of something wrong in society because these are tests for the believers. But when conflict arises and no one recognizes the conflict, and no one feels the obligation to mediate to solve the conflict in accordance with fairness and justice, then there is something wrong with society.

There are times in life when we all need some help—some mediation when we are in conflict with others. But if there is no attempt to resolve the conflict and honor the sense of brotherhood, then hearts rage, anger boils, and violence and hatred increases.

Respect the dignity of others

يَٰٓأَيُّهَا ٱلَّذِينَ ءَامَنُوا۟ لَا يَسْخَرْ قَوْمٌ مِّن قَوْمٍ عَسَىٰٓ أَن يَكُونُوا۟ خَيْرًا مِّنْهُمْ وَلَا نِسَآءٌ مِّن نِّسَآءٍ عَسَىٰٓ أَن يَكُنَّ خَيْرًا مِّنْهُنَّ ۖ وَلَا تَلْمِزُوٓا۟ أَنفُسَكُمْ وَلَا تَنَابَزُوا۟ بِٱلْأَلْقَٰبِ ۖ بِئْسَ ٱلِٱسْمُ ٱلْفُسُوقُ بَعْدَ ٱلْإِيمَٰنِ ۚ وَمَن لَّمْ يَتُبْ فَأُو۟لَٰٓئِكَ هُمُ ٱلظَّٰلِمُونَ ﴿١١﴾

O you who believe! let not one people laugh at another people, perchance they may be better than them; and nor let women at women, perchance these women may be better than them. And do not slander your own people; nor call one another by nicknames. An unflattering name is ungodliness after belief. And whoever does not turn, then these are themselves the wrongdoers. (49:11)

As in other examples, the ayāh begins by drawing the attention of the believers: *O you who believe!* The ayāh prohibits Muslim men and women from ridiculing one another. The act of ridiculing another is distasteful conduct, but the reason mentioned here is the one who is being ridiculed is likely to be morally superior to the one who ridicules. The word *sakhira* (سخر, literally, to mock, to laugh at, to make fun of). Ridiculing may be verbal, it can also be a gesture, or both.

Pay attention to the wording of the ayāh. It does not restrict this guidance to men only. Women are separately addressed to emphasize that from Allāh's ﷻ perspective, the value of a person is not restricted by gender, wealth, nationality, religion or race.

Do not slander your own people. The distinction between men and women is dissolved halfway through the ayāh, as it now uses the word *anfusakum*, meaning "yourselves." Thus the act of ridiculing others actually slanders oneself. How? By slandering others, one has actually displeased Allāh ﷻ and debased oneself.

After prohibiting ridiculing and slandering—both are clearly acts of showing contempt for others—the ayāh goes on to prohibit name-calling. Calling others a mean name is another form of showing contempt for others. Name-calling can be done verbally and through gestures. We should understand that ridiculing and slandering others may give rise to suspicion and hatred, while name-calling openly ignites animosity and disgust. Both are unacceptable to Allāhﷻ.

An evil name is an [act of] ungodliness after belief. This means that after becoming a believer, one should not only avoid all forms of wicked acts, but also drive away any thoughts of wickedness from one's mind. One should avoid an "evil name" (*bi'sa-l ismu*)—that is, the word itself or the idea of wickedness. In Islam, belief and wickedness are two disjointed acts, poles apart from each other.

If one unintentionally, or due to human weakness, commits one of the acts prohibited in the ayāh, then he or she should express repentance to Allāhﷻ. Only those who refuse to express repentance will be considered wrongdoers.

Avoid suspicion and backbiting

يَٰٓأَيُّهَا ٱلَّذِينَ ءَامَنُوا۟ ٱجْتَنِبُوا۟ كَثِيرًا مِّنَ ٱلظَّنِّ إِنَّ بَعْضَ ٱلظَّنِّ إِثْمٌ ۖ وَلَا تَجَسَّسُوا۟ وَلَا يَغْتَب
بَّعْضُكُم بَعْضًا ۚ أَيُحِبُّ أَحَدُكُمْ أَن يَأْكُلَ لَحْمَ أَخِيهِ مَيْتًا فَكَرِهْتُمُوهُ ۚ وَٱتَّقُوا۟ ٱللَّهَ ۚ إِنَّ ٱللَّهَ
تَوَّابٌ رَّحِيمٌ ﴿١٢﴾

O you who believe! shun most of the suspicions, because some suspicions are sins indeed; and do not spy; and do not back-bite one another. Do any one of you like to eat the flesh of his dead brother? Surely you loathe it! Therefore, revere Allāh. Certainly Allāh is oft-Returning, most Rewarding. (49:12)

Again, the ayāh begins by drawing the attention of the believers: *O you who believe!* It does not befit the believers to prejudge other believers or have prejudices against them. Unfounded suspicion damages the stability of a family, society, and nation. Some legitimate suspicion is allowed, because without careful and intelligent reservations, some social or political evils will go unnoticed. However, snooping into the affairs of others is strictly prohibited. The act of spying takes the suspicion one step further. Suspicion is the root of all mistrust.

Back-biting is a common tendency of men and women, but the Qur'ān strictly prohibits such conduct. The Qur'ān offers the analogy of a back-biter and a predator. Upon smelling a dead animal, a predator approaches it, and feeling secure, the predator starts nibbling on the flesh. The Qur'ān presents the imagery of the victim as a dead animal, whose flesh is devoured by the predator with shameless pride and a sense of immunity from the consequences of the action.

The end of the ayāh calls upon the believers to fear Allāhﷻ and refrain from committing the acts forbidden in this chapter. However, if at any time they commit such prohibited actions, then they must turn in repentance to Allāh ﷻ, for *He is oft-Returning, most-Rewarding.*

Achieve taqwā—the determinant of a true believer

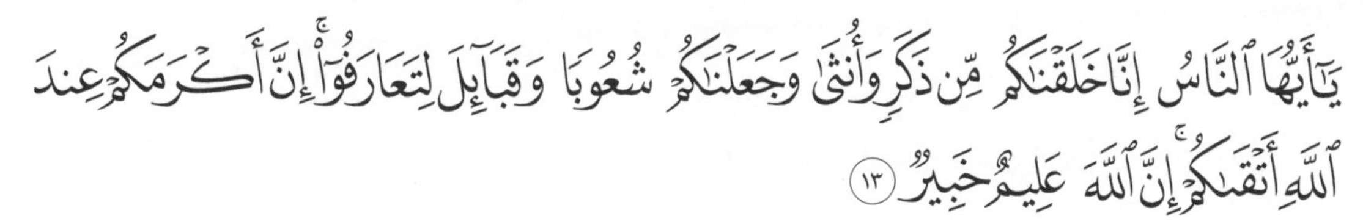

O you mankind! We have surely created you out of a male and a female, and We have made you into nations and tribes that you may recognize one another. Surely the noblest of you in the presence of Allāh is the most reverential of you. Truly Allāh is all-Knowing, all-Aware. (40:13)

All the verses in this chapter address the believers except this ayāh, which addresses all of mankind. According to the Qur'ān, all human beings are descendants from a common source. Through the forces of speciation, Allāh ﷻ made His creation diverse in terms of looks, language and culture, and then further divided humans into tribes and families. This was done so that people could establish their identities and deal with one another in a harmonious manner. Diversity was not intended to divide us but to help us create attachments with one another and recognize each other. Thus, diversity was intended to be functional criterion, nothing more.

The ayāh points out that the cultural, social or anthropological superiority of one nation or tribe is meaningless to Allāh ﷻ. To Him, the superiority of human beings depends upon piety and god consciousness (*taqwā*).

In conclusion, we can see that all the verses discussed in this chapter demonstrate how much importance Islam gives to having a strong, harmonious, and cohesive society. These verses provide a cure for some prevalent diseases in our society. The cures suggested in these verses are from the Almighty, and these suggestions are the best way to achieve healthy social cohesion.

Homework

1. Which sūrah in the Qur'ān discusses a selfish slanderer and defamer who is concerned with nothing but money?

A. Sūrah Inshirah.
B. Sūrah Humazah.
C. Sūrah an-Naziat.
D. Sūrah 'Abasa.
E. Sūrah Balad.

2. According to the ayāh 6 in sūrah Hujurat, we need to ascertain the truth of news conveyed by certain type of person. What type of person is mentioned in the ayāh?

A. A spy.
B. A beggar.
C. A traveler.
D. A businessperson.
E. A corrupt person.

3. What incident led to the revelation of ayāh 6 in sūrah Hujurat, where believers are advised to check the truth of news conveyed to them?

A. An invasion of Banu Qurayzah.
B. An attack on the Byzantine army.
C. News brought by a Jewish traveler.
D. A failed attempt to collect zakāt from Banu Mustaliq.
E. A dispute between two married couples from Banu Mustaliq.

4. What three immoral vices are mentioned in ayāh 7 in sūrah Hujurat, that lead people to their ruin?

A. Nonbelief, greed, and excessive hoarding.
B. Greed, pride, and backbiting.
C. Wickedness, homicide, and spying.
D. Nonbelief, wickedness, and disobedience.
E. Rebellion, corruption, and self-glorification.

5. A scuffle between two tribes led to the revelation of ayāh 9 in sūrah Hujurat. What were these two tribes?

A. ____.

B. ____.

6. According to sūrah Hujurat, why did Allāh ﷻ create nations and tribes in the world?

A. To help them maintain their country.
B. To show divine creativity.
C. To establish separate government and leadership.
D. To help people recognize each other.
E. To stabilize the nations of the world.

7. When two parties are involved in a serious dispute or fight, believers are required to establish peace between the two parties. In order to do this, the Qur'ān recommends taking four steps. What are these four steps?

1. ____.
2. ____.
3. ____.
4. ____.

8. Read ayāh 49:11 in the Qur'ān. What is the specific message of the ayāh?

A. Maintain integrity.
B. Uphold community relationships.
C. Support each other with money and labor.
D. Achieve taqwā.
E. Respect the dignity of others.

9. According to the Qur'ān, what is the main criterion used to distinguish a superior human beings?

A. His or her ethnic status.
B. His or her social status and education.
C. His or her religious commitment.
D. His or her level of taqwā.
E. His or her compassion for other human beings.

True Piety: *A Synthesis of Belief, Practice, and Conduct*

Objective of the Lesson:

The Qur'ān has a beautiful ayāh in sūrah Baqarah that summarizes the meaning of piety or righteousness. The ayāh points out piety is not about certain mechanical, ritual function believers are accustomed to, but it is much more. In doing so, the Qur'ān explains piety has two major aspects—belief and right practice. The lesson discusses the Qur'ānic interpretation of true piety.

If someone would like a complete overview of Islam from a single ayāh in the Qur'ān, he or she will find it in sūrah Baqarah, ayāh 177. This ayāh is sometimes called "the verse of piety," or "*Ayātul Birr.*" The reason this ayāh is known by this name is because "piety" or "righteousness" is the central theme of the ayāh.

Webster dictionary defines piety as "the quality or state of being pious," or as "an act inspired by piety." Oxford dictionary defines piety as "the quality of being religious or reverent." The Arabic word *birr* carries a much deeper meaning. The word *birr* has an essence of carrying out an obligation faithfully. For example, the word is used to denote such actions as fulfilling an oath, keeping a promise, or upholding someone's trust. The word also used to denote doing a meritorious duty, for example treating parents with compassion, helping a destitute and so forth. All these actions require commitment, honesty and faithful discharge of duty. *Birr* is therefore, not a dry, callous, or spiritless duty done for the sake of doing. We will see from the rest of the lesson that *birr*, as explained in the Qur'ān, is a true piety reflected through a synthesis of right belief, right practice and right conduct. Before proceeding further, let us read the ayāh 2:177.

۞ لَّيْسَ ٱلْبِرَّ أَن تُوَلُّوا۟ وُجُوهَكُمْ قِبَلَ ٱلْمَشْرِقِ وَٱلْمَغْرِبِ وَلَٰكِنَّ ٱلْبِرَّ مَنْ ءَامَنَ بِٱللَّهِ
وَٱلْيَوْمِ ٱلْءَاخِرِ وَٱلْمَلَٰٓئِكَةِ وَٱلْكِتَٰبِ وَٱلنَّبِيِّـۧنَ وَءَاتَى ٱلْمَالَ عَلَىٰ حُبِّهِۦ ذَوِى ٱلْقُرْبَىٰ وَٱلْيَتَٰمَىٰ
وَٱلْمَسَٰكِينَ وَٱبْنَ ٱلسَّبِيلِ وَٱلسَّآئِلِينَ وَفِى ٱلرِّقَابِ وَأَقَامَ ٱلصَّلَوٰةَ وَءَاتَى ٱلزَّكَوٰةَ
وَٱلْمُوفُونَ بِعَهْدِهِمْ إِذَا عَٰهَدُوا۟ ۖ وَٱلصَّٰبِرِينَ فِى ٱلْبَأْسَآءِ وَٱلضَّرَّآءِ وَحِينَ ٱلْبَأْسِ ۗ أُو۟لَٰٓئِكَ
ٱلَّذِينَ صَدَقُوا۟ ۖ وَأُو۟لَٰٓئِكَ هُمُ ٱلْمُتَّقُونَ ﴿١٧٧﴾

There is no piety in that you turn your faces towards the East and the West, but piety is in him whoever believes in Allāh and the Last Day, and the angels, and the scripture, and the nabis; and who gives wealth out of love for Him to the near of kin, and to the orphans, and the needy, and the wayfarers, and the beggars, and to those in captivity; and who establishes the Salāt, and pays the Zakāt; and those who fulfill their contract when they make a contract; and those who persevere in hardship and injury, and during stress. These are those who have proven truthful; and these are themselves the god-fearing. (2:177)

What piety is not

The ayāh opens with a statement describing what piety is not about. It is not about turning one's face east or west—that is, facing one or another qiblah at the time of salāt. The issue of qiblah became a contested topic in 624 C.E., when a revelation asked the Muslims to face the direction of the Ka'bah. The performance of daily salāt had already been made obligatory during the late Makkah period. Muslims had been performing salāt facing the direction of Jerusalem—making it their qiblah. Muslims continued this practice after arriving in Madīnah. The Jewish community took pride in noticing the Muslims venerate their own holy place—Jerusalem—and this gave them a sense of superiority over the Muslims. But a revelation asking the Muslims to make the Ka'bah their qiblah suddenly damaged Jewish pride. The Jewish people became the most vocal critics of this decision. In response to their criticism, the Qur'ān points out that all directions belong to Him, and He is free to change the direction of prayer from one direction to another.

The opening statement not only admonishes the Jewish community, but also the Muslims. Just because the Ka'bah has now became their qiblah, they should not feel complacent in facing the direction of the Ka'bah, because there is more meaning involved to it than merely facing a particular direction. Facing a particular direction is only an outward motion. There is much

Points to Remember

The qiblah is the direction of the Ka'bah. Muslims face the direction of the Ka'bah during prayer.

Originally Muslims faced the direction of Masjid al-Aqsa in Jerusalem during their prayers.

After his migration to Madīnah, the Messenger ﷺ continued to face Jerusalem during prayers.

In 624 C.E., 17 months after migration, during the dhuhr prayer in a masjid, a revelation was sent asking the believers to make the Ka'bah the qiblah.

Upon receiving the revelation, Rasūlullāh ﷺ turned toward the Ka'bah, while he was in the middle of the dhuhr prayer. This masjid where the incident happened later came to be known as "the Masjid al-Qiblatain," or the Masjid with two Qiblah.

more to religion than outward or superficial ritual. If the Muslims think that they achieved piety simply because God appointed a qiblah for them, they are mistaken. Piety is not about mechanical, outward motions. It is about synthesis of right belief, right practice, and right conduct. This point is further illustrated in the rest of the ayāh.

Points to Ponder

If there are two young men in front of us—one wearing jeans and a shirt, and the other wearing a Middle Eastern white thobe and a black and white keffiyeh on his head—most of us would tend to think the second person is more religious. The truth may be just the opposite, or it may be that both are equally religious or non-religious. However, we tend to make quick decisions based on external show or appearance.

The first element: Right belief

After pointing out that piety is not about certain mechanical ritual functions, the ayāh proceeds to name the first element of piety—right belief—that includes five articles of faith.

> *...virtue is in him whoever believes in Allāh and the Last Day, and the angels, and the scripture, and the nabis...*

These five articles define the faith of a Muslim. The elements of piety relating to faith are as follows:

1. Belief in Allāh عَزَّ وَجَلَّ by acknowledging His oneness and by submitting to His will;
2. Belief in the Hereafter and being held accountable for every deed done in this world, and consequently receiving due recompense;
3. Belief in angels who are entrusted with various responsibilities, particularly bringing revelations to the messengers and inspiring humankind in general;
4. Belief in the divine books, primarily the Qur'ān, but also to the divine origin of all earlier genuine books; and
5. Belief in all the messengers of the world, whether or not they are mentioned by name in the Qur'ān.

The second element: Right practice

After stating the first element of piety, the ayāh now focuses on the second element of piety—right practice. Right practice includes three sub-elements: the use of one's financial resources, the two most important religious duties in Islam—salāt and zakāt, and fulfilling contractual agreements.

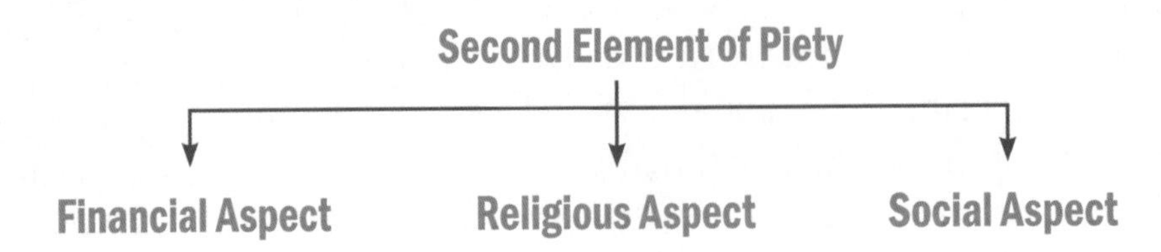

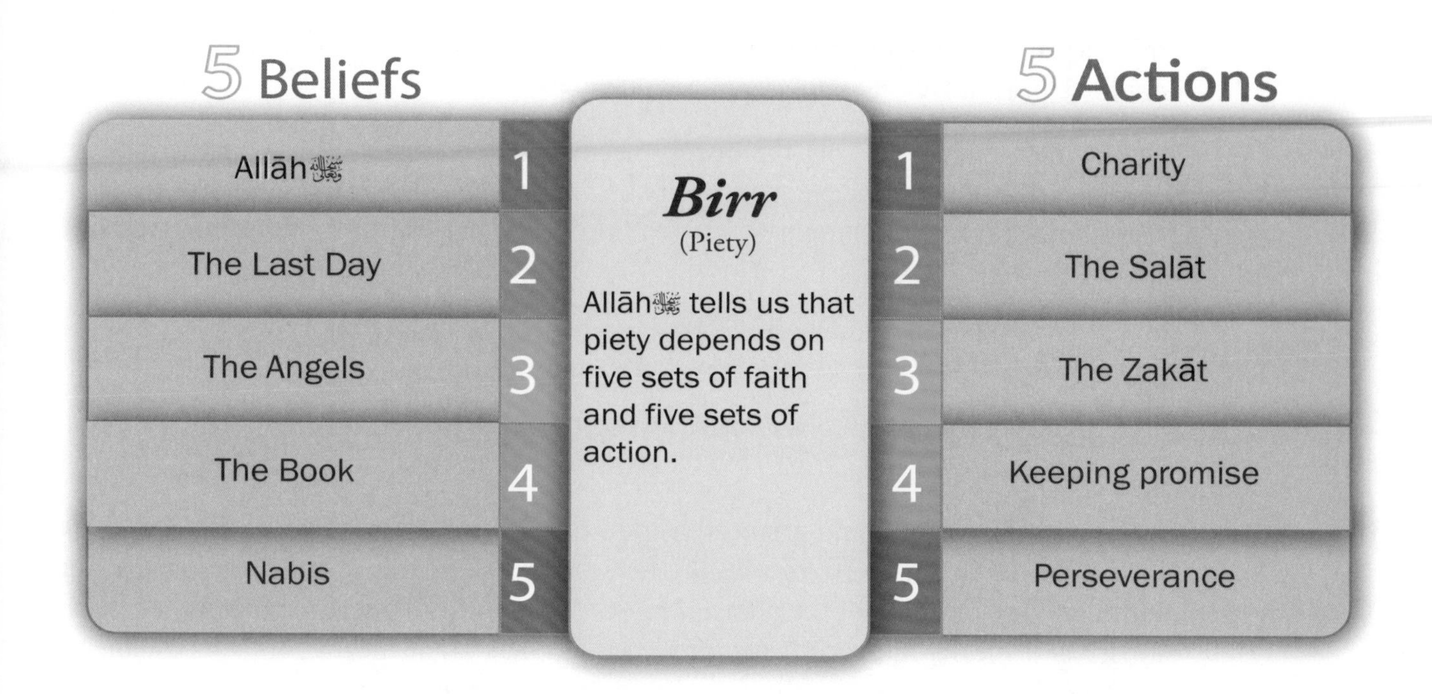

...and who gives wealth out of love for Him to the near of kin, and to the orphans, and the needy, and the wayfarers, and the beggars, and to those in captivity; and who establishes the Salāt, and pays the Zakāt; and those who fulfill their contract when they make a contract...

In the first element, the ayāh focused on faith, which is an abstract, inner thought. Islam always teaches faith alone will not suffice until one translates faith into righteous action. For this reason, many verses speak of righteous deeds immediately after belief. For example,

those who believe and do good

Financial aspect: In the above ayāh, in translating faith into action, the short command "do good" is expanded into three broad aspects. The first aspect concerns the use of financial resources. Here, spending wealth does not mean gratifying personal desires by means of extravagance. The focus is to spend wealth in a manner that directly benefits some of the prescribed beneficiaries. These beneficiaries, in order of preference, are: (1) needy close relatives, (2) orphans, (3) needy people, (4) travelers, (5) beggars, and (6) prisoners.

Before we discuss each category of people, let us understand the phrase: *who gives wealth out of love for Him*. Some commentators translated the word *hubbihi* as "love of it," implying the phrase means "in spite of love for it," that is, love for money. This version indicates people's love for wealth is not necessarily an evil motive, rather it can be a source of much good. Love for wealth is quite natural, and having wealth is not blameworthy, as long as people remember to use wealth to benefit the poor. But a majority of the commentators translated the word as "love for Him," that is, they spend out love for Allāhﷻ.

The first beneficiary on the list is needy close relatives. This is prescribed in consideration of the principle that charity begins at home. This command is repeated in several other āyāt, for example:

وَءَاتِ ذَا ٱلْقُرْبَىٰ حَقَّهُۥ وَٱلْمِسْكِينَ وَٱبْنَ ٱلسَّبِيلِ وَلَا تُبَذِّرْ تَبْذِيرًا ﴿٢٦﴾

And give to the near of kin his due, and to the needy and the wayfarer, and do not squander wastefully. (17:26)

The command to extend financial help to the close relatives is repeated in āyāt 2:83, 215; 4:36; 16:90; 24:22; 30:38 as well. The word *qurbā* literally means "relationship," or "affinity." The meaning of the phrase *dhil qurbā* varies from one jurist to another. Most jurist say it means "near kin," however, many others say it means "one's fellow men," because of universal values reflected in this and similar āyāt.

The next category of people to whom Muslims should extend financial help is orphans—particularly those who are underage, have no skill to earn a living, and depend on others for their overall welfare. Orphans should not be treated as burdens, but should be cared for just like close relatives. In the past, societies typically placed orphans living in one's household or in the same village. For this reason, welfare of orphans is mentioned immediately after the welfare of close relatives.

The needy people (*masākīn*, pl.) are not to be confused with beggars. Needy people have some resources, but they are not able to earn a living. From their appearance, it is difficult to tell they are needy. One might think they are rich because they do not ask for help. However, it is possible to recognize their difficult financial position from looking at their faces.[2:273] For example, a farmer with 100 acres of crop land but three years of draught leaves him with no earnings. What good is the land if there is no income from it? In another example, a man is the only income earner in the house, but he falls sick and is unable to work for an extended period of time. One must recognize a needy person in society and help him or her, as this is part of achieving piety.

The expression *ibn as-sabīl* (lit. son of the road) describes any person who is away from home and stranded due to lack of money, a job or a political reason. Today if a person is stranded in a foreign land due to lack of money, transferring money to the person electronically is possible, yet there might be situations when a traveller needs financial help. The traveller might not be able to communicate with his or her family to send money, or the family might not be in a position to send money. Under these circumstances, one must help the traveler who is stranded due to lack of money,

The word *sā'ilīna* (lit. those who ask) refers to those who actually ask for help or money. In other words, they are the beggars. Just as needy people deserve help, the beggars too have a right on the wealth of the affluent people. When beggars ask for money or help, we are obligated to give them. However, the beggars should not be

Time to Review

1. What is the Qur'ānic meaning of the word miskin?
2. Why does the Qur'ān uses the word "neck" to describe the slaves?
3. What are some of the meanings of the word ibn as-sabil in today's context? What problems do present-day ibn as-sabil face?

tempted with liberal alms making them take up begging as a profession. The Qur'ān teaches us to cooperate in riotousness and taqwā, but not in sin and transgression.[5:2]

The word *riqāb* (lit. a neck) is a metaphor for a slave in the sense that the yoke of slavery hangs on the neck of the person. The expression *fi-r riqāb* denotes freeing or ransoming of a slave. By including the act of freeing or ransoming a slave in the list of essential acts of piety, the Qur'ān indicates the abolition of slavery is one of the social objectives of Islam. The Qur'ān and the sunnah of the Messenger ﷺ particularly stresses freeing of a slave. It is considered a meritorious act to atone for a sin (4:92; 58:3; 90:13).

Religious aspect: The second sub-element of right practice is performing the two most important rituals in Islam—salāt and zakāt. Salāt is a form of worship that shows submission to God on one had, and on the other, it is a tool to benefit the worshipper. As mentioned in ayāh 29:45, *Surely the salāt restrains from indecency and evil*. True piety cannot be achieved by neglecting salāt.

The Qur'ān stresses salāt as a duty that needs to be established rather than merely observed. The root word *qāma* means "to stand still," "to stand firm," "to observe," "to keep up," "to institute" or "to appoint." Therefore, in order to achieve true piety, one should not only observe the devotional dedication in its true spirit, but also encourage others to do the same.

One of the right practices of achieving true piety is doing work that benefits others. Giving zakāt is one meritorious action that directly benefits poor people and serves other social causes. Zakāt, a mandatory act of charity, is obligatory for people who have surplus income. In this ayāh, zakāt is mentioned separately from spending one's wealth on close relatives, orphans, and others, because if spending on those categories of people are deemed voluntary, then linking it with zakāt makes it obligatory. Furthermore, paying zakāt can fund social causes that are not mentioned in the ayāh.

The Qur'ān frequently mentions salāt and zakāt together because salāt is the elemental form of worshipping Allāh ﷻ, and doing so displays one's spiritual responsibility, while giving zakāt is the person's social responsibility. Salāt purifies one's soul while spending purifies one's possessions. Giving zakāt could very well be categorized under the social aspect, but we categorize it here under the religious aspect because the Qur'ān frequently refers to salāt and zakāt together.

Social aspect: After stating the religious aspect of piety, the ayāh states that fulfilling one's commitment is part of achieving true piety. The word used here is *'ahd*, which literally means "to protect" or "to care for something." Therefore, a promise that should be fulfilled is called *ahd.*

...and those who fulfill their contract when they make a contract...

A commitment made to fellow human beings is considered a commitment made to God. The resolution can also be made to society or to oneself. Thus, the word *'ahd* carries the implication of the word "covenant," which God makes with human beings. The Arabic particle *idhā*, translated as "when" has the force of the conjunction "once"—that is, "as soon as," or "after." Thus the ayāh implies that as soon as people make a commitment or resolution, first they are aware of the responsibility attached to the commitment, and second, they are obligated to fulfill the commitment. Only through proper fulfilment of the commitment can they be considered on the path of achieving true piety.

The third element: Right conduct

Towards the end of ayāh 2:177, three qualities are mentioned. These are classified under the right conduct expected of those who wish to achieve true piety.

وَٱلصَّٰبِرِينَ فِي ٱلۡبَأۡسَآءِ وَٱلضَّرَّآءِ وَحِينَ ٱلۡبَأۡسِۗ

...and those who persevere in hardship and injury, and during stress...

The clause requires people to remain steadfast or persevere during three critical times in life:

1. In times of hardship—for example, hunger, setback, poverty, a financial stress, emotional trauma, and so forth.
2. During illness—for example, a chronic ailment, physical disability or any form of illness that causes pain and suffering.
3. During war—the word *b'asi* means "stress," but in classical Arabic it is also used to mean "war."

From the analysis above we can see that Qur'ānic piety is not an abstract concept, but a visible quality in some people. Thus, if someone wants to know the meaning of piety, instead of looking in the dictionary, he or she should look at those people who are the embodiment of piety.

The last word in ayāh 2:177 is *muttaqūn*, which is translated as "God-fearing." The entire ayāh discusses the qualities of people who are the embodiment of piety, yet their another feature is God-fearingness. Instead of simply translating the word *muttaqūn* as pious, the action of piety is connected with being God-fearing—both qualities complement each other.

Homework

1. In order to explain the meaning of true piety, ayāh 2:177 in the Qur'ān mentions that piety is not bout turning one's face in two directions. Which two directions are mentioned?

A. North and south.
B. Directions of Makkah and Jerusalem.
C. East and west.
D. Directions of Makkah and Madīnah.
E. Directions of heavens and earth.

2. In which year was the Qiblah established as the direction of the Ka'bah?

A. In 622 C.E.
B. In 624 C.E.
C. In 625 C.E.
D. In 626 C.E.
E. In 628 C.E.

3. What is the overall message of true piety as described out in ayāh 2:177 in the Qur'ān?

A. The importance of the direction of prayer.
B. The synthesis of right belief, right practice, and right conduct.
C. The spread of Islam in all directions.
D. Reducing the importance of Jerusalem as the Qiblah.
E. Distinguishing between true and false religions.

4. What is the significance of the second element of true piety as pointed out in ayāh 2:177 in the Qur'ān?

A. To explain that Islam is the true religion.
B. To explain that salāt and zakāt are important.
C. To emphasize that faith must translate into righteous action.
D. To demonstrate how to perform righteous actions.
E. To explain the five articles of faith.

5. Ayāh 2:177 in the Qur'ān details the financial aspects of true piety. According to the ayāh, who should be the first two beneficiaries of our charity?

1. ____.

2. ____.

6. According to the Qur'ān, who is an ibn as-sabīl?

A. A son born on the street.
B. A traveller.
C. A person who is in dire need of money.
D. A beggar on the street.
E. A slave waiting to be freed from bondage.

7. Ayāh 2:177 in the Qur'ān describes the social aspect of true piety. According to the ayāh, what should be fulfilled?

A. One's commitment.
B. One's religious duties.
C. One's duty to close relatives.
D. One's obligation to traveler.
E. One's obligation to one's parents.

8. Ayāh 2:177 in the Qur'ān describes the social aspect of true piety. The lesson mentions three critical times we must persevere in life. What are the three critical times?

1. ______________________________.
2. ______________________________.
3. ______________________________.

Ayātul Qurʾsi: *The Throne Verse*

Objective of the Lesson:

The Throne Verse is one of the greatest verses in the Qur'ān. It describes God's action, knowledge, majesty, power and dominion. Many considers this ayāh the equivalent of one-third of the Qur'ān because monotheism is the main theme of the ayāh. This lesson discusses the meaning of the ayāh in detail.

If someone would like to choose a single ayāh in the Qur'ān that describes God's action, knowledge, majesty, power, and dominion over the universe, he or she would have to choose ayāh 255 in sūrah Baqarah. This ayāh is sometimes called as "the Throne Verse," or "*Ayātul Qurʾsi.*" The ayāh is known by this name because *qurʾsi*, or "throne" is the central theme of the ayāh.

Many theologians consider the Throne Verse the greatest ayāh in the Qur'ān. Muslims memorize the ayāh and recite it on a variety of occasions. It is a favorite ayāh for Muslim calligraphers. Artists add inscriptions of the ayāh on a variety of objects, and these objects become welcome decor in many Muslim houses.

Although the central theme in ayāh 2:255 is God's throne, the ayāh contains several secondary themes. When we analyze all these themes, we will understand this ayāh is indeed the greatest ayāh about the Exalted One. Scholars say the gravity of this ayāh is equivalent to one-third of the Qur'ān because monotheism is the main theme of the ayāh. The other two themes, as we will learn, are the prophecy of Judgment Day and life after death.

The Throne verse

Before we proceed further, let us read the ayāh. We will refer to specific words and phrases in the ayāh throughout the chapter.

ٱللَّهُ لَآ إِلَٰهَ إِلَّا هُوَ ٱلْحَىُّ ٱلْقَيُّومُ ۚ لَا تَأْخُذُهُۥ سِنَةٌ وَلَا نَوْمٌ ۚ لَّهُۥ مَا فِى ٱلسَّمَٰوَٰتِ وَمَا فِى
ٱلْأَرْضِ ۗ مَن ذَا ٱلَّذِى يَشْفَعُ عِندَهُۥٓ إِلَّا بِإِذْنِهِۦ ۚ يَعْلَمُ مَا بَيْنَ أَيْدِيهِمْ وَمَا خَلْفَهُمْ ۖ وَلَا
يُحِيطُونَ بِشَىْءٍ مِّنْ عِلْمِهِۦٓ إِلَّا بِمَا شَآءَ ۚ وَسِعَ كُرْسِيُّهُ ٱلسَّمَٰوَٰتِ وَٱلْأَرْضَ ۖ وَلَا يَـُٔودُهُۥ حِفْظُهُمَا ۚ
وَهُوَ ٱلْعَلِىُّ ٱلْعَظِيمُ ﴿٢٥٥﴾

Allāh—there is no deity but He, the ever-Living, the self-Subsisting; slumber does not overtake Him nor sleep. To Him belongs whatever is in the heavens and whatsoever is on the earth. Who is there to intercede in His presence except with His authority? He knows what is in front of them and what is behind them. And they do not encompass anything of His knowledge except what He pleases. His Throne of Power extends over the heavens and the earth, and the management of these both does not tire Him; and He is the most High, the Supreme. (2:255)

Allāh—there is no deity but He

The ayāh begins by making a fundamental statement about God by God—*there is no deity but He*. This formulaic phrase is identical to the Islamic phrase used to declare faith—*Lā ilāha illā llāh*—there is no god but God. This phrase appears in other verses in the Qur'ān as well. For example, in verses 2:163 and 3:2.

وَإِلَٰهُكُمْ إِلَٰهٌ وَٰحِدٌ ۖ لَّآ إِلَٰهَ إِلَّا هُوَ ٱلرَّحْمَٰنُ ٱلرَّحِيمُ ﴿١٦٣﴾

And your God is the One God, there is no god but He, the most Gracious, the most Rewarding. (2:163)

This simple, much-repeated statement in ayāh 2:255 and similar statements affirm that no being, object, power, or concept other than Allāhﷻ can be a deity. The Godhead of Allāhﷻ is such that it cannot admit plurality of the divine in any form whatsoever. Therefore God cannot be reduced to images, idols, or statues. The concept of His representation in human or other terrestrial forms—for example, baboon and lion gods of ancient Egypt; cow, boar, monkey, owl or hundreds of other animal gods of Hindus; a dragon god of Mesopotamia and China—is absolutely impossible. For this reason, He is the only one worthy of worship. There is no god but He—therefore, He cannot beget nor is He begotten.[112:3] Plurality of Godhead is not an indication of any imperfection in His Godhead, but not allowing plurality is unique with Him. This key theme of the oneness of God is conveyed in each of the ten sub-elements of this ayāh. These ten sub-elements are listed at the end of the lesson.

Ever-Living, self-Subsisting

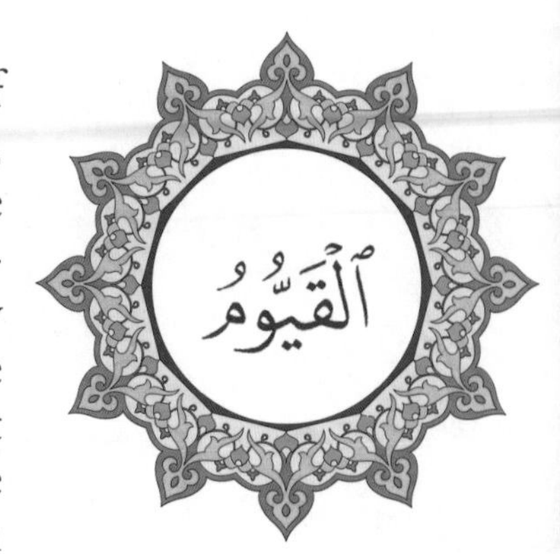

Allāh ﷻ is a living being in the sense that He exists and will exist by Himself in His own right. He cannot die. None of the Aztec, Babylonian, Celtic, Chinese, Egyptian, Greek, Hellenistic, Hindu, Roman or other deities are alive or self-subsisting. Jesus, Mary, Buddha, and Krishna are neither living nor self-subsisting. The limitations of these deities, only prove that there is no deity but Him. The word *qayyum* means one who is self-sustaining as well as one who is a maintainer, that is, one who manages affairs. All other deities cannot sustain themselves, nor can they sustain others. Even if alleged human-gods are credited with sustaining others, they cannot do so without receiving help from external sources. In other words, *al-qayyum* is one whose existence is absolute, whereas the existence of everything else is contingent upon Him.

Slumber does not overtake Him nor sleep

Sleep and slumber are key biological needs of the human body, without which a person would exhaust all or most motor functions and become hysterical. During slumber, one is partially unconscious, and during sleep one is metaphorically dead. During sleep, our body heals itself and restores its chemical balance. The brain forges new connections and improves memory retention. Sleep helps us rejuvenate and re-energize.

Allāh ﷻ does not need to rejuvenate, re-energize, or restore His chemical balance. Sleep and slumber would not only impair Allāh's ﷻ ability to sustain Himself, but also impair His ability to sustain the universe. The purpose of stating that Allāh ﷻ is above and beyond any of the human biological functions is to emphasize His uniqueness. It also attests that Allāh ﷻ is never unmindful or neglectful of His creations.

Interesting Facts

During sleep, the body heals itself and restores its chemical balance. The brain forges new connections and improves memory retention.

Lack of adequate sleep can cause serious problems. The long-term effects of sleep deprivation can create more serious health issues.

Lack of sleep can affect judgment, learning ability, and the ability to retain information. It can also cause serious accidents and injury.

Chronic sleep deprivation can cause obesity, diabetes, a stroke, heart problems, suicidal thoughts, and early death.

To Him belongs everything

Allāh ﷻ is the creator, sustainer, and controller of all things in the universe. Therefore, it is logical that whatever is in the heavens and on the earth belongs to Him. Because of this, it is impossible for other alleged deities to claim ownership of any part of the universe, let alone control any part of it.

This point is reiterated throughout the Qur'ān. Sometimes this concept is poised as a question to the reader, for example:

أَلَمْ تَعْلَمْ أَنَّ ٱللَّهَ لَهُۥ مُلْكُ ٱلسَّمَٰوَٰتِ وَٱلْأَرْضِ

Do you not know that surely Allāh,—to Him belongs the sovereignty of the heavens and the earth? (2:107; 5:40)

أَلَآ إِنَّ لِلَّهِ مَا فِى ٱلسَّمَٰوَٰتِ وَٱلْأَرْضِ ۖ

Is it not that to Allāh belongs whatsoever is in the heavens and the earth? (24:64)

At other times, the Qur'ān simply states: *To Him belongs whatever is in the heavens and whatever is on the earth.* The purpose of stating this fact over and over again is simple: We must believe there is one God in the universe and He is in control of everything. The idea that some subordinate god or gods manage a particular part of the universe is not only foolish but also impossible. Ironically, a vast majority of people in the world adamantly subscribe to this false notion.

Who can intercede with Him?

The theory of intercession on Judgment Day is a much-discussed and misunderstood topic in Islamic theology. A large number of Muslims pin their hopes on receiving salvation through the process of intercession. In fact a practice has emerged in many parts of the world where people surrender to religious authorities who are believed to have some power to act as an intercessor.

Before discussing the issue of intercession, we need to understand the basic purpose of Judgment Day—to reward each soul for what it has earned in a just and equitable manner. The Qur'ān says:

This Day every soul will be rewarded according to what it earned. No injustice this Day! Surely Allāh is Swift in Reckoning. (40:17)

[The Day of Judgment will happen] so that Allāh may requite every soul as it has earned. Surely Allāh is quick in reckoning. (14:51)

Towards Him is the return of you—all together. The Promise of Allāh is true. Surely He originates a creation, then He reproduces it, so that He may reward with justice those who believe and do good... (10:4)

And guard yourselves against a Day—no soul will avail from another soul anything at all, nor will any intercession be accepted on its behalf, nor will any compensation be taken from it, nor will they be helped. (2:48)

These āyāt and a large number of others indicate that no form of intercession will benefit anyone. The Throne Verse rightfully raises a question: *Who is there to intercede in His presence except with His permission?* The logical answer to this question is simple: none. On Judgment Day, only Allāh ﷻ will pass judgment. No one can influence, override or overthrow the judgment. Furthermore, Allāh's ﷻ knowledge encompasses everything, therefore, an intercesssor cannot provide Him any information that He does not already possess. Another question arises about the issue of permission in the Qur'ān. While it would be an honor to be Allāh's ﷻ chosen person to speak on behalf of another, this person could not override the judgment. The possibility of any intercession on Judgment Day will not contradict the principle of justice. Therefore, no intercession will change Allāh's ﷻ decision.

He knows what is in front and back

Human beings have very limited knowledge, constrained by their social, psychological, and physical limits. Human societies will remain more ignorant than knowledgeable because humans do not know even half of what is knowable. In contrast, Allāh's ﷻ knowledge is comprehensive and perfect (6:3; 13:9; 20:7; 50:16; 21:28). The phrase *mā bayna aydīhim* indicates things that lie in the future as well as those that are perceivable and known; similarly, *wa mā khalfahum* indicates things that happened earlier and long gone as well as those that are beyond one's perception. With so many limitations on knowledge, human beings cannot acquire even part of Allāh's ﷻ knowledge except what He allowed, and what He might allow in the future.

Throne of Power

His Throne of Power extends over the heavens and the earth. Commentators have different views about the meaning of the term *kursi* (lit. chair, footstool). Typically the Qur'ān uses the term *'arsh* to mean throne. In this instance, *kursi* is rendered the Throne of Power to emphasize some of the significance, yet no one or two words in any language can adequately explain the meaning of the word. In reality, God cannot be limited to a physical body necessitating a physical "seat," therefore any human characterization of God would be fallacious. Why would He need a "seat" when He does not tire of managing His dominion? For centuries, humans have become accustomed to visualizing a king sitting on a throne. To imagine that Allāh ﷻ has a body that needs to "sit" on a throne is an idolatrous concept and contradicts the theme of the Throne Verse. The imagery of angels bearing the Throne, as mentioned in ayāh 69:17, is a metaphorical allusion to their continued obedience and glorification of Allāh ﷻ.

A classical scholar, Ibn 'Arabi, interpreted the meaning of *kursi* as knowledge. Rāzī and Zamakhsharī explained *kursi* is used to describe Allāh's ﷻ greatness and exaltation. Syyid Qutb defined the word as Allāh's ﷻ dominion. Allāh's ﷻ *kursi* extends over heaven and earth, implying His authority encompasses everything in the universe.

Interesting Facts

How big is the universe? Our Solar System is located in the center of Milky Way galaxy. The size of this galaxy is 100,000 to 180,000 light-years. This galaxy has an estimated 100 billion planets.

The observable or visible universe has an estimated 2 trillion galaxies. It is estimated that there are more stars in the universe than all the grains of sands on earth.

Nothing overwhelms God

To feel tired is a human condition. Feeling tired is a form of weakness. In order to overcome feeling tired, human beings need periodic rest—on a bed, chair, or sofa. Human beings can suffer from physical and mental fatigue. Prolonged fatigue is a medical condition. Allāh ﷻ does not suffer from fatigue of any type. He actively manages the entire universe and does not need any assistance in carrying out His tasks.

He is Exalted, most High

Allāh ﷻ is the most High, the Supreme. These two attributes of Allāh ﷻ complement each other. He is most High in the sense that He is above all imperfection. He is too exalted to depend on anyone else, and He is the possessor of all perfection. He is too

Supreme to be judged by our ordinary standards which we use to evaluate or judge our fellow human beings.

Contemporary scholar, Dr. Mustansir Mir, from Yougstown, Ohio, has pointed out the Throne Verse has ten components. All of these components emphasize monotheism. These ten components are as follows:

1. Allāh ﷻ *alone* is the deity.
2. Allāh ﷻ *alone* is the living deity.
3. Allāh ﷻ *alone* is free from the need of sleep or slumber.
4. Allāh ﷻ *alone* is the owner and master of everything in the universe.
5. Allāh ﷻ *alone* has the power to judge.
6. Allāh ﷻ *alone* knows everything in the universe.
7. Allāh ﷻ *alone* is the source of any knowledge possessed by human beings.
8. Allāh ﷻ *alone* has jurisdiction over all that exists.
9. Allāh ﷻ *alone* takes care of all of existence.
10. Allāh ﷻ *alone* is the Exalted One, the Supreme.

In conclusion, we can say the Throne Verse is the equivalent of one-third of the Qur'ān because monotheism is the main theme of the ayāh. The other two themes are the prophecy of Judgment Day and life after death.

Homework

1. What are the three major themes in Ayātul-Qurʾsi, as explained in the lesson?

    1. ____.

    2. ____.

    3. ____.

2. In Ayātul-Qurʾsi, what is the second sub-element of Allāh'sﷻ attributes, after stating that there is no deity but He?

    A. Allāh'sﷻ knowledge
    B. Allāh'sﷻ sovereignty.
    C. Slumber does not overtake Allāhﷻ.
    D. Allāhﷻ is Ever-Living, self-Subsisting.
    E. Allāhﷻ is most-Merciful, most-Rewarding.

3. Which of the following terms explains one whose existence is absolute, whereas the existence of everything else is contingent upon Him?

    A. Al-Hayy.
    B. Al-Qayyum.
    C. Al-Khabīr.
    D. Ar-Raqīb.
    E. Al-Mughnī.

4. Which of the following statements about the basic purpose of Day of Judgment as emphasized in the Qur'ān is correct?

    A. To reward each soul with a life in Jannah.
    B. To distinguish truth from falsehood and to establish the Qur'ān.
    C. To end the world.
    D. To demonstrate the absolute power of Allāhﷻ.
    E. To reward each soul with what it has earned in a just and equitable manner.

5. What is the teaching in the Qur'ān about intercession on the Day of Judgment?

    ____

    ____.

6. What is the expanse of Allāh's 'Arsh?

A. It is all over the world.
B. It is located in the seventh heaven.
C. It extends over the heavens and the earth.
D. It is hidden behind a curtain.
E. It lies only in water.

7. Which two phrases in Ayātul-Qursi provide a glimpse of Allāh's absolute knowledge?

A. Hayyul Qayyum.
B. Mulkus Samāwat wal-ardh.
C. Yashfa'u 'indahu.
D. Bayna aydīhim wa mā khalfahum.
E. 'Aliyyu-l 'azhīm.

Unit 2: Knowing the Messenger ﷺ

After learning about the Creator, the next-most important topic is the Messenger ﷺ who brought the message from the Creator. Throughout the Weekend Learning series, we have studied the life and mission of the Messenger ﷺ at great length. This unit first discusses Muhammad ﷺ, the person—what made him so distinguished, praiseworthy, and an excellent role model for the Muslims. The next chapter describes the significance of the Farewell Pilgrimage and the memorable speech delivered at the gathering. In our attempt to know the Messenger ﷺ, it is important to understand that he was the final Messenger; no new messengers will be sent. Our final lesson in this unit is intimately connected with the Messenger ﷺ. The topic is about hadīth—focusing on the collection process and classification.

*Unit 2: Knowing the Messenger*ﷺ

The Person Muhammadﷺ

This lesson offers an intimate look at Muhammadﷺ as a person—focusing on some of his unique qualities. He was born into a noble family, and he was raised in a noble manner. Allāhﷻ prepared him so that when he became the Messenger, no one could find a single stain on his character. Everything that Nabi Muhammadﷺ did was exemplary, and there is much to learn from his action and behavior.

Farewell Pilgrimage

The Farewell Pilgrimage is remembered as a significant event in the history of Islam. Rasūlullāhﷺ delivered a famous sermon during the pilgrimage. This sermon summarizes the key responsibilities of Muslims. This lesson introduces students to the sermon and provides an overview of the Farewell Pilgrimage.

Finality of Prophethood

The Qur'ān and Hadīth confirmed that Muhammadﷺ is the final messenger, yet during the past 1,000 years, several people have claimed to be prophets. Students will learn that it is not possible for any new prophets to come. Muhammadﷺ is the final messenger in Islam.

Hadīth: *Collection and Classification*

Hadīth are not only the sayings of Rasūlullāhﷺ—they are much more than that. Students will learn about the structure, types, purpose, and classification of hadīth. They will also learn about the collectors of hadīth.

The Person Muhammad ﷺ

Objective of the Lesson:

This lesson offers an intimate look at Muhammad ﷺ as a person—focusing on some of his unique qualities. He was born into a noble family, and he was raised in a noble manner. Allāh ﷻ prepared him so that when he became the Messenger, no one could find a single stain on his character. Everything that Nabi Muhammad ﷺ did was exemplary, and there is much to learn from his action and behavior.

When we speak of Muhammad ﷺ, the Messenger of Allāh, we usually speak about his life as the Messenger and the Qur'ān. We also speak about his sayings and actions recorded in the books of hadīth. However, the Qur'ān and hadīth provide a wealth of information about Muhammad ﷺ as a person. In addition, there is a large number of authentic biographies of Muhammad ﷺ, some from the early period of Islam, that document his entire life.

From all these sources, we can obtain an intimate view of the life and actions of Nabi Muhammad ﷺ. In this lesson, we will learn a few specific details about our Nabi ﷺ to get a glimpse of the type of person he was as an individual and as a messenger.

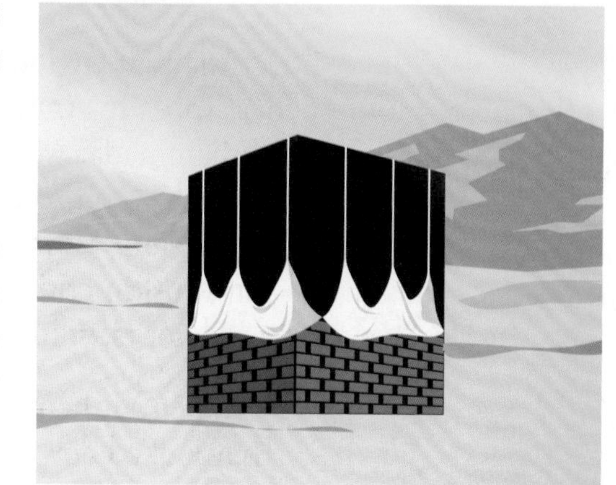

The name

From time to time, Allāh prompted the names of messengers and righteous people. For example, Nabī Yahyā's (A) name was prompted by Allāh.[19:7] The Qur'ān does not mention how the name "Muhammad" was chosen, but biographers have noted that Aminah was prompted to use the name. She had faith that in the true spirit of the name "Muhammad," people would continue to praise him in years to come. The name was uncommon and unusual at that time because the name was not connected to any of his ancestors.

The name "Muhammad" is derived from the root word "hamd" (lit, to praise) meaning "praised one." 'Abd al-Muttalib named him "Ahmad," also derives from the root word "hamd." Much later, the Qur'ān was revealed and disclosed that Nabī 'Isā (A) had predicted that a new messenger would be named "Ahmad."[61:6]

The lineage

It was a divine plan that Rasūlullāh ﷺ would be born into a family with the best lineage in Arabia. The word "lineage" means family tree, family roots, or the ancestry of a person. The study of lineage establishes a relationship between a person and his or her ancestors. Such relationships are typically formed through marriage and having children. The study of lineage reveals not only who the parents were, but also, importantly, who the grandparents and great-grandparents were and their history.

Let us review Rasūlullāh's ﷺ immediate ancestors. His father was Abdullāh and his mother was Aminah. Abdullāh was the youngest son of 'Abd al-Muttalib, the chief of the Quraish tribe. Aminah was the daughter of Wahb ibn 'Abd Manaf ibn Zuhrah, the chief of the Zuhrah tribe.

Rasūlullāh's ﷺ grandfather, 'Abd al-Muttalib, belonged to the Quraish tribe and the Hāshim clan. A clan is a group of people united by immediate family ties. A tribe, on the other hand, is a much larger social group consisting of several clans that have some kinship ties. For example, under the Quraish tribe, there were several clans and sub-clans, such as Banu Zuhra, Banu Makhzum, Banu Hāshim, Banu Asad, Banu Nawfal and so forth.

Nabī Muhammad ﷺ belonged to the Banu Hāshim clan. The name of the clan was derived from his great-grandfather, who was known as "Hāshim," an Arabic name that means "destroyer of evil." Hāshim was not his real name. His real name was 'Amr al-'Ula ibn Abd Manaf. The Banu Hāshim clan originated from the off spring of Hāshim.

The lineage of Muhammad ﷺ reaches furhter back than Hāshim—all the way to Fihir, back to Ismā'īl (A) and to Ibrāhīm (A). According to the Qur'ān, Ibrāhīm (A) helped his second wife, Hājar, and his first son, Ismā'īl (A), settle in Arabia.[14:37] Nabī Muhammad ﷺ was a direct descent of Ismā'īl (A).

Allāh's ﷻ divine wisdom determined that Muhammad ﷺ would be born among the best tribes in Arabia and belong to the best clan. It was also Allāh's ﷻ grand plan that Muhammad ﷺ would have the best lineage. During the course of his life as a messenger of Allāh ﷻ, on several occasions, people questioned his lineage in order to undermine his mission. However, they could not taint his lineage. When Islam spread in Europe, non-Muslim critics tried to depict Muhammad ﷺ in disrespectfully, but even then they could not taint his lineage.

When Muhammad ﷺ was born, Arabs were very critical of a person with poor lineage. They looked down on people who did not have a good lineage. They respected someone

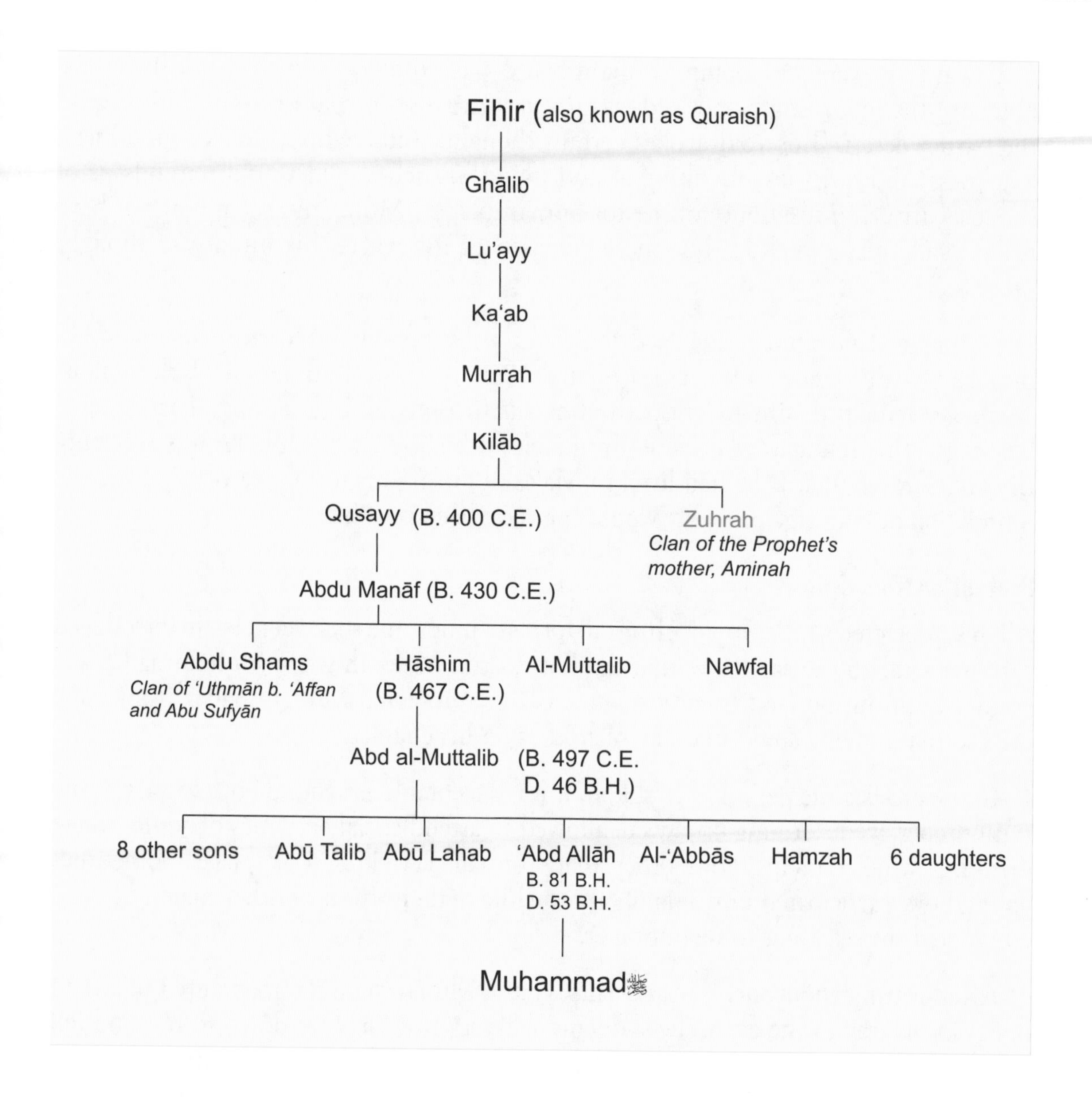

if he or she had a good lineage. If Muhammad ﷺ did not have the best lineage, then the Arabs would have argued that he wanted to attain a higher social status by claiming to be a prophet. They would have further argued that Muhammad ﷺ was trying to change the social structure because he wanted a better social position and recognition.

Childhood

In pre-Islamic Arabia, education was not emphasized. Very few children in Arabia received even an informal education. Few learned how to read and write as adults. Even though Muhammad ﷺ did not have formal schooling, which is the reason he remained unlettered, almighty God educated him in a different manner. Every event that happened to him, from birth, was a form of education.

This unusual education process began soon after Muhammad's ﷺ birth, when Aminah sent him to a nurse-mother named Halīmah. For the next four years, he lived among the Sa'd ibn Bakr tribe in the Arabian desert. As a toddler, while his senses and awareness were developing, Muhammadﷺ was exposed to the difficult life of the nomads. The first thing he noticed was the vast expanse of void in front of his eyes—the barren desert. This void evokes certain thoughts and feelings, such as emptiness, loneliness, and quietness. Looking at and living in such a void would reminds us of the insecurity and instability of life for human beings. Muhammadﷺ might not have realized all this as a child, but these experiences influenced his mind and thought process.

Living in Tā'if among the Sa'd ibn Bakr tribe provided Muhammadﷺ another important early lesson. Desert life offered him the basic foundation of the Arabic language. It helped him to grasp the fine distinctions and variations of the Arabic language. This foundation became invaluable in his life later, while he was receiving the divine revelation. If he had lived in Makkah during his formative years, this basic foundation of language probably would not have been possible.

Protection from evil

Allāhﷻ protected Muhammadﷺ from all forms of moral and social evil. Islam introduced certain moral and social values that did not exist in Makkah when Muhammadﷺ was young. Even during Islam's early stages, Allāhﷻ protected Muhammadﷺ from these evils so that nobody could find any blemishes on his character.

In the pre-Islamic period in Makkah, it was acceptable for young boys to participate in improper events. Young boys were allowed to attend social activities of adults where drinking wine, dancing, and other inappropriate activities took place. Sometimes young boys participated in fun and games while nude in front of other males. No one considered these actions to be improper.

After hearing about such social events, young Muhammadﷺ once wanted to attend one. On his way to the event, he suddenly felt very tired. He sat down to rest and fell asleep. The next morning, the heat of the sun woke him. This seemingly simple incident indicates how Allāhﷻ protected the future messenger from participating in social and moral evils that were common in Makkah.

Sometimes childhood fun and frolic can cross the boundaries of decency. Once Muhammad ﷺ was playing with some boys who decided to carry stones from one place to another. They took off their clothes to put stones on them to make the stones easier to carry. When Muhammad ﷺ was about to take off his clothes, he felt a hard punch and a voice told him to put on his garment. Instead of taking off his garment, he wrapped it around him tightly. Thus, he was the only boy carrying stones and wearing clothes.

On another occasion, when the Ka'bah was being repaired, young men were carrying stones on their shoulders. Some men took off their lower garments and put them on their shoulders as a cushion to carry the stones. Muhammad's ﷺ uncle, Al-'Abbās, advised him to do the same to protect his shoulders. When he was about to take off his lower garment, he fell on the ground unconscious. When he regained consciousness, he carried on with his work without removing his clothes.

Never worshipped idols

Allāh ﷻ protected Muhammad ﷺ from involvement with idol worshipping. While Muhammad ﷺ was growing up, he never bowed to an idol, he never swore using their names, he never offered anything to them, and he never ate anything that was offered to an idol.

When Muhammad ﷺ was a member of his uncle Abū Tālib's household, he noticed their dedication to idols. Abū Tālib always attended the festivals in honor of an idol. He asked his nephew to attend the festivals, but Muhammad ﷺ declined. His uncle and aunt tried to persuade him to attend the festivals and scolded him for not attending. Once, he reluctantly went to such a festival but he returned horrified. He did not touch any offerings for an idol. Several other reports indicate that Allāh ﷻ always kept him away from pagan worship.

Always truthful

The Messengerﷺ was always truthful in his words and conduct—in all situations—during war and peace time. Long before Muhammadﷺ became a Nabi, he was truthful, trustworthy, and honest. Out of appreciation for his truthfulness, the Quraish lovingly named Muhammadﷺ **al-Amīn**, meaning "the truthful one."

He was truthful with everyone—with close acquaintances and strangers, with men and women, and with friends and enemies. The Messengerﷺ was truthful when buying and selling merchandise, when playing or relaxing, when signing contracts or treaties, when telling stories or giving instructions, and when discussing serious legal matters or political issues. He was a living example of Qur'ānic teachings:

> *O you who believe! revere Allāh and remain with the truthful. (9:119)*
>
> *Allāh will say: "This is the Day on which their truthfulness will benefit the truthful. For them are Gardens beneath which flow the rivers, abiding in it all the time." Allāh is well-pleased with them, and they are well-pleased with Him. This is the great achievement. (5:119)*
>
> *And whoever obeys Allāh and the Rasūl, then they are with those upon whom Allāh has bestowed favors—from among the nabis, and the truthful, and the witnesses, and the righteous. And what goodly friends are they! (4:69)*

The Messengerﷺ forbade Muslims from lying, even if they were telling a simple joke. He discouraged people from lying, even if they did it with a gesture, a signal or a wink of an eye.

Always patient

During good times in life, we do not realize the value of patience. During bad times in life, we often become restless, impatient, and we lose hope. When we look Nabi Muhammad'sﷺ life, we find that in every aspect of his life, and in every stage of his mission, he was patient. He was not a superman by any means, but he remembered the Qur'ānic teaching about patience:

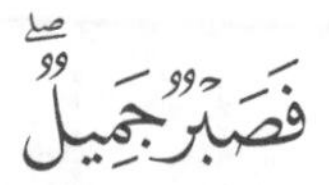

Therefore patience is elegant. (12:18; 12:83)

This statement in mentioned in sūrah Yūsuf by Ya'qūb (A) when he exercised patience after his sons returned home with the news that a wolf ate Yūsuf (A) and when Binyamin was arrested for an alleged theft.

Every time Rasūlullāhﷺ faced difficulties and challenging situations in life, he remembered the following teaching:

فَٱصۡبِرۡ كَمَا صَبَرَ أُوْلُواْ ٱلۡعَزۡمِ مِنَ ٱلرُّسُلِ

Therefore bear you with patience, as did the messengers of strong determination ... (46:35)

Rasūlullāhﷺ faced difficult times during his entire life. When the pagan Quraish ridiculed and tortured Muslims in Makkah, he was patient. When most people rejected his message, he was patient. When Muslims had to migrate to Abyssinia, he was patient. When the Quraish exiled the Banū Hashim clan, he was patient. When his beloved wife and uncle Abū Tālib died, he was patient. When people spread rumors about his wife 'Ā'ishah (ra), he was patient. In short, during all the difficulties in his life, Rasūlullāhﷺ was patient. He always demonstrated the following teachings in the Qur'ān:

ٱلَّذِينَ إِذَآ أَصَٰبَتۡهُم مُّصِيبَةٞ قَالُوٓاْ إِنَّا لِلَّهِ وَإِنَّآ إِلَيۡهِ رَٰجِعُونَ ١٥٦

أُوْلَٰٓئِكَ عَلَيۡهِمۡ صَلَوَٰتٞ مِّن رَّبِّهِمۡ وَرَحۡمَةٞۖ وَأُوْلَٰٓئِكَ هُمُ ٱلۡمُهۡتَدُونَ ١٥٧

Who, when a misfortune confronts them, say: "Surely we belong to Allāh and to Him invariably we do return." These are those upon whom are blessings from their Rabb and mercy, and these are themselves the guided. (2:156–157)

Example of mercy

All his life, Rasūlullāhﷺ was an example of mercy. Everything he did or said reflected mercy. He was equally merciful towards his family, friends, and strangers. He was not only merciful towards Muslims, but also to people of all religions. For this reason, Allāhﷻ says He sent Rasūlullāhﷺ as a mercy for all the worlds.[21:107]

وَمَآ أَرۡسَلۡنَٰكَ إِلَّا رَحۡمَةٗ لِّلۡعَٰلَمِينَ ١٠٧

And We have not sent you but as a mercy for all the worlds. (21:107)

A large number of examples abound in hadīth and Rasūlullāh'sﷺ seerah about his exemplary mercy. He loved to prolong congregational salāt, but when he heard the a baby crying, he would shorten the salāh only to make it easier for the mother and the baby. He advised his companions, "When someone among you leads people in prayer, then let him shorten the length of salāh, for among the people are the elderly, young, sick, and the ones who have important errands to run."

The laughter of the Messengerﷺ

In a large number of biographies about Rasūlullāhﷺ, one fact is often ignored. This is the laughter of Rasūlullāhﷺ. He is often portrayed as a serious man—always worshipping, advising, and talking about religion. The lighter side of his personality is often understated.

Rasūlullāhﷺ was a man with a loving demeanor. When he was in the company of his wives and family, he smiled, laughed, and joked around. He made the home environment lively and pleasant. When he joked or said something funny, he only told the truth. He never lied to make others laugh. When he joked with his companions, he provided a new sense of energy and spirit for their souls.

Even in his laughing and joking, Rasūlullāhﷺ was always moderate. He laughed when it was appropriate to laugh, but he never laughed loudly and uncontrollably, as we sometimes do. He never laughed needlessly, but he always maintained a good sense of humor.

A great military leader

Another fact not often emphasized in biographies about Rasūlullāhﷺ is his exemplary military leadership. Rasūlullāhﷺ had no formal military experience. During his childhood, he was not trained in basic warfare. He did not learn archery, sword fighting, wrestling, or any other combat training that many Arab fathers taught their sons. He also did not participate in any tribal warfare.

When Rasūlullāhﷺ was compelled to engage in defensive wars, he quickly recognized the strategic advantage, on a battlefield and made the best use of that advantage. He could see the "big picture" and worked towards achieving major objectives.

Along with beginning a social, political, and religious revolution in Arabia, Nabi Muhammadﷺ also began a military revolution. Without a formal defense budget, Rasūlullāhﷺ was able to build an army that was not only motivated, but that was also committed to the cause of Islam. He transformed the army from tribes raiding caravans into an organized cadre capable of large-scale combat operations. Based on his methodologies, years later, Muslim leaders were able to conquer other neighboring countries, such as Byzantine and Persia.

Example of humility

Most of us live in a society where humility is often seen as a weakness and boldness is considered a sign of strength. Using the modern version of "survival of the fittest," people often think aggressive, assertive, bold, or pretentious individuals are most likely to succeed. Sometimes people express humility due to low self-esteem and fear of uncertainty. But humility is really the opposite of being arrogant, haughty, and proud. The secret of success might very well lie in one's ability to express humility in everything he or she does in life.

When we look at Nabi Muhammad'sﷺ life, we find him humble in all his conduct. He was humble in awe of the greatness and mightiness of his Rabb. Knowing that Allāhﷻ is the Greatest and all-Powerful, the Messengerﷺ understood that it would be foolish to walk with an aura of arrogance or a sense of superiority.

The Messengerﷺ forbid people from standing up to meet or greet him. If he arrived at a gathering, he did not make his way to a prominent position at the gathering; instead, he would sit where there was available space.

One of the Messenger'sﷺ neighbors was his uncle Abū Lahab, who opposed Islam and the Muslims. Out of extreme hatred for the Messengerﷺ, Abū Lahab's wife routinely threw garbage in his compound. Without becoming angry, upset or annoyed, the Messengerﷺ cleaned up the garbage. This was possible for him because he was humble.

The Messenger ﷺ showed mercy and compassion for the poor, the needy, and the orphans. He was full of compassion for the weak and sick people. He played with children, joked with his family, and always remained accessible to others. He did not mind sitting on dirt, sleeping on the ground, or using straw as a pillow. He spoke gently to women, and used kind words with them. He addressed strangers with a tone of love and compassion.

The Messenger ﷺ was always content with whatever Allāh ﷻ decreed for him. He never aspired for status, recognition, power, wealth or any material objects. Yet he was not an ascetic who rejected the good things in life.

Homework

1. 'Isā (A) predicted the name of a new messenger. According to the Qur'ān, what name did 'Isā (A) use to refer to the future messenger?

A. Rasūlullāh.
B. Ahmad.
C. Karimullāh.
D. Al-Amin.
E. Al-Farūq.

2. Who was an ancestor of Nabi Muhammadﷺ?

A. Harithah.
B. Hāshim.
C. Al-Abbās.
D. Zuhrah.
E. Sufyān.

3. What did Rasūlullāhﷺ do when he heard a baby cry during salāt?

A. He first determined whether the baby's mother was present.
B. He stayed in sujūd position for long until they baby stopped crying.
C. He shortened the salāt.
D. He ended the salāt and finished it later.
E. He told the mother not to bring the baby next time.

4. What is the meaning of the phrase *'Innā Lillāhi Wa 'Innā 'Ilayhi Rāji'ūn*?

A. These are those who are guided.
B. Surely we are going to be raised after death.
C. Surely patience is elegant.
D. Surely to Allāh we belong and He is merciful.
E. Surely to Allāh we belong and to Him do we invariably return.

5. In the Qur'ān, which nabi expressed the phrase *Faṣabrun Jamīlun* twice?

____

6. During all defensive battles, what military strategy did Rasūlullāhﷺ adopt?

A. Attack in the middle of the night when his enemies were unprepared.
B. Assemble a large military force quickly.
C. Use gunpowder to attack and scatter his enemies.
D. Invite the enemy leaders to a dinner for a friendly discussion.
E. Recognize strategic advantage on a battlefield and make the best use of it.

7. Nabi Muhammadﷺ forbade Muslims from doing what even when telling a simple joke?

A. Telling a joke about animals.
B. Telling a joke that was too hilarious.
C. Telling a joke about the ruler of the country.
D. Telling a lie.
E. Telling a joke that nobody understands.

Farewell Pilgrimage

Objective of the Lesson:

The Farewell Pilgrimage is remembered as a significant event in the history of Islam. Rasūlullāh ﷺ delivered a famous sermon during the pilgrimage. This sermon summarizes the key responsibilities of Muslims. This lesson introduces students to the sermon and provides an overview of the Farewell Pilgrimage

The Farewell Pilgrimage refers to the famous pilgrimage, or Hajj, made by Nabi Muhammad ﷺ in the year 10 A.H./632 C.E. This was the only Hajj performed by Rasūlullāh ﷺ. Soon after the Hajj, he passed away. For this reason, this Hajj is widely known as the Farewell Pilgrimage. In Arabic, this pilgrimage is called **Hijjat-al-Widah**. A few important events happened during the pilgrimage—involving Rasūlullāh's *khutbah,* or sermon. Therefore, it is important for us to learn about the pilgrimage and the sermon delivered during the pilgrimage.

During the pilgrimage, Rasūlullāh ﷺ delivered a sermon to the pilgrims. This sermon was the final one delivered by Rasūlullāh ﷺ. In Arabic, this sermon is called **Khutbatul Widah**. In English, it is usually called The Last Sermon or The Farewell Sermon. The details of the sermon are mentioned in almost all the books of Hadīth. Minor details vary among the books, but the major details and the core message of the Sermon is the same.

Preparation for Hajj

According to several ahādīth, angel Jibril (A) appeared to Nabi Muhammad ﷺ every year to recite the entire Qur'ān with him. In the tenth year of Hijrah, 632 C.E., Jibril (A) visited him twice. Because of this, Rasūlullāh ﷺ deduced that he would not live very long. During the month of Dhu al-Qa'dah, Rasūlullāh ﷺ let all of his companions know that he intended to perform Hajj. On two previous occasions he had performed ‘Umrah, but he had not performed Hajj. The rituals of Hajj needed to be established and demonstrated in their entirety to the Muslims, so Muslims can learn them and teach them to generations to come.

Corrupt practices must end

Before the final Hajj, some of the rituals of Hajj were done in a corrupt way. For example, the Quraish felt that certain parts of Hajj were not necessary for them because they were the custodians of the Ka‘bah. They also required pilgrims from outside of Makkah wear *ihrām* garments made in Makkah or to be naked during *tawāf*. There were a few other traces of polytheism in some of the rituals. The previous year, Rasūlullāh ﷺ sent Abū Bakr to perform Hajj and to stop all the corrupt practices.

Preparation for Hajj

Hajj was one of the acts of worship that the Muslims had not seen Rasūlullāh ﷺ perform. Hajj is an important part of Islam. The message of Islam would not be complete unless Rasūlullāh ﷺ himself performed it and demonstrated its proper procedures. For this reason, he spread the word to everyone in Madīnah, and other parts of Arabia that he intended to perform Hajj. He welcomed anyone who wished to perform Hajj with him.

Everybody understood that it would be Rasūlullāh's ﷺ final pilgrimage. For the first time, a large number of Muslims gathered for Hajj. It is reported that over 70,000 people assembled for Hajj. By the time Hajj began, more than 100,000 Muslims entered Makkah to perform *tawāf* and other rituals.

Date and place of delivery

On the 9th day of Dhu al-Hajj, 10.A.H./632 C.E., Rasūlullāh ﷺ led the pilgrims through the valley of Mina to the Mountain of Arafat and stopped at the **Valley of Uranah**. There, he sat on a camel and delivered the sermon that is known as the Farewell Sermon. As you can imagine, it was very difficult to address a crowd of 120,000 people without a loudspeaker. During Hajj, Rasūlullāh ﷺ did not feel well and his voice could not reach all those who were present. Therefore, he asked his companion, **Rab'ah Ibn Umayya Ibn Khalaf**, who had a loud beautiful voice, to repeat the sermon after him. Rab'ah Ibn Khalaf carefully repeated Rasūlullāh's ﷺ sermon, sentence by sentence, so that everyone could hear.

The Last Sermon

The Last Sermon can be read as a continuous speech or broken down into individual parts. For the sake of understanding the message of the speech, we have divided the Sermon into individual parts. Each part requires careful attention.

First, Rasūlullāh ﷺ praised and thanked Allāh ﷻ. Then he said:

1. People! Lend me an attentive ear, for I know not whether after this year, I shall ever be amongst you again. Therefore, listen to what I am saying to you very carefully, and take these words to those who could not be present here today.

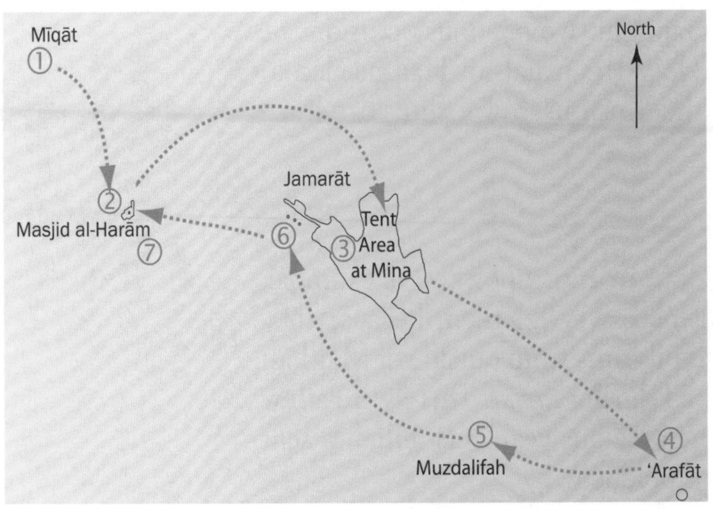

2. O People! Just as you regard this month, this day, this city as sacred, so regard the life and property of every Muslim as a sacred trust. Return the goods entrusted to you to their rightful owners. Hurt no one so that no one may hurt you. Remember that you will indeed meet your Lord, and that He will indeed reckon your deeds. Allāh ﷻ has forbidden you to take usury; therefore, all usurious interest obligations shall henceforth be given up. Your capital, however, is yours to keep. You will neither inflict nor suffer any injustice.

3. Allāh ﷻ has judged that there shall be no usury and that all usurious interest due to Abbās Ibn Abd al Muttalib [Rasūlullāh's ﷺ uncle] shall henceforth be waived.

4. Beware of Shaitān for the safety of your religion. He has lost all hope that he will ever be able to lead you astray in big things, so beware of following him in small things.

5. O People! It is true that you have certain rights in regard to your women, but they, too, have rights over you. Remember that you have taken them as your wives, only under Allāh's ﷻ trust and with His permission. If they abide by your right, then to them belongs the right to be fed and clothed in kindness. Do treat your women well and be kind to them, for they are your partners and committed helpers. And it is your right that they do not make friends with anyone of whom you do not approve, as well as never be unchaste.

6. O People! Listen to me in earnest: worship, say your five daily prayers (Salāh), fast during the month of Ramadan, and give your wealth in Zakāt. Perform Hajj if you can afford it.

7. All mankind is from Adam and Eve; an Arab has no superiority over a non-Arab, nor does a non-Arab have any superiority over an Arab; also, a white has no superiority over a black, nor does a black have any superiority over a white—except by piety and good action. Learn that every Muslim is a brother to every Muslim and that the Muslims constitute one brotherhood. Nothing shall be legitimate to a Muslim, which belongs to a fellow Muslim, unless it was given freely and willingly. Do not, therefore, do injustice to yourselves.

8. Remember that one day, you will appear before Allāh ﷻ and answer for your deeds. So beware—do not stray from the path of righteousness after I am gone.

9. O People! No prophet or apostle will come after me and no new faith will be born. Reason well, therefore, O people, and understand the words which I convey to you. *I leave behind two things, the Qur'ān and the Sunnah,* and if you follow these, you will never go astray. All those who listen to me shall pass on my words to others and those to others again; and may the last ones understand my words better than those

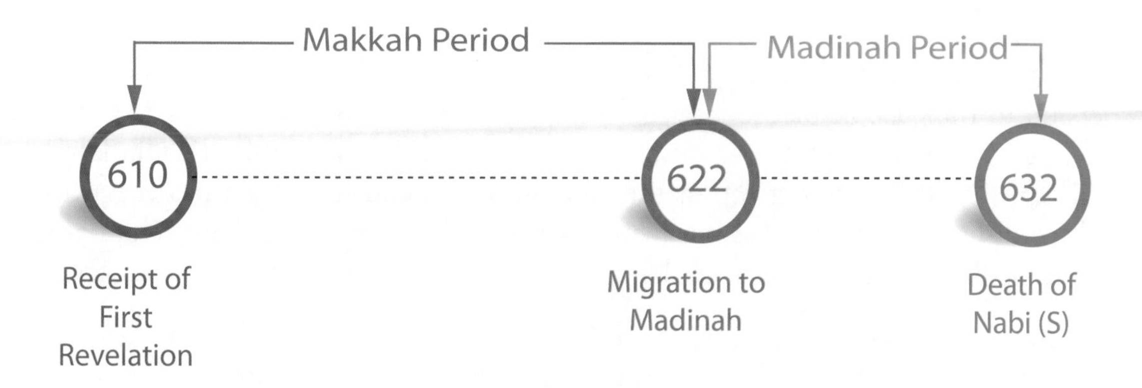

who listened to me directly. Be my witness, O Allāh, that I have conveyed your message to your people.

Toward the end of his sermon, Nabi Muhammad asked three times: "O people, have I faithfully delivered unto you my message?" The entire congregation replied in a loud voice, "By Allāh, yes!" In Arabic, they said, "Allāhumma na'am." The loud response filled the sky like thunder. Then Rasūlullāh raised his forefinger and said: "Be my witness, O Allāh, that I have conveyed your message to your people."

Revelation of āyah 5:3

Towards the end of the sermon, Allāh revealed āyah 5:3. This āyah supplements the Last Sermon and serves as a conclusion of the sermon. This āyah says:

ٱلْيَوْمَ أَكْمَلْتُ لَكُمْ دِينَكُمْ وَأَتْمَمْتُ عَلَيْكُمْ نِعْمَتِي وَرَضِيتُ لَكُمُ ٱلْإِسْلَٰمَ دِينًا

...This day I have perfected for you your religion, and completed upon you My blessing, and have accepted for you ISLAM as the religion ... (5:3)

Variations

There are at least three different variations of the sermon available in hadīth. These variations pertain to some of the minor details, but these differences are significant. Most of the variations involve details mentioned at the end of the sermon. One report states Rasūlullāh said: "I leave behind two things, the Qur'ān and the Sunnah." Another version says he said: "I leave behind two things, the Qur'ān and **Ahl-al-bayt**." The word Ahl-al-bayt means "the family of the House," implying the family of Rasūlullāh. A third version of the statement is: "I leave with you the Qur'ān, you shall uphold it."

Meaning of the variations

Although it appears that the variations are small, the significance is enormous. Muslims have deep disagreements about these details. The cause of the rift between the Sunnis and the Shī'ahs began with this statement. The Sunnis believe Rasūlullāh said: "I leave behind two things, the Qur'ān and the Sunnah." The Sunnis believe they follow the sunnah, or the practice of Rasūlullāh. These practices were reported by the companions of Rasūlullāh.

The Shī'ahs believe in the second version of the statement: "I leave behind two things, the Qur'ān and Ahl al-Bayt." According to them, Rasūlullāh ﷺ gave legitimate leadership to the "people of the House," implying 'Ali and his descendants. 'Ali was Rasūlullāh's ﷺ cousin and son-in-law. The Shī'ites believe that after Rasūlullāh ﷺ passed away, legitimate leadership of the community should have been passed on to 'Ali. According to them, the Muslims made a serious mistake by nominating Abū Bakr as the immediate successor and then 'Umar and 'Uthmān as the next two successors.

The Sunnis dispute this argument. According to them,120,000 pilgrims listened to the Farewell Sermon and they could not be wrong. A few days after the sermon, Rasūlullāh ﷺ passed away. The memory of the Sermon was fresh in the minds of the Muslims. If Rasūlullāh ﷺ had said "the people of the House," all the senior and highly respectable companions would have been wrong.

A third version states that Rasūlullāh ﷺ said: "I leave for you the Qur'ān, you shall uphold it." According to this view, Rasūlullāh ﷺ did not say "Sunnah." He only advised them to follow the Qur'ān and nothing else. People who believe in this version reject hadīth altogether.

Regardless of any variations you might read or hear about the Farewell Sermon of Rasūlullāh ﷺ, the core message is that people must adhere to the Qur'ān and the sunnah of Rasūlullāh ﷺ as the guiding principles in their lives.

Five principles

The Farewell Sermon outlines five basic principles of the Islamic code of action. Two of these principles apply on an individual level, and three apply to Islamic society. The two principles that apply on an individual level are: (1) all links of ignorance, idol-worshipping, usurious transactions, erroneous ways of the past, and so forth are removed from Islam, so that the Muslims could start fresh, (2) individuals should guard against Shaitān and his attempts to seduce people. Sins are more dangerous than battles because sins can destroy a person in this life and in the Hereafter.

The three principles on which an Islamic society should lay its foundation are: (1) maintaining ties of Islamic brotherhood because such ties make one Muslim a patron of another, (2) supporting the weaker members of society, including the poor, women, and children, so they do not become a burden on the strong and do not cause society to crumble, (3) cooperation between an Islamic government and society so that together, they can work for the betterment of society.

The core message of the Last Sermon is also discussed in the Qur'ān. Rasūlullāh ﷺ simply pointed out some of these same messages in the sermon. The Last Sermon is one of the best summaries of our rights and duties as Muslims. May Allāh ﷻ help us and guide us to live in the spirit of Islam.

Homework

1. How many pilgrimages were performed by Nabi Muhammad ﷺ after 10 A.H./632 C.E.?

A. 1 pilgrimage.
B. 2 pilgrimages.
C. 3 pilgrimages.
D. 5 pilgrimages.
E. No other pilgrimages were performed.

2. Where was the Farewell Sermon delivered?

A. In the valley of Badr.
B. In the valley of Uranah.
C. In the valley of Uhud.
D. In the valley of Hijjaz.
E. In the valley of Khaybar.

3. According to most authorities, which āyah of the Qur'ān was revealed during the Farewell Sermon?

A. Āyah 2:286.
B. Āyah 5:3.
C. Āyah 4:5.
D. Āyah 5:100.
E. Āyah 96:1–5.

4. Which of the following is a message delivered in the Last Sermon?

A. All Arabs have superiority over all non-Arabs.
B. Men and women have certain rights over each other.
C. All usurious practices should be given up.
D. All of the above.
E. Only (b) and (c).

5. Sometimes people disagree with a certain part of the Last Sermon. Which part of the Last Sermon is disputed?

A. Whether men and women have certain rights over each other.
B. Whether men can accept interest.
C. Whether Rasūlullāh ﷺ left behind his sunnah or Ahl al-Bayt in addition to the Qur'ān.
D. Whether all mankind was created from Adam and Eve.
E. Whether new prophets will appear after Muhammad ﷺ.

6. According to the Last Sermon, on what basis can a person have superiority over another?

A. On the basis of skin color.
B. On the basis of whether he or she is of Arab origin.
C. On the basis of piety and good action.
D. On the basis of the language spoken.
E. On the basis of wealth.

7. In the Last Sermon, Rasūlullāhﷺ advised us to be careful of Shaitān regarding certain things. What was he referring to?

A. Eating an apple from the tree.
B. Temptation in small matters.
C. Feeding and clothing poor people.
D. The Muslim Brotherhood.
E. Revolting against kings.

8. At the end of the Farewell Sermon, what did Rasūlullāhﷺ tell everybody to pass on to others?

A. His words.
B. His rule.
C. His family values.
D. Ahl al-Bayt to those who do not follow it.
E. The teachings of Ahlul Kitāb.

9. In the Farewell Sermon, Rasūlullāhﷺ hoped that the last people to hear the sermon after it had been passed on would do something. What did Rasūlullāhﷺ hope they would do?

A. Ignore the message.
B. Write it down.
C. Commit it to memory.
D. Understand it better than those who listened to it directly.
E. Edit it and make changes to it.

Finality of Prophethood

Objective of the Lesson:

The Qur'ān and Hadīth confirmed that Muhammad ﷺ is the final messenger, yet during the past 1,000 years, several people have claimed to be prophets. Students will learn that it is not possible for any new prophets to come. Muhammad ﷺ is the final messenger in Islam.

According to accepted Islamic belief, the tradition of prophethood ended with Nabi Muhammad ﷺ. Muslims all over the world believe in this concept. At least two Qur'ānic ayāt and several ahādīth confirm this belief. Only a small minority believes that Nabi Muhammad ﷺ is the most important messenger, but not the "last" messenger. They think new messengers may come or have already come after Nabi Muhammad ﷺ. The purpose of this lesson is to explain, through analytical study, that Nabi Muhammad ﷺ is "the Last Prophet" and the tradition of prophethood ended with him.

Āyah 33:40: As mentioned previously, at least two Qur'ānic ayāt indicate that Nabi Muhammad ﷺ is the Last Prophet. The first āyah is from sūrah Al-Ahzāb, āyah number 40. Let us read the āyah and analyze its messages.

مَّا كَانَ مُحَمَّدٌ أَبَآ أَحَدٍ مِّن رِّجَالِكُمْ وَلَٰكِن رَّسُولَ ٱللَّهِ وَخَاتَمَ ٱلنَّبِيِّـۧنَ ۗ وَكَانَ ٱللَّهُ بِكُلِّ شَىْءٍ عَلِيمًا ﴿٤٠﴾

Muhammad is not the father of any of your men; but he is a messenger of Allāh, and the Seal of the prophets. And Allāh is ever-Knowing of all things. (33:40)

This āyah show three themes:

(1) Muhammad ﷺ is not the father of any of your men,
(2) He is the messenger of Allāh ﷻ, and
(3) He is the seal of the prophets.

Reason for revelation

This āyah above was revealed to answer the criticism of Rasūlullāh's ﷺ marriage with Zainab (Ra) (see the Level 9 book in this series for details). Zainab was Rasūlullāh's ﷺ cousin. At first, Rasūlullāh ﷺ arranged the marriage of his adopted son Zaid (R) to Zainab. From the very beginning, this marriage had difficulties. The couple could not get along. Eventually Zaid divorced her. Then, following a divine instruction, Rasūlullāh ﷺ married her. This created a lot of controversy because in the Arab culture, it was improper for men to marry their son's wife. The āyah was revealed to state that Muhammad ﷺ was not the father of any man; therefore, Zaid could not have been his "son." Since Zaid was not his son, there was no reason to dispute Rasūlullāh's ﷺ marriage to Zainab.

Not the father of any man

In many cultures in the past, a person's lineage continued through his son or sons. It was no different in Arabia during Rasūlullāh's ﷺ time.

Rasūlullāh ﷺ did not have any adult sons, only adult daughters. His three sons died during their infancy or early childhood. The people in Arabia at that time knew that. Yet the Qur'ān states this fact so that, later on, no man could say he had a biological connection to Rasūlullāh ﷺ. By pointing out that Rasūlullāh ﷺ was not the father of any men, the Qur'ān rejects the possibility of any man claiming to be his son and continuing the institution of prophethood.

You might remember that many past messengers had sons who grew up to be messengers. For example, Ibrāhīm (A) had two sons, who grew up to be messengers. Ibrāhīm's (A) grandson Ya'qūb (A) was a messenger. Ya'qūb's (A) son Yūsuf (A) was a messenger. Dāwūd's (A) son Sulaimān (A) was a messenger. Zakariyyā's (A) son Yahyā (A) was a messenger. But Nabi Muhammad ﷺ did not have an adult son. Therefore, no one could claim to be a nabi or rasūl by virtue of his birth in Nabi Muhammad's ﷺ family. Thus, the Qur'ān carefully eliminated the possibility of continuing the institution of prophethood after Nabi Muhammad ﷺ.

Interesting Facts

Rasūlullāh ﷺ had seven sons and daughters.

His wife Khadījah gave birth to six children. His wife Mariah gave birth to one son.

No other wives of Rasūlullāh ﷺ gave birth to any children.

All of his sons died during childhood or infancy.

Only his daughters grew up to become adults. They all married. All of them except Fātimah died before Rasūlullāh ﷺ passed away.

Fātimah lived six more months after Rasūlullāh ﷺ passed away.

Seal of the prophets

Āyah 33:40 also states that Muhammad ﷺ was the messenger of Allāh ﷻ and **the seal** of the prophets. Two words are very important in this āyah. One is **khātam** and the other is **nabiyyīn**. The meaning of the word khātam is "to seal." The word is used in the Qur'ān in other places with the same meaning.

The following examples illustrate this point.

خَتَمَ ٱللَّهُ عَلَىٰ قُلُوبِهِمْ وَعَلَىٰ سَمْعِهِمْ ۖ وَعَلَىٰٓ أَبْصَٰرِهِمْ غِشَٰوَةٌ ۖ وَلَهُمْ عَذَابٌ عَظِيمٌ ٧

*Allāh has set a **seal** [khātam] upon their hearts, and upon their hearing, and upon their sight is a veil; and for them is a great chastisement. (2:7)*

قُلْ أَرَءَيْتُمْ إِنْ أَخَذَ ٱللَّهُ سَمْعَكُمْ وَأَبْصَٰرَكُمْ وَخَتَمَ عَلَىٰ قُلُوبِكُم مَّنْ إِلَٰهٌ غَيْرُ ٱللَّهِ يَأْتِيكُم بِهِ ۗ
ٱنظُرْ كَيْفَ نُصَرِّفُ ٱلْءَايَٰتِ ثُمَّ هُمْ يَصْدِفُونَ ٤٦

*Say: "Do you see, if Allāh were to take away your hearing and your sight, and put a **seal** [khātam] upon your hearts, which deity other than Allāh would bring these to you?" See how We explain in varieties the Messages, yet they do turn back! (6:46)*

وَأَضَلَّهُ ٱللَّهُ عَلَىٰ عِلْمٍ وَخَتَمَ عَلَىٰ سَمْعِهِۦ وَقَلْبِهِۦ وَجَعَلَ عَلَىٰ بَصَرِهِۦ غِشَٰوَةً

*...And Allāh has left him straying with knowledge; and has put a **seal** [khātam] upon his hearing and his heart, and he has placed a veil over his sight...(45:23)*

The word *khātam* is used in the sense of sealing something by bringing closure to it—like sealing an envelope, sealing a gift box, or sealing a door after it has been shut. In āyah 2:7, the sealing of hearts indicates a closing of the hearts by using a symbol of closure. The hearts of some people had to be sealed because they did not apply reasoning to understand truth. On the other hand, if we say sealing the heart meant a "stamp" was placed on the heart to document its authenticity, the meaning would be confusing and misleading.

Some people erroneously say *khātam* means "seal" in the sense of an emblem, stamp, or hallmark. If this opinion is accepted, then it appears that Allāhﷻ places an emblem on the hearts of hypocrites (see ayāh 2:7). But think about it. How does placing an emblem help the hypocrites, who are actually closing their hearts from understanding the message of Islam? Obviously, there is a mistake in this conclusion.

People also argue that Allāhﷻ made Nabi Muhammadﷺ a seal of all the messengers in the sense of making him the hallmark of all the messengers. He is certainly the greatest of all the messengers. These people think that Nabi Muhammadﷺ is a hallmark of all the messengers, but the institution of sending messengers was not closed or "sealed." This erroneous interpretation makes them believe that more prophets could come or have already come after Nabi Muhammadﷺ.

Khātam and khatim debate

People who say that Nabi Muhammadﷺ is not the "final" prophet argue that the word used in āyah 33:40 is *khātam*, not *khatim*. The word *khatim* would more commonly mean "final" or "last." According to them, the word *khatim* was not used, therefore more prophets could come or have already come.

The reason Allāh ﷻ used the word *khātam* rather than *khatim* is to show that the tradition of sending chains of prophets was "sealed" by bringing closure to it. The word *khātam* serves a dual purpose:

(a) to indicate closure of the tradition of sending new prophets, and

(b) to indicate Muhammad ﷺ was most eminent of all the prophets.

Āyah 5:3

The second Qur'ānic āyah to indicate Muhammad ﷺ was the last prophet is āyah 5:3. Let us read part of this long āyah.

This day I have perfected for you your religion, and completed upon you My blessing, and have accepted for you ISLAM as the religion. (5:3)

In this āyah, the Qur'ān clearly states that the religion was perfected and completed—and the religion of Islam is a way of life for all of us. Because the religion was perfected and completed, there is no purpose for any other prophet to come. A new prophet would not bring any new law or new guidance because the Qur'ān already contains guidance for all of mankind. The Qur'ān is complete in itself.

Those who believe new prophets are possible say the new prophets would only "revive" the religion from falling into obscurity. Why is a prophet needed to do that? This would create more disagreements and rifts among the ummah. Hundreds of scholars of Islam at different periods of time "revived" the religion by providing intelligent studies or directions for Muslims. None of these scholars claimed to be prophets.

Last Sermon about finality of prophethood

In the previous lesson, we studied the Farewell Sermon, also known as the Farewell Khutba. During the Last Sermon, Rasūlullāh ﷺ reminded us in clear words:

*"O People, **no prophet or apostle will come after me** and no new faith will be born. Reason well, therefore, O People, and understand the words which I convey to you. I leave behind me two things, the Qur'ān and my example, the Sunnah, and if you follow these you will never go astray."*

The Last Sermon also eliminates the possibility of new prophets in the future. Islam has been perfected and Allāh's ﷻ favor has been completed. We are given the Qur'ān and the Sunnah to follow. Islam has already been perfected, so there is no need for new messengers.

No new faith will be born

In the Last Sermon, Rasūlullāh ﷺ declared that no new faith will be born. This statement indicates that any new faith would be artificial faith, with little or no divine source. After Rasūlullāh's ﷺ death, hundreds of new faiths or faith-based ideologies evolved in Buddhism, Christianity, Hinduism, Islam, and Judaism. Hundreds of individuals claimed to be prophets, gods, God's reincarnation or avatar—but all such claims are false. Some of these artificial faiths do have good teachings, but that do not make them a divine faith worthy of following.

Hadīth on finality of prophethood

There are many ahādīth that conclusively prove that Nabi Muhammadﷺ was the final prophet.

Abū Huraira narrated that Rasūlullāhﷺ said, "The Children of Israel used to be ruled and guided by prophets: Whenever a prophet died, another would take over his place. There will be no prophet after me, but there will be Caliphs who will increase in number." The people asked, "O Allāh's Apostle! What do you order us [to do]?" He said, "Obey the one who will be given the pledge of allegiance first. Fulfill their [the Caliphs] rights, for Allāhﷻ will ask them about [any shortcoming] in ruling those Allāhﷻ has put under their guardianship." (al-Bukhārī 4:661; Sahih Muslim 20:4543.)

In another hadīth, Abū Huraira narrated: Allāh'sﷺ messenger said, "My similitude in comparison with the other prophets before me, is that of a man who has built a house nicely and beautifully, except for a place of one brick in a corner. The people go about it and wonder at its beauty, but say: 'Would that this brick be put in its place!' So I am that brick, and I am the last of the Prophets." (Sahih Bukhārī Vol. 4, Book 56, #735 and Sahih Muslim Book 30, #5,673.) This hadīth is also narrated by Jabir bin Abdullah in Sahih Bukhārī and Muslim.

In another hadīth, 'Ā'ishah (Ra) narrated: Rasūlullāhﷺ said "Prophethood will not continue after me, except the harbingers of good news." They asked "What are the harbingers of good news, O Messenger of Allāh?" He replied: "Virtuous and pious dreams that a Muslim sees or that are shown to him." (Musnad of Imam Ahmad ibn Hanbal.)

The following hadīth was narrated by Ismā'īl: I asked Abi Aufa, "Did you see Ibrāhīm, the son of Rasūlullāhﷺ?" He said, "Yes, but he died in his early childhood. Had there been a prophet after Muhammadﷺ, then his son would have lived, but there is no prophet after him." (al-Bukhārī 8.214.)

Interesting Facts

Hundreds of faiths and faith-based idealogies emerged in the last 1,000 years. Some of these are:

- Arya Samaj
- Babism
- Bahaism
- Bhakti Movement
- Branch Davidians
- Deen-e Elahi
- Jehovah's Witness
- Namdhari
- Nations of Islam
- Nation of Yahweh
- Seventh-day Adventists
- Sikhism

In conclusion, we can say that Islam has always stated that Muhammadﷺ is the final Messenger and no prophet will come after him. After Rasūlullāh'sﷺ death, many people claimed they were prophets. In the past 200 years, more people claimed they were prophets. Such claims are only innovations. Any innovation in the Islamic religion is bad. There is no harm in analyzing these claims, but we must not fall into the trap of endless arguments in favor of new prophets. The Qur'ān and the Sunnah of Rasūlullāhﷺ disputes the need for any new prophets.

Homework

1. Which āyah in the Qur'ān discusses the Finality of Prophethood?

A. Āyah 30:33.
B. Āyah 33:55.
C. Āyah 33:40.
D. Āyah 40:33.
E. Āyah 40:44.

2. Why does the āyah on the Finality of Prophethood state Muhammad ﷺ "is not the father of any of your men"?

A. To settle the dispute about Zaid being the son of Muhammad ﷺ.
B. To settle the dispute about Zaid's marriage with Zainab.
C. To settle the dispute about the father of Muhammad ﷺ.
D. To settle the dispute about the sons of Muhammad ﷺ.
E. To settle the dispute about sūrah al-Ahzāb.

3. According to the lesson, which of the following choices about the Seal of the Prophet is correct?

A. The seal was an ornament or emblem, but nothing else.
B. The seal was primarily the closure of the prophethood tradition.
C. The seal was an approval of God.
D. The seal was an approval of new prophets to come.
E. The seal was Rasūlullāh's ﷺ approval of past and future prophets.

4. Many ayāt in the Qur'ān mention the sealing of the hearts of non-believers. What Arabic word is used to indicate such a sealing?

A. Khatim.
B. Khalifah.
C. Khashiya.
D. Khātam.
E. Khosrow.

5. According to the lesson, for how long have some people spread the idea that new prophets could come after Nabi Muhammad ﷺ?

A. Since the time of Rasūlullāh ﷺ.
B. Since the time of the Khalifas.
C. Since the time of Jesus.
D. Within the last 500 years.
E. Within the last 1,000 years.

6. Some people say a particular Arabic word was not used to confirm that Nabi Muhammad ﷺ is not the final prophet. Which word do they mention in support of their argument?

A. Nabiyyin.
B. Rasūl.
C. Khatim.
D. Imām.
E. Khalifah.

7. Based on the Finality of Prophethood lesson, which of the following statements is correct?

A. Those who claim to be prophets after Nabi Muhammad ﷺ are false prophets.
B. Those who claim to be prophets after Nabi Muhammad ﷺ are genuine prophets.
C. Those who claim to be prophets after Nabi Muhammad ﷺ are his descendants.
D. Those who claim to be prophets after Nabi Muhammad ﷺ are misleading people.
E. Only (a) and (d).

8. Which of the following choices is correct about the statement that Nabi Muhammad ﷺ is the Final Messenger?

A. Only a minority of Muslims believe in the statement.
B. The vast majority of Muslims believe in the statement.
C. Only a minority of Muslims do not believe in the statement.
D. Only (a) and (c).
E. Only (b) and (c).

9. According to the lesson, people who claim that new prophets can come after Muhammad ﷺ say the new prophets would do something specific. What would the new prophets do?

A. Bring new revelations.
B. Revive the religion.
C. Create a new religion.
D. Revive all lost religions.
E. Do nothing.

WEEKEND 10 Classwork

Hadīth: *Collection and Classification*

Objective of the Lesson:

Hadīth are not only the sayings of Rasūlullāh ﷺ—they are much more than that. Students will learn about the structure, types, purpose, and classification of hadīth. They will also learn about the collectors of hadīth.

Throughout the Islamic Studies curriculum, we have learned about various aspects of hadīth (singular) and ahādīth (plural). This year, we will study hadīth again to review some of the aspects we learned earlier and to extend our knowledge and understanding of ahādīth.

Collectors of hadīth

Formal collection of hadīth did not begin until about 200 years after Rasūlullāh ﷺ passed away. The period between 200 A.H. and 300 A.H. was the most significant in terms of the collection of ahādīth. During this century, after several attempts to collect hadīth, six collections eventually emerged as the most authentic. Over a period of time, these six collections earned the name **Sahih Sittah,** or Six Correct Books. They became the standard works of hadīth. These six collections eventually became known by the names of the collectors.

The six collectors are as follows:

Name	Birth	Death
Bukhārī	194 A.H	256 A.H
Muslim	204 A.H.	261 A.H.
Ibn Majah	202 A.H.	275 A.H.
Tirmidhī	209 A.H.	279 A.H.
Nasā'ī	214 A.H.	303 A.H.
Abū Dawūd	202 A.H.	275 A.H.

Classification of hadīth

During and after collection of all the ahādīth by the six collectors, many early writers devoted their time and effort to studying the collections. Such analysis continued for several decades. During this analysis, early writers raised questions about some of the collections. After careful and methodical study, they classified all the ahādīth into two broad categories. One classified all ahādīth by various **degrees of authenticity.** Another classified ahādīth by the **number of transmitters**.

Based on the degree of authenticity, all ahādīth can be classified into one of four categories. These categories are:

1. **Sahih, or genuine hadīth**: These are the most reliable hadīth that have no weakness in the chain of narrators (**isnad**) or in the text of the narrations (**matn**). These ahādīth uphold the teachings of the Qur'ān. A large number of ahādīth are in this category.
2. **Hasn, or fair hadīth:** According to some experts, some of the narrators are less reliable or weaker in memory compared to the narrators of sahih hadīth. The issue here is not as much about the authenticity of the ahādīth, but as the individuals who transmitted them.
3. **Dhaif, or weak hadīth:** When the hadīth were being collected, there was a large number of spurious and doubtful hadīth in circulation. The collectors inadvertently included some of these hadīth, but upon further study, these hadīth appeared questionable. Further study revealed that there might be disagreement about the text or the content of the same hadīth collected by various collectors. It is also possible that one or two transmitters might have been questionable, making the entire hadīth questionable.
4. **Maudu, or forged hadīth:** These are ahādīth that are totally fabricated.

As questions were raised about the authenticity of several ahādīth, there were attempts to find out how many transmitters actually reported the same hadīth. If a large number of transmitters reported the same hadīth, it was considered authentic. Thus, based on

the number of transmitters during the first three generations of Muslims, all ahādīth can also be divided into several types. They are:

1. **Mutawatir:** The word *mutawatir* means "consecutive." A *large number* of the first three generations of Muslims transmitted a particular hadīth, so there is no doubt about the authenticity of the hadīth. It is not clearly explained what a "large number" of transmitters means, but anywhere from four to 70 transmitters is considered a large number.

2. **Mashhur:** The word *mashhur* means "famous." This types of ahādīth originally transmitted by a few of the first-generation transmitters, but, subsequently, these were transmitted, on their authority, by large number of second- or third-generation transmitters. Even though these ahādīth are widely known, they may not be authentic.

3. **Ahad:** The word *ahad* means "single." This type of hadīth was transmitted during the first three generations of Muslims by only one to four transmitters. If the transmitters was more than four, then the hadīth would be categorized as a *mutawatir*.

4. **Gharib:** The *ahad* hadīth can also be classified as *gharib*, meaning "strange." These hadīth are considered strange because only one transmitter reported it.

5. **Aziz:** This is another form of *ahad* hadīth. The word *aziz* means "strong." These ahādīth were transmitted by only two narrators, but the text of the hadīth appears very convincing.

Compilation of ahādīth

The compilation of ahādīth took place over a long period of time. During this time, some of the close companions of Rasūlullāhﷺ, or the immediate followers of the companions, were alive. The companions narrated many ahādīth that were eventually collected by dedicated followers of Islam. Based on the sources of the ahādīth and the period when they were collected, we can identify four main periods of collection.

1. **Period of Rasūlullāhﷺ:** During this period, Rasūlullāhﷺ was alive. This period lasted until 10 A.H., or 632 C.E.

2. **Period of companions:** The second period lasted approximately 89 years, between 11 A.H. and 100 A.H. During this period, most of the companions of Rasūlullāhﷺ were alive.

3. **Period of Tābi'īn:** The third period lasted approximately 99 years, between 101 A.H. and 200 A.H. During this period, all the companions had died, but the descendants and followers of the companions, called Tābi'īn, were alive.
4. **Period of Taba Tābi'īn:** The fourth period lasted from 200 A.H. to 300 A.H. The followers and descendants of the actual Tābi'īn lived during this time period.

Collection during the time of Rasūlullāh ﷺ

During the time of Rasūlullāh ﷺ, there was no formal collection or compilation of ahādīth. In fact, Rasūlullāh ﷺ discouraged collection of ahādīth—he did not want people to confuse the text of the Qur'ān with his sayings. For this reason, we do not find ahādīth collected by Abū Bakr, 'Umar or 'Uthmān although they were close to Rasūlullāh ﷺ. Also people did not feel the necessity to write down ahādīth because what Rasūlullāh ﷺ said was fresh in their memory and Rasūlullāh ﷺ was alive to clarify any doubt. During this period, most ahādīth were orally transmitted.

Collection during the time of the companions

After Rasūlullāh ﷺ passed away, people continued to show interest in what Rasūlullāh ﷺ said or did about a particular matter. New and unique circumstances began to surface every day as Muslims conquered new territories and more and more people accepted Islam. The four rightly guided Khalifās expanded the territories of Muslim rule beyond Arabia. During this period, Muslims wanted to know what Rasūlullāh ﷺ had done or would do under such circumstances. Moreover, many new socio-political circumstances developed that necessitated knowing Rasūlullāh's ﷺ response to similar situations.

During this period, there were not many regular or methodical compilations. People collected ahādīth, but they did not compile them. Compilation took place much later, during the periods of Tābi'īn and Taba Tābi'īn.

Collection during the period of Tābi'īn

Significant progress was made during this period in the formal collection and compilation of ahādīth. After the death of most of the companions, the Tābi'īn devoted their time and effort to collecting and compiling ahādīth. During this period, all four Imams who formulated madhāhib were born, worked, and some also died. The chart below provides the birth and death dates of the Imams. Compare this chart to the chart of the birth and death dates of the six hadīth collectors in the beginning of this chapter. The six hadīth collectors were born and worked several decades after the four Imāms had already served the Muslim ummah.

	Birth	Death
Abū Hanifa	80 A.H	150 A.H
Malik Ibn Anas	94 A.H.	178 A.H.
As- Shāfi'ī	150 A.H.	204 A.H.
Ahmad Ibn Hanbal	163 A.H.	240 A.H.

The collection of ahādīth during this period was mostly conducted independently. For example, Abū Hanifa collected ahādīth independent of Imam Malik and Imam Shāfi'ī and vice versa. If all of them had collected the same ahādīth, there would not have been separate madhāhib.

Collection during the period of Taba Tābi'īn

This was the most significant period of ahādīth collection. This period lasted from 200 A.H. to 300 A.H. All six of the ahādīth collectors lived and worked during this period. The monumental works of the collectors provided a definitive resource for understanding Islam through ahādīth. They established a uniform methodology about how hadīth would be collected.

In order to identify and classify a genuine hadīth, the collectors devoted time and energy to examining the chain of narrators (*isnad*).

First, they determined whether the chain was authentic and reliable. Then they determined if the text of the hadīth was free of any contradictions. They also examined whether the people who transmitted the particular hadīth had meaningful connections to one another. In other words: When and where was each transmitter born? When and where did they live and die? Was it geographically possible for the transmitters to meet? Above all, were they trustworthy and did they have a good memory?

In order to accomplish this enormous task, all six ahādīth collectors traveled to various parts of the region and interviewed a large number of people. Eventually, they compiled a large number of ahādīth and eliminated many others that seemed unreliable.

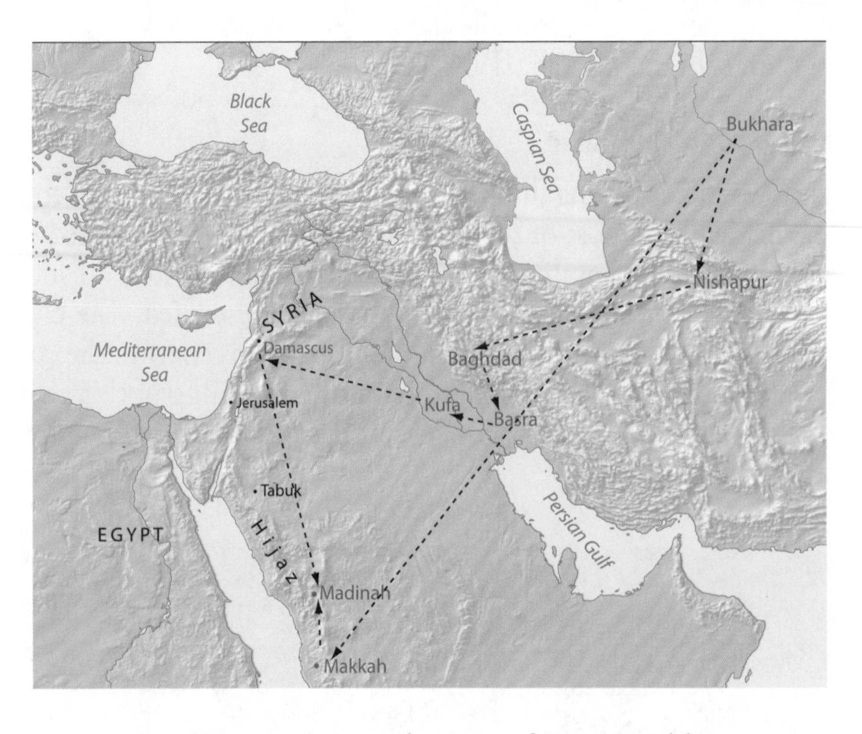

Map showing the travel routes of Imām Bukhārī

Homework

1. What was the predominant mode of transmitting ahādīth during Rasūlullāh's ﷺ time?

A. Oral transmission.
B. Written transmission.
C. No transmission of hadīth occurred during Rasūlullāh's ﷺ time.
D. Through formal religious schools.
E. Through print media.

2. Which of the following choices is correct about the phrase "Sahih Sittah"?

A. It refers to the six books of Imam Bukhārī.
B. It refers to the six books of Imam Nawawi.
C. It refers to collections of hadīth by six main compilers.
D. It refers to the last six Juz of the Qur'ān.
E. It refers to the collection of hadīth by four Khalīfas.

3. According to the lesson, how many broad periods of ahādīth collection can be identified based on the sources of the ahādīth and the time period when they were collected?

A. Three periods.
B. Four periods.
C. Seven periods.
D. Nine periods.
E. One period.

4. According to the lesson, which period of ahādīth collection lasted from 200 A.H. to 300 A.H.?

A. The period of the companions.
B. The period of the Taba Tābi'īn.
C. The period of Tābi'īn.
D. The period of the Imams.
E. The period of the Khalīfas.

5. According to the lesson, which period was the most significant in terms of the methodical collection of hadīth and their formal compilation?

A. The period during Rasūlullāh's ﷺ lifetime.
B. The period immediately after Rasūlullāh ﷺ passed away.
C. The period between 200 A.H. and 300 A.H.
D. The period between 40 A.H. and 100 A.H.
E. The period of the Rightly Guided Khalīfas.

6. Why did people begin to show interest in ahādīth?

A. People wanted to know what Rasūlullāh ﷺ would do about a particular matter.
B. New territories were conquered and new circumstances developed, which made people want to find answers.
C. New socio-political situations necessitated finding answers in Rasūlullāh's ﷺ conduct.
D. All of the above.
E. Only (a) and (b).

7. Which of the following statements about the compilation and collection of ahādīth during the time of the companions is correct?

A. Hadīth were extensively compiled and collected.
B. Hadīth were extensively compiled by the four Imams.
C. No hadīth were collected or compiled.
D. Most of the hadīth were compiled into books.
E. Hadīth were collected but were not compiled.

8. What is the prominent feature of ahādīth collected during the time of the Tābi'īn?

A. The collection was mostly conducted independently.
B. The collection was comprehensive.
C. The collection was mostly assimilated into other volumes.
D. Only (b) and (c).
E. Only (a) and (c).

9. In order for a hadīth to be sahih, or genuine, which of the following criteria must be met?

A. Hadīth should be reliable with a strong isnad and matn.
B. Only a reliable matn is necessary; the isnad is secondary in importance.
C. Only the isnad must be reliable; the matn is not important.
D. If a hadīth is collected, the isnad or matn is not important.
E. If some of the narrators are reliable, the hadīth is sahih.

Unit 3: Challenges in Madīnah

Throughout the Weekend Learning Series, we have covered the important events that happened in Madīnah after Nabi Muhammad ﷺ migrated there in 622 C.E. In Madīnah, a new group of Muslims emerged that vacillated between belief and non-belief. Known as munāfiq, these groups were the hypocrites who had dual standards about belief. They symbolically entered Islam from one side and exited from the other at their convenience. The first chapter in this unit describes the hypocrites. Elements of hypocrisy was evident in some of the major developments in Madīnah, as we will note in the events described in all the chapters in this unit. Three chapters describe Rasūlullāh's ﷺ interactions with three prominent Jewish tribes in Madīnah. These tribes plotted to kill Nabi Muhammad ﷺ and conspired against the Muslims. Nabi Muhammad ﷺ had to deal with the tribes in a manner that would positively shape the future history of Islam; and would give new direction to the newly emerging Muslim society in Madīnah. On one hand, the tribes were treated with great deal of compassion; and on the other hand, a sense of justice was never violated. The lessons highlight these issues to allow us to fully comprehend the challenges in Madīnah. Another challenge in Madīnah was to mobilize a large army to thwart a possible Roman attack on Arabia. The chapter about the Mission to Tabūk discusses the difficulties of forming an army and the trials and tribulations faced by the army. Although there was no battle, there is an important lesson to learn from the mission.

Unit 3: Challenges in Madīnah

Hypocrites

The hypocrites mentioned in the Qur'ān were actually Muslims, but their commitment to Islam remained questionable. Hypocrites are difficult to identify because their hypocrisy resides deep in their hearts. Students will learn how they can protect themselves from their own hypocrisy and the hypocrisy of others. May Allāh ﷻ protect us from hypocritical conduct. May Allāh ﷻ save us from the evil activities of hypocrites in our society.

Banu Qaynuqa: *Threat Within Madīnah*

Soon after the Battle of Badr, the Jewish tribe Banu Qaynuqa began conspiring against the Muslims. The tribe challenged the Muslims to fight. Muslim efforts to restore peace were foiled. The Muslims had no other choice but to expel the tribe from Madīnah. This lesson explains these events with the proper historical perspective.

Banu Nadīr: *Treachery Within Madīnah*

Soon after the Battle of Uhud, the Jewish tribe Banu Nadīr was expelled from Madīnah. Banu Nadīr had violated the peace treaty with the Muslims. What caused the tension between the tribe and the Muslims? Students will learn the historical truth about one of the cruel conspiracies against the Muslims.

Banu Qurayzah

Banu Qurayzah nearly destroyed the Muslim community when they conspired with the polytheist Quraish to attack the Muslims. Before they could launch the attack, a misunderstanding caused a rift between the Jewish tribe and the polytheists. The Muslims were saved from an imminent attack. Soon after the Battle of the Trench, some members of Banu Qurayzah were punished for their treachery. This chapter exposes the truth behind these events.

Mission to Tabūk: *A Test of Steadfastness*

The expedition to Tabūk challenged the Muslims to a severe test. Many of them failed the test and many others emerged successful. The Muslims did not have to fight the Byzantines, but the expedition proved to be a show of force to others. When the Muslims began conquering outlying areas at a later time, the experience of Tabūk helped them. This lesson discusses the expedition and the twists and turns of these historical events.

Hypocrites

Objective of the Lesson:

The hypocrites mentioned in the Qur'ān were actually Muslims, but their commitment to Islam remained questionable. Hypocrites are difficult to identify because their hypocrisy resides deep in their hearts. Students will learn how they can protect themselves from their own hypocrisy and the hypocrisy of others. May Allāh ﷻ protect us from hypocritical conduct. May Allāh ﷻ save us from the evil activities of hypocrites in our society.

While living in Makkah, Rasūlullāh ﷺ had to confront just one group of people—the idolaters among the Makkan Quraish. After he migrated to Madīnah, his challenges magnified and diversified. He had to confront several ethnically and religiously disparate groups of people. They were Jews and Christians. As a result, many Madīnan sūrahs address issues and challenges arising from interactions with these two groups.

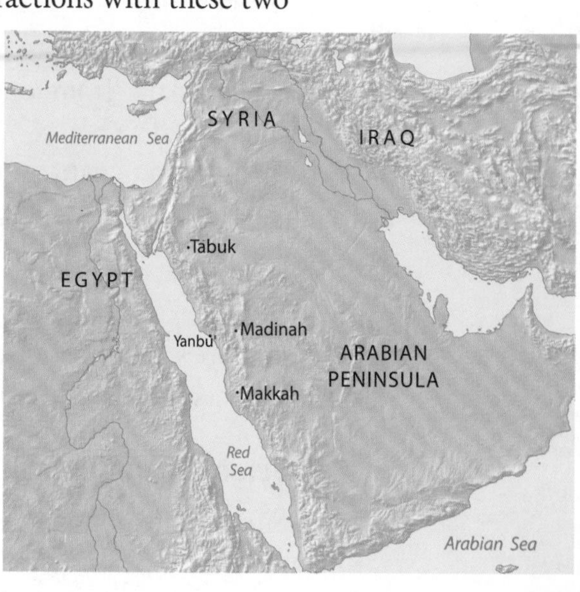

When many local people began accepting Islam, a new group emerged among the Muslims. They were the **Munāfiq**, meaning "the hypocrites." This group of people was led by certain affluent, influential individuals who hoped to dominate local politics. They realized that their political and economic interests could be preserved and enhanced only if they accepted Islam rather than oppose it. They suspected Islam would not emerge as a powerful ideology or faith. They figured that working against Islam from within might allow them to destabilize the faith and retain their political and economic aspirations. This new Madīnan phenomenon became a much-discussed topic in the Qur'ān.

Diversity in Madīnah

Before discussing the hypocrites further, we should first understand the socio-political condition in Madīnah. The city was distinctly different from Makkah in many ways. For example, the cultures and faiths of its inhabitants were significantly different. As a result, life in Madīnah was more complex and full of challenges. In contrast, people in Makkah practiced one faith and belonged to one large community. Their main source of income was from commerce. The main profession of the people in Madīnah was agriculture.

When Muslims arrived in Madīnah, they noticed the political environment was tense, and interclan rivalry was visible. Madīnah and its immediate 20-square-mile surroundings included 11 tribes living in and around the fertile volcanic soil and water sources. Three of the tribes were Jewish, with an adult male population of more than 2,000. The other eight tribes were Arab.

The munāfiq

A munāfiq is a hypocrite who has dual standards about belief. He or she symbolically enters Islam from one side and exits from the other. Hypocrites are never fully committed to Islam. When Islam benefits them, they pretend to be Muslims. But when the situation changes, they quickly condemn Islam and break away from Muslims.

The word munāfiq derives from the root word "*nafaq*," which means an underground burrow or passageway that opens at both ends. A chipmunk, mouse, or other animal can enter one side of the burrow and exit through the other. Hypocrisy, in general, describes the practice of claiming to have certain standards or beliefs but acting in a manner that is contradictory to those standards or beliefs.

Sūrah Baqarah on munāfiq

Sūrah Baqarah begins by describing some of the key attributes of believers and nonbelievers. In ayāh 8, a third category of people are discussed—the hypocrites.

However, the sūrah never mentions the term "munāfiq." It simply introduces their mode of approach regarding faith. The reason it explained this way is simple. Hypocrisy cannot be detected from a person's appearance. Therefore, the Qur'ān gives people the benefit of doubt, because it is nearly impossible to identify a hypocrite. Some hypocrites knowingly and intentionally practice hypocrisy, while others unknowingly practice it. The characteristics of these hypocrites are described in further detail sūrah 9 and 63. For simplicity, we will discuss āyāt 8-16 from sūrah Baqarah.

Verses 8–20 from sūrah Baqarah

> **8.** *And of mankind there are some who say: "We believe in Allāh and in the Hereafter", but they are not at all Believers.* **9.** *They pretend that they deceive Allāh and those who believe. But they do not deceive any except themselves, and they do not perceive.* **10.** *In their hearts is a disease, so Allāh increased to them the disease, and for them is a painful punishment because they have been belying.* **11.** *And when it is said to them: "Do not make mischief in the earth," they say: "Surely we are indeed peacemakers."* **12.** *Is it not that they themselves are the mischief-makers? But they do not perceive.* **13.** *And when it is said to them: "Believe as the people believe," they say: "Shall we believe as the fools have believed?" Is it not that surely they are themselves the fools? But they do not know.* **14.** *And when they meet those who believe, they say: "We believe." But when they are alone with their Shaitān, they say: "We are really with you, we by ourselves were only mocking."* **15.** *Allāh throws back the mockery to them, and leaves them alone in their trespasses blindly wandering on.* **16.** *These are those who buy Error for Guidance, so their trade does not bring profit, and they are not guided.*

Āyāt 8-10

The hypocrites' statement, "We believe in Allāh and in the Hereafter" is a verbal declaration. This verbal declaration gives the impression that they are genuine believers. True believers have no reason to doubt the hypocrites' intention, therefore, believers must accept the hypocrites as their own. But this causes a problem for believers for they are not aware of the motives of the hypocrites. Using the duplicity of their intention, the hypocrites are determined to destroy Islam. However, Allāh ﷻ knows what is in everyone's heart.[4:63; 33:51] A verbal declaration of faith has no value, because there is no commitment to faith. Therefore, Allāh ﷻ informs them right away that *they are not at all believers.*

Hypocrites are under assumption that these false statements will go undetected. They are convinced they can deceive Allāh ﷻ and the believers. The irony is that they do not understand that they are actually deceiving themselves by such conduct. In any action of deception (*khada'a*), the perpetrator intends to derive benefit by tricking or harming others. Hypocrites intentionally want to deceive Muslims, but their acts of deception do not harm Muslims—only themselves.

These people are understood as having a spiritual disease (*marada*) in their hearts. Here the heart (*qalb*) is used as a metonymy for a force within human beings that sustains their intellect. This impairment of qalb is self-inflicted; therefore, according to the law of cause of consequence, Allāh ﷻ increases the disease for them. Here the word *kānu* is in past tense, and *yakdhibūn* (the act of lying) is in present tense—combination of past and present tense indicates that falsification and lying is a persistent nature.

The criminal codes of all countries include the principle of punishing a criminal. It is universally accepted that the punishment should fit the crime. In the Qur'ān, the acts of disbelief, gross injustice and tyranny are always viewed seriously. Here, the crime of nurturing and exacerbating spiritual disease—a form of disbelief—is considered a serious crime, therefore, the divine punishment (*'adhāb*) for such a crime will be painful.

Āyāt 11-14

The act of corruption (*fasāda*) is the cause of many troubles on earth. In most cases, corruption is perpetrated by those in power or those who have authority to change or influence the course of an action. The identity of the speaker who says, "*Do not make corruption...*" is intentionally unclear, because the victim or victims of corruption can come from any walk of life. The speaker can be a collective voice of victims against those in power.

The theme of the passage is a spiritual matter, therefore, *fasāda* indicates acts of corruption in the matter of faith. These acts tat are intended to confuse and vitiate the faith of te believers through friendly overtures. However hypocrites do not realize that they, themselves, are the cause of dissension.

Most of the early believers in Madīnah struggled financially and they did not have any political power. These conditions led the hypocrites and nonbelievers to ridicule the Muslims as fools who believed blindly. When the hypocrites met the believers, they said, "*We believe*" with the intention of deceiving them. But when they were with their own group of people, they said, "*We are really with you, we by ourselves were only mocking.*" Here, their own group of people is called *shayātin* (pl. of Shaitān) to denote those evil people whose faith and conduct run counter to what is good and true. The plural *shayātin* is used to indicate there is a number of evil people indulging in this corruption.

Āyāt 15-16

Mocking Muslims gives the hypocrites temporary satisfaction, but Allāh uses this mockery to hurt them. First, Allāh leaves the hypocrites to their transgression, (*tughyān*, transgression, being exceedingly wicked) for a while. As a result, the believers will have to experience the effect of their nefarious activities for some time. However, contempt for the truth never harms, rather, over time it recoils on those who showed contempt. This is in accordance with the law of Allāh (Sunan Allāh—see Chapter 2) which states that recompense for any evil act is proportionate to the evil act (6:161; 27:90; 28:84; 37:39; 40:40; 53:31; 66:7; 78:26). The word *yastahzi'u* (lit. he derides, he mocks) is used in the sense of imposing penalty, indicating Allāh will bring disgrace and ignominy upon the hypocrites.

Many Qur'ānic teachings are illustrated figuratively with trading activities. When the moral of a teaching was presented using terms such as profit, loss, barter, balance, and loan, people from all walks of life could relate to it. In trading activities a person spends his or her assets to acquire another asset. Misguided people are described as trading on their assets—in this case, their reasoning, understanding, willingness, and efforts—to purchase error.

End notes

From the preceding discussion we now have an illustrative description of the hypocrites. It is also clear that identifying hypocrites is very difficult because the condition arises in their heart. This portrait of hypocrites is as valid today as it was during Rasūlullāh's ﷺ time. Let us summarize the key features of hypocrites:

When hypocrites are with Muslims:

1. They claim they believe in Allāh ﷻ and the Hereafter.
2. They claim they are the peacemakers.
3. They claim they believe in Islam.

When hypocrites are with their own people:

1. They do not believe "like the fools believe."
2. They support their own people, and claim they were only mocking Islam.

What hypocrites truly are and what they face:

1. They are not believers.
2. They only deceive themselves.
3. They suffer from their own self-imposed spiritual disease.
4. They will face painful punishment.
5. They are the actual troublemakers.
6. They remain entangled in their own blind circle.
7. Their activities do not benefit them and they buy error.

May Allāh ﷻ protect us from adopting hypocritical conduct. May Allāh ﷻ save us from the evil activities of hypocrites in our society.

Homework

1. What is the meaning of the word "nafaq?"

____

2. Which of the following statements about hypocrisy is correct?

A. It is entirely about faith in Islam and working against Islam.
B. It is about one's standards and level of faith in religion.
C. It is about Jews and Muslims in Madīnah during Rasūlullāhs time.
D. It is about certain standards and beliefs about anything and acting in a manner opposite to it.
E. It is about a type of Muslim whose heart is impure.

3. Which of the following statements about hypocrisy is correct?

A. It is a disease that affects one's brain cells, making the person non-Muslim.
B. It cannot be detected in the person's appearance.
C. It is about Muslims who refuse to believe anything.
D. It is about people who abandon religion and adopt another one.
E. It is about Muslims who say they believe in Allāh and the Hereafter.

4. Why does Allāh say, "They are not at all believers," even though they declare "We believe in Allāh and the Hereafter," as mentioned in āyāt 2:8–10 of sūrah Baqarah?

A. Because they did not declare their faith in a masjid.
B. Because they supported Jewish tribes in Madīnah.
C. Because Allāh knows their verbal declaration contains no commitment to faith.
D. Because they would not perform salāt.
E. Because they refused to help the Muslims who migrated to Madīnah.

5. What is the significance of the word *qalb* (meaning heart) used in āyāt 2:8–10 of sūrah Baqarah ?

A. It is a physical organ in one's body.
B. It is the part of the heart that triggers a heart attack.
C. It is the subconscious part of one's brain.
D. It is a figure of speech for a force within a person that sustains intellect.
E. It is a burrow or passageway that opens at both ends.

6. How does the Qur'ān identify hypocrites' own group of people with whom they attest that they are actually mocking the Muslims?

A. Brethren.
B. Wali.
C. Imām.
D. Soothsayer.
E. Shayātin.

7. How did the hypocrites in Madīnah refer to Muslims?

A. As fools.
B. As hypocrites.
C. As confused.
D. As animals.
E. As slaves.

8. According to the Qur'ān, misguided people trade guidance to buy something else. What do they buy?

A. Hell.
B. Punishment.
C. Failure.
D. Error.
E. Disgrace.

9. What sort of punishment are reserved for hypocrites, as mentioned in the Qur'ān?

____

10. Hypocrites only harm themselves by their actions. Write three things that hypocrites experience as a result of their hypocrisy.

1. ____

2. ____

3. ____

Banu Qaynuqa: *Threat Within Madīnah*

Objective of the Lesson:

Soon after the Battle of Badr, the Jewish tribe Banu Qaynuqa began conspiring against the Muslims. The tribe challenged the Muslims to fight. Muslim efforts to restore peace were foiled. The Muslims had no other choice but to expel the tribe from Madīnah. This lesson explains these events with the proper historical perspective.

In Level 4 we studied Rasūlullāh's ﷺ migration to Madīnah. In Level 5 we studied several battles Muslims fought after they migrated to Madīnah. The first one was the Battle of Badr, which was fought two years after the migration. In that battle, a poorly prepared Muslim army of 313 men defeated a Makkan army of 1,000 men.

The Muslim victory in the Battle of Badr created new challenges in Madīnah. The victory of a small contingent of Muslims against the mighty forces of Makkah was sensational. Most residents of Madīnah recognized the Muslims as a major power. They realized that they would have to live with this new power. Opposing the Muslims would not be a wise choice. The residents realized the leadership of Rasūlullāh ﷺ was unlike any other they had experienced in the past. Whether or not it was a result of this victory, more and more Arabs began accepting Islam. While Islam was making inroads in Madīnah, the Jews of Madīnah were clearly not happy to see this progress. They became a new challenger for the Muslims.

Misinformation continues

There is a large amount of misinformation and misinterpretation circulating even today about Muslim and Jewish interaction in Madīnah. The Internet promotes such misinformation and half-truths about how Muslims dealt with the Jewish challenge in Madīnah. If you are uninformed or misinformed about the Jewish tribes in Madīnah, particularly Banu Qaynuqa, you might easily accept the viewpoint of certain interest groups on the Internet.

The main reason we are learning about Banu Qaynuqa is to understand what truly happened in Madīnah shortly after the Battle of Badr. But first let us review the historical accounts of Jewish settlement in Madīnah.

Jewish settlement in Madīnah

After the Romans destroyed Jerusalem in 70 C.E., a large number of Jews migrated to other parts of the world. Three of the largest tribes settled in and around Madīnah. They chose to live in Madīnah because they believed a new Messenger would come and settle in the region. They hoped they would be the first to follow him. With his support, they would establish a new kingdom, similar to that of David and Solomon.

Banu Qaynuqa was one of the three major Jewish tribes. They lived within the city limits of Madīnah. They had a serious rivalry with the two other Jewish tribes—Banu Nadīr and Banu Qurayzah. Due to this mutual rivalry, the Jewish tribes in Madīnah could never form a central authority to govern Madīnah. Instead, they paid an annual tribute to other Arab tribes, so they would not be attacked and would be protected in the event of inter-tribal warfare.

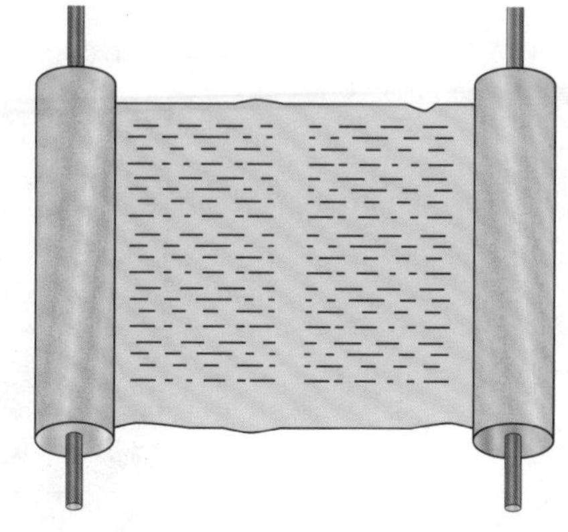

About five years before Rasūlullāh's ﷺ hijrat to Madīnah, these three Jewish tribes incited Arab hostility by provoking two Arab tribes—the 'Aws and the Khazraj—to fight. The Arab tribes fought the ferocious Battle of Bu'āth, in which the Jewish tribes sided against each other.

Constitution of Madīnah

After Rasūlullāh ﷺ migrated to Madīnah in 622 C.E., one of the first things he did was establish a pact with various Madīnite tribes. The pact involved two main Arab tribes in Madīnah, the Aws and the Khajraz, who were bitter enemies, and three Jewish tribes that lived inside or on the outskirts of Madīnah.

The main clauses of the Constitution were designed to establish a meaningful administrative policy of the city and establish guidelines to deal with different inter-community relations. The main areas covered by the pact were:

1. Agreement pertaining to Muslim affairs
2. Agreement pertaining to non-Muslim Arabs
3. Agreement pertaining to Jews
4. Agreement involving everybody in Madīnah

The pact required all tribes in and around Madīnah to boycott the Makkan Quraish and not offer them any assistance. The pact also required that if any of the Madīnan tribes were attacked by a third party, every other tribe would support that tribe. Furthermore, if the city of Madīnah was attacked by other tribes, all of the Madīnan tribes should defend the city.

Trouble in Madīnah

Banu Qaynuqa was a Jewish tribe that lived within the city limits of Madīnah. Within two years of the Muslims migrating from Makkah to Madīnah, the relationship between Banu Qaynuqa and the Muslims went from bad to worse. Particularly after the Battle of Badr, the relationship deteriorated due to several unfortunate events.

Banu Qaynuqa was secretly opposed to the Muslims. They were jealous of and angry with Nabi Muhammadﷺ for claiming to be a prophet. For nearly two years, they continued to ridicule the Muslims and belittle them for their misery and refugee status. There were several small skirmishes between the Muslims and the Jews. The Jews admitted that if it were not for the Constitution of Madīnah, they would have dealt sternly with the Muslims long ago.

The Muslims faced another dilemma. On many occasions, they had borrowed money from the rich Jewish people at high interest rates and fell victim to their unfavorable lending practices.

Hatred after the Battle of Badr

Banu Qaynuqa was not required to participate in the Battle of Badr. They were required to remain neutral in the battle and not to side with the Makkan Quraish. The battle was purely an issue between the Muslims and the Quraish.

However, Banu Qaynuqa was unhappy with the Muslim victory in the Battle of Badr. They openly expressed their disappointment. They had believed the Muslim army would not be able to defeat the mighty Quraish.

The Jews and hypocrites in Madīnah understood that Muslim power increased after the battle. They realized that two years before, these Muslims came to Madīnah as refugees, poor and weak. After the Battle of Badr, they were in a position to command respect and attention. In the past, these immigrants only influenced other Muslims. Now Muslim authority seemed to apply to the entire city of Madīnah. The Jews and hypocrites were not pleased.

One day, a Muslim woman went to a Jewish jewelry shop, where the shop owner mischievously pinned her robe to the wall. When the woman moved to leave, her robe pulled away from her body, leaving her naked. The shop owner burst into laughter, thinking he played a good joke on the woman. This incident sparked a huge commotion. A Muslim man jumped on the shopkeeper and killed him. Within moments, other Jews cornered the Muslim man and killed him.

One murder was committed and others retaliated against the murderer. According to tribal norms of the time, justice was served. But soon, sporadic violence broke out between the Muslims and Banu Qaynuqa. Rasūlullāh ﷺ intervened. He publicly asked the Jews to stop the skirmishes and respect the covenant of mutual peace and security. Nobody listened to his appeal.

Challenge by Banu Qaynuqa

When Rasūlullāh ﷺ asked them to maintain peace, someone replied: "O Muhammad, you seem to think that we are your people. Do not deceive yourself because you defeated an army of Quraish that had no knowledge of war and you got the better of them; for, by God, if we fight you, you will find that we are real men, and that you have not met the likes of us."

The tribe had openly challenged Rasūlullāh ﷺ and the Muslims. After this, the Muslims had no choice but to fight Banu Qaynuqa. But the Muslims did not respond immediately. They did not want to fight Banu Qaynuqa over a verbal challenge, so they gave the tribe time to pacify the situation. Because Banu Qaynuqa provoked the situation, it would have been useful if their chief came forward and try to diffuse the situation. However, the chief of the Jewish tribe failed to do several things:

1. He did not come forward to restrain the violent people who challenged the Muslims
2. He did not reconfirm the tribe's allegiance to the peace treaty
3. He did nothing to calm the tension created by the verbal challenge

The failure to take any of these measures indicated that the chief supported the opinion of the violent people: "If we fight you, you will find that we are real men, and that you have not met the likes of us."

Blockade of Banu Qaynuqa

Despite the peace initiative made by the Muslims, Banu Qaynuqa did not respond. As a result, the Muslims began to barricade Banu Qaynuqa in their quarters. During this period, the tribe did not send any representative to indicate they would comply with the peace initiative. Day after day passed by, but the tribe did not offer peace. The blockade lasted for 15 days. Then the tribe finally came forward and surrendered.

During the blockade, Banu Qaynuqa truly wanted to fight the Muslims. They were waiting for other Jewish tribes to come to their rescue and then they would fight. They also hoped that one of their strongest Arab allies, Abdullah Ibn Ubayy, the chief of the Khazraj tribe, would extend help.

After the blockade

Banu Qaynuqa surrendered on the conditions that they would give up all their wealth, and they would be allowed to keep their women and children. Rasūlullāh ﷺ ordered that all men should be taken captives. At this point, Abdullah Ibn Ubayy came forward to appeal for the tribe. He said that in the past, members of the tribe protected him during tribal warfare. He felt that he had an obligation to save the tribe as an expression of his gratitude towards them.

Rasūlullāh ﷺ granted them mercy. He also wanted a definitive ending to Jewish animosity. He believed this could only happen if the tribe left Madīnah. Abdullah Ibn Ubayy continued to appeal to let them stay in Madīnah, but the companions stopped him from making any more requests. At this point, Banu Qaynuqa voluntarily agreed to leave Madīnah for good. As the agreement required, they surrendered all their wealth and left in exile to Syria.

Fair judgment

It is often argued that the Muslims should not have banished the tribe from Madīnah for such a "small" offense. The offense in and of itself might have been small, but for two long years, Banu Qaynuqa had showed hatred and anger toward the Muslims. Even during the blockade, there was no indication that the tribe was willing to reaffirm peace. They were waiting for outside support to arrive so that they could launch an attack on the Muslims.

Rasūlullāh ﷺ was kind enough not to punish the tribe harshly, but he required that the tribe vacate their dwellings inside Madīnah. This step was necessary to ensure the safety and security of the Muslims. It was actually the Jewish chief who made the decision to leave Madīnah.

WEEKEND 12

Homework

1. Search for the tribe "Banu Qaynuqa" on the Google website. How many results did you find? Bring a copy of the search results to class.

____

2. Which of the following choices about Banu Qaynuqa and the Battle of Badr is correct?

A. The tribe sided with the Quraish in the battle.
B. The tribe remained neutral in the battle.
C. The tribe sent a secret army to kill the Muslims.
D. The tribe obstructed the Muslims from fighting.
E. None of the above.

3. After which battle did the relationship between Banu Qaynuqa and the Muslims become bitter?

A. Battle of Badr.
B. Battle of Uhud.
C. Battle of Khandaq.
D. Battle of Siffin.
E. Battle of the Camel.

4. How did Banu Qaynuqa react when they learned about the Muslim victory in the Battle of Badr?

A. They were very happy.
B. They were very disappointed.
C. They celebrated the victory.
D. They organized a victory parade in Madīnah.
E. They composed poems praising the Muslims.

5. Which of the following statements about the pact between by Nabi Muhammadﷺ with different tribes in Madīnah is correct?

A. All tribes were free to support any tribe that attacked Madīnah.
B. All tribes must support the powerful army coming from the south.
C. Some Madīnan tribes could remain neutral if Madīnah was attacked.
D. All tribes in and around Madīnah should boycott the Makkan Quraish.
E. Only (b) and (c).

6. Rasūlullāhﷺ asked Banu Qaynuqa to participate in the Battle of Badr. True / False

7. What three things did the chief of Banu Qaynuqa fail to do after some of his people challenged the Muslims?

A. ______________________________

B. ______________________________

C. ______________________________

8. The Muslims enforced a blockade upon Banu Qaynuqa for how many days?

A. 10 days.
B. 15 days.
C. 20 days.
D. 25 days.
E. 1 month.

9. After the blockade, who intervened on behalf of Banu Qaynuqa to ask for a lighter punishment?

A. A Jewish tribe named Banu Nadir.
B. Abū Sufyān.
C. Ka'b Ibn Ashraf.
D. Abdullah Ibn Ubaay.
E. The wife of a Jewish goldsmith.

10. Who ultimately decided that Banu Qaynuqa should go into exile after the tribe surrendered?

____

____

Banu Nadīr: *Treachery Within Madīnah*

Objective of the Lesson:

Soon after the Battle of Uhud, the Jewish tribe Banu Nadīr was expelled from Madīnah. Banu Nadīr had violated the peace treaty with the Muslims. What caused the tension between the tribe and the Muslims? Students will learn the historical truth about one of the cruel conspiracies against the Muslims.

The Jewish tribe Banu Nadīr played an important role in shaping the early history of Muslims in Madīnah. In this chapter, we will learn about interactions between Banu Nadīr and the Muslims. Banu Nadīr lived near Madīnah. Two other prominent Jewish tribes lived in Madīnah. Banu Qaynuqa lived in Madīnah and Banu Qurayzah lived just north of Madīnah. All three tribes shaped the early history of Muslims in one way or another. Muslim interaction with the different Jewish tribes was so important that the chapters of the Qur'ān revealed in Madīnah dealt extensively with Jewish heritage and various issues of Judaism.

Treaty with Rasūlullāhﷺ

After Rasūlullāhﷺ migrated to Madīnah, initially the Jewish tribes were not opposed to his relocation. However, over the course of time, as Rasūlullāhﷺ continued preaching Islam and more Jews learned about Islam, Jewish opposition to Islam and Muslims generally increased.

Rasūlullāhﷺ was aware that two prominent local Arab tribes, the 'Aws and the Khazraj, were involved in vicious infighting. Three Jewish tribes in Madīnah participated in the conflict by siding with one of the tribes. The Jewish tribe Banu Qurayzah sided with the 'Aws, while Banu Qaynuqa and Banu Nadīr, sided with the Khazraj. After assessing the local alliances, Rasūlullāh ﷺ realized it was very important to earn the confidence of all the tribes and maintain peace with them. He entered into a series of treaties with the tribes emphasizing neutrality during any war and non-interference in each other's affairs. These treaties were a far-sighted approach by Rasūlullāh ﷺ, because he thought the Quraish would soon wage war against the Muslims. If any of the Madīnan tribes supported the Quraish during war, his chances of winning would be seriously jeopardized. Also, Rasūlullāh ﷺ had already dealt with enemies in Makkah, and he did not want to create or face new enemies in Madīnah.

Banu Qaynuqa

As we previously learned, Banu Qaynuqa was the first Jewish tribe to break the treaty of neutrality and non-interference. This tribe lived within the city limits of Madīnah and interacted with the Muslims daily. In 3 A.H./625 C.E., Banu Qaynuqa staged an unsuccessful rebellion against Rasūlullāh ﷺ. Armed street battles began in Madīnah between the Muslims and the Jewish tribe. Muslims were able to contain the rebellion. As punishment for staging the rebellion against the Muslims, the tribe was expelled from Madīnah in accordance with the Arab custom.

Banu Nadīr

After Banu Qaynuqa was expelled from Madīnah, Rasūlullāh ﷺ reassured the other Jewish tribes and made a special treaty with them to maintain peace and neutrality. During the Battle of Badr, Banu Nadīr did not break the peace agreement with the Muslims.

However, during the Battle of Uhud, the tribe secretly conspired with the Makkan polytheists. During the battle, the Quraish obtained support from Banu Nadīr; in return, the Quraish promised to extend support to them in the future.

Collection of blood money

If a man belonging to one tribe was killed by another tribe, the second tribe had to pay "blood-money" to compensate for the killing.

In the same year the Battle of Uhud was fought, a Muslim man killed two non-Muslim men. These two men were under Muslim protection. Muslims were obligated to pay blood-money to the victims families. The amount of blood-money was more than the Muslims had. Rasūlullāh ﷺ felt it was his obligation to collect and pay the blood-money. He went to Banu Nadīr personally to request they contribute to the collection. Abū Bakr, 'Umar, and 'Ali accompanied Rasūlullāh ﷺ. Most of the members of Banu Nadīr were willing to contribute money. However, their chief, **Huyayy Ibn Akhtab**, was opposed to contributing. Upon further discussion, he agreed to pay the money.

The tribe requested that Rasūlullāh ﷺ and the others stay until a meal could be served. However, several members whispered to one another in the presence of the Muslims. Huyayy joined them and then the group withdrew inside a house. Rasūlullāh ﷺ sat down, leaning against the outside wall of the house. The Muslims were under the impression that the men went inside to collect some money and prepare the meal for their guests.

Conspiracy to assassinate

The Jews were actually whispering about killing Rasūlullāh ﷺ, who appeared to be an easy target. Once inside the house, they conspired to drop a big boulder on Rasūlullāh's ﷺ head from the top of the house. A strong Jewish man volunteered to do the job.

In the meantime, angel Jibril came to Nabi Muhammad ﷺ and told him that the Jews were planning to kill him, and, he must return to Madīnah immediately. Without saying a word, Rasūlullāh ﷺ left the house and returned to Madīnah. The companions who were waiting there thought he would return soon. After some time had passed and Rasūlullāh ﷺ did not return, the companions decided to leave. They went to Rasūlullāh's ﷺ house to find out what happened. Rasūlullāh ﷺ explained what angel Jibril told him.

The Muslims sent a messenger to Banu Nadīr to explain in detail that their plot to kill Rasūlullāh ﷺ had been discovered. He also told them that due to this conspiracy, the peace agreement was nullified and they had to leave Madīnah within ten days. The tribe did not deny the accusation, indicating that it was true. They also did not show any regret for the plot.

Preparation to leave

Most members of Banu Nadīr began preparations to leave Madīnah. However, Abdullah Ibn Ubayy, the hypocrite leader in Madīnah, sent a message to the Jewish tribe asking them not to leave. The hypocrites promised to extend their support to the tribe. They even said that if the tribe was expelled from Madīnah, they would go with the tribe. After hearing this assurance, Huyayy Ibn Akhtab decided to postpone his decision to leave Madīnah. He also hoped that the other powerful Jewish tribe, Banu Qurayzah, would come to their rescue. The tribe sent a message to Rasūlullāh ﷺ that said: "We shall not leave our dwellings and our possessions, so do what you want to do." The Qur'ān mentions this development in the following ayāh:

Have you not observed those who practice hypocrisy,—they say to those of their brethren who have disbelieved from among the people of the scripture: "If you are expelled, we shall certainly go out with you, and we shall not obey against you anyone any time; and if you are fought against, we shall certainly help you"? And Allāh bears witness that surely they are indeed liars. (59:11)

The blockade

After receiving this message, Rasūlullāh ﷺ decided to stage a blockade of Banu Nadīr's territory. A large number of Muslims gathered around the fortresses of the Jewish settlement. Both sides shot arrows and stones at each other. As the days passed by, the tribe hoped that Abdullah Ibn Ubayy would come to their aid. They also wanted their allies, the Ghatafān, to help. In addition, they hoped their brethren from Banu Qurayzah would fight alongside them. However, no help came from any quarter. In the meantime, internal conflict among the tribal members increased. This situation is mentioned in the Qur'ān:

If they are expelled, they will not go out with them; and if they are fought against, they will not help them; and even if they help them, they will certainly turn back; and then they will not be helped. (59:12)

After about ten days, Rasūlullāh ﷺ ordered all the palm trees around the dwellings of the tribal members to be cut down. This indicated that a fierce battle was about to begin. The Qur'ān mentions this development in the following ayāh:

Whatever palm-tree you cut down or leave it standing upon its roots, it is with the permission of Allāh, and that He might disgrace the evildoers. (59:5)

The ground was prepared for archers to shoot arrows and for warriors to fight. On the 15th day of the blockade, Banu Nadir surrendered. They knew fighting the Muslims would be much too dangerous. The Muslims allowed the tribe to take whatever they could load on their camels except weapons.

The tribe left Madīnah and settled further north in a place called Khaybar. Some members of the tribe migrated to Syria and settled there.

Conspiracy from Khaybar

After their expulsion from Madīnah, Banu Nadīr looked for an opportunity to get revenge against the Muslims. They continued to keep in touch with the Makkan polytheists. Their leader, Huyayy Ibn Akhtab, went to Makkah and provoked the Quraish to attack the Muslims. He advised them to raise the largest possible army to defeat the Muslims. Banu Nadīr promised to assist the Quraish in the battle. The tribe also assured the Quraish that the Jewish tribe Banu Qurayzah, still living in Madīnah, could be provoked to attack the Muslims.

As a result of these diplomatic contacts with the Quraish, a mighty force was eventually mobilized against the Muslims. This mighty force advanced Madīnah to fight a battle that became known as the Battle of Khandaq.

Homework

1. Why did Rasūlullāh ﷺ enter into a treaty of neutrality and peace with the different Jewish tribes in Madīnah?

A. Rasūlullāh ﷺ wanted to force the tribes to accept Islam.
B. Rasūlullāh ﷺ wanted to banish them from the city.
C. Rasūlullāh ﷺ wanted to make them second-class citizens by limiting their civil rights.
D. Rasūlullāh ﷺ did not want to have internal enemies in Madīnah.
E. Rasūlullāh ﷺ wanted to learn about Judaism from the tribes.

2. Which Jewish tribe lived within the city limits of Madīnah?

A. Banu Qaynuqa.
B. Banu Qurayzah.
C. Banu Nadīr.
D. Banu Asad.
E. Banu Hashim.

3. Which of the following Jewish tribes first staged an armed rebellion against Rasūlullāh ﷺ in Madīnah?

A. Banu Qaynuqa in 3 A.H.
B. Banu Qaynuqa in 7 A.H.
C. Banu Qurayzah in 3 A.H.
D. Banu Qurayzah 7 A.H.
E. Banu Nadīr in 7 A.H.

4. Banu Nadīr decided to leave Madīnah, but then stayed back, hoping to receive help from certain people. Whose help were they hoping for?

A. Abdullah Ibn Ubayy, the Ansars, and the Muhajirs.
B. Abdullah Ibn Ubayy, the Ghatafān, and Banu Qurayzah.
C. Banu Qurayzah, the Ansars, and the Quraish.
D. The Quraish, Banu Tamim, and Banu Qaynuqa.
E. Banu Qaynuqa, Banu Qurayzah, and Banu Asad.

5. Banu Nadīr surrendered to the Muslims after how many days of blockade?

____

6. Banu Nadīr conspired with the Makkan Quraish to wage war against the Muslims. In which two battles did they conspire against the Muslims?

A. Battle of Badr and Battle of Khandaq.
B. Battle of Uhud and Battle of Tabuk.
C. Battle of Uhud and Battle of Khandaq.
D. Battle of Khandaq and Battle of the Camel.
E. Battle of Muta and Battle of the Camel.

7. According to the conditions of surrender, Banu Nadīr was allowed to take some assets with them. According to the lesson, what was the tribe NOT allowed to take?

____

8. A Banu Nadīr chief played an important role in the tribe's resistance and conspiracy against the Muslims. What was his name?

A. Abdullah Ibn Ubayy.
B. Abdullah Ibn Masud.
C. Sa'd Ibn Mu'adh.
D. Huyayy Ibn Akhtab.
E. Abu Jahl.

9. According to the lesson, where did Banu Nadīr settle after they were exiled from Madīnah?

A. Only in Khaybar.
B. Only in Syria.
C. In Khaybar and Syria.
D. In Uhud and Tabuk.
E. In Tabuk and Jerusalem.

10. When did Rasūlullāhﷺ decide to barricade Banu Nadīr to punish them?

A. After they composed poems praising the Quraish.
B. After they refused to obey the treaty of neutrality.
C. After they decided to settle in Khaybar.
D. After they conspired to assassinate Rasūlullāhﷺ.
E. After they protested the expulsion of Banu Qaynuqa.

Banu Qurayzah

Objective of the Lesson:

Banu Qurayzah nearly destroyed the Muslim community when they conspired with the polytheist Quraish to attack the Muslims. Before they could launch the attack, a misunderstanding caused a rift between the Jewish tribe and the polytheists. The Muslims were saved from an imminent attack. Soon after the Battle of the Trench, some members of Banu Qurayzah were punished for their treachery. This chapter exposes the truth behind these events.

Soon after the Battle of the Trench, a series of events occurred in Madīnah involving the Jewish tribe Banu Qurayzah. Because of the tribe's treachery during the battle, the Muslims punished them. Some of their men were captured and killed. The rest of the people were allowed to leave Madīnah on similar terms that were granted to other Jewish tribes who went into exile. Let us review these events and the actual punishment.

The morning after the storm

During the Battle of the Trench, the Makkan army attempted to attack Madīnah. They could not attack Madīnah because the Muslims had dug a wide trench around the city boundary, preventing enemies from crossing over. After 25 days of siege, one night a violent winter storm destroyed the Quraish camp. The storm uprooted their tents, destroyed their belongings, let loose their animals, and drenched the Quraish army during bitter cold temperatures. As a result, the siege of Madīnah ended.

The Muslims woke up the following morning to find no trace of the enemies on the other side of the trench. Only scattered belongings, uprooted tents, and dead animals remained. The prospect of a fierce battle dissipated not because of any human effort, but because of divine intervention. The Muslims were relieved.

After evaluating the aftermath of the storm, Rasūlullāh ﷺ and the Muslims returned to their homes in Madīnah. However, at noon, angel Jibril went to Rasūlullāh ﷺ and told him to march to the quarters of Banu Qurayzah to deal with the tribe's intended betrayal during the siege on Madīnah.

The blockade

A large number of Muslim forces marched to the quarters of Banu Qurayzah. The tribe did not expect the Muslims to arrive so quickly after the end of the storm and the departure of the Makkan coalition army. When the Muslims arrived, they found Banu Qurayzah in a defiant mood, provoking the Muslims with insults. Banu Nadīr's leader, Huyayy ibn Akhtab, was among them, probably to lend support and rally them to challenge the Muslims. He reviled Rasūlullāh ﷺ and uttered insulting words to his wives. These were daring acts, knowing that they were outnumbered by the Muslims.

The Muslims barricaded the Qurayzah Jews inside their quarters. Nobody was allowed to leave their quarters. As the days passed by, there was no sign of the Muslims relaxing their siege or the Jews attempting to surrender.

An offer to leave Madīnah

After several days, the Qurayzah Jews sent an offer to Rasūlullāh ﷺ, requesting to receive treatment similar to what Banu Nadīr had received. This was probably Huyayy ibn Akhtab's idea. Banu Nadīr had been allowed to leave Madīnah in honor with their women, children, and wealth. Banu Qurayzah offered to leave Madīnah if they were given similar terms.

Rasūlullāh ﷺ rejected these terms. He reasoned that the crimes perpetrated by each tribe were significantly different. Banu Nadīr had conspired to kill Rasūlullāh ﷺ. They did not form an alliance with the enemies, and they did not conspire to annihilate the entire Muslim community. However, Banu Qurayzah conspired with the enemies, and they participated in the plan to annihilate the entire Muslim community. Considering the gravity of these two crimes, Rasūlullāh ﷺ did not believe the two tribes should be treated as if they were on an equal footing.

The surrender

The barricade of Banu Qurayzah lasted for 25 days. The Muslims could have simply invaded and killed the tribe without cordoning it off, but they wanted the tribe to surrender. The defiant Banu Qurayzah would not surrender.

However, over time, Banu Qurayzah's morale waned. Their chief offered his people three choices to end their hopeless condition: (1) embrace Islam; (2) kill their own women and children, then attack the Muslims in face-to-face combat, in which case they would certainly die; or (3) launch a surprise attack on Saturday, the day of the Sabbath, when, by mutual understanding, no fighting would take place. None of these choices were accepted. After about 25 days of siege, Banu Qurayzah finally decided to surrender unconditionally. They accepted Rasūlullāh ﷺ judgment.

Intervention of 'Aws Muslims

The 'Aws Muslims of the Ansārs wanted to treat the prisoners leniently because of their past ties of friendship. They requested Rasūlullāh ﷺ to show mercy. Because of this request, Rasūlullāh ﷺ offered to allow the 'Aws to judge Banu Qurayzah's case. The Qurayzah were happy with this offer because they thought if Muhammad ﷺ or other Muslims judged their case, they would be killed. Rasūlullāh ﷺ told the 'Aws to let the Qurayzah choose someone from the 'Aws tribe to arbitrate their case. They chose the chief of the 'Aws, Sa'd Ibn Mu'ādh. He was well respected by the Qurayzah as a good friend, having wisdom and a keen sense of judgment.

The judgment

Sa'd Ibn Mu'adh asked the Qurayzah leaders if they wanted to be judged according to Muslim law or Jewish law. The tribe chose judgment according to Jewish law, believing that Jewish law was better. However, Jewish law clearly states a specific punishment for the crime of treachery. **Deuteronomy** 20:12–14 says: "Now if the city will not make peace with you, but makes war against you, then you shall besiege it, and when the Lord your God delivers it into your hands, you shall strike every male in it with the edge of the sword, but the women, the little ones, the livestock ... you shall plunder for yourself..."

Sa'd Ibn Mu'adh pronounced his verdict that all fighters from Banu Qurayzah should be killed, their property should be distributed, and their women and children should be taken as prisoners.

The Jewish tribe was shocked by the judgment. They did not expect such harsh treatment from their close friend and ally. However, they had given their solemn pledge to abide by any judgment. As the first step, Sa'd Ibn Mu'adh ordered the men to be handcuffed and separated from the women and children. All handcuffed men were taken to Usāmah Ibn Zayd's house, and all women and children were taken to Kayysah bint Hārith's house.

How many Jews were killed?

A few of the biographies of Rasūlullāh ﷺ mention "all" adult males of Banu Qurayzah were killed and "all" women and children were enslaved. Several reports mention 700 adult males were killed. This number appears to be exaggerated. It is important for us to understand whether the report of 700 Jewish men killed is accurate.

The Qur'ān provides a brief but insightful account of all the major battles, including all key events in Madīnah. The Qur'ān mentions the situations involving Banu Nadīr, including their conspiracy to kill Rasūlullāh ﷺ,[5:11] joining the allied forces,[33:9] support extended by 'Abdullah ibn Ubayy,[59:11–12] and their expulsion from Madīnah.[59:2] Similarly, the Qur'ān provides an account of Banu Qurayzah joining the allied forces[33:9] and their punishment.[33:26–27]

In ayāh 33:26, Allāh says, "*some you slew and some you captured.*" Clearly not all Qurayzah men were captured and killed. Sa'd Ibn Mu'ādh's judgment stated that "all fighters from Banu Qurayzah should be killed." Obviously "all fighters" does not include all male members of the tribe. Several ahādīth reported by Bukhārī and Muslim also clearly mention that Sa'd said "all warriors" or "all fighters" should be killed. (See Bukhārī 58:148; 59:447; 74:278; Muslim 19:4364; 19:4368; 19:4370). The number of "fighters" was no more than 25, and they were killed.

How big was the house?

It is reported that handcuffed Qurayzah men were held in Usāmah Ibn Zayd's house and all women and children were placed in Kayysah bint Hārith's house. If there were 700 male prisoners, there would have been 300 to 400 women and more than 1,000 children. The question is: How big were their houses? Could these houses accommodate 700 men and hundreds of women and children? The answer is no. They were poor Muslims and their houses were not big. Evidently, not all Qurayzah men were handcuffed, imprisoned, and executed.

Example of mercy

During the entire 23-year mission of Rasūlullāh, he was the epitome of the Qur'ānic testimony, "*and We have not sent you but as a mercy for all the worlds.*"[21:107] Rasūlullāh lived by this testimony, and his actions provide the evidence that he lived by this statement. At different times many individuals attempted to kill him, but he pardoned all of them. After his painful experience in Ta'īf, where children pelted rocks at him, making him bruised and bloodied, angels asked his permission to destroy the entire city of Ta'īf. But Rasūlullāh did not permit this to happen. When Rasūlullāh liberated Makkah, he had the power to punish the Quraish people for their hostility, but he forgave them. Based on a careful analysis of his actions and personality, it is not possible that he would have allowed 700 men to be killed.

No proof of mass killing

According to the Qur'ān, "some" were captured and "some" were killed. The property of those captured and killed was distributed among the Muslims. If 700 men were killed, where were they buried? The history of Madīnah contains no record of a mass grave of Jews. If 700 men were killed, the Qur'ān would have provided justification or at least mentioned it. Islam does not advocate punishing an entire community for the crime of one individual or a few. In the matter of retaliation, the Qur'ān prescribes "*life for life, and eye for eye, and nose for nose, and ear for ear, and tooth for tooth.*"[5:45] With regard to Banu Qurayzah, only their leaders and a few other men of influence conspired together. The majority of tribal members played no role except to go along with their leaders. They had no voice in the decision making. It is justified that the Qur'ān uses the word "some" to describe the number of men who were killed.

For additional reading, see Adil Salahi, *Muhammad: Man and Prophet*, United Kingdom, The Islamic Foundation, 1995.

Homework

1. Why did the Muslims take action against Banu Qurayzah?

A. Banu Qurayzah participated in the Battle of the Trench against the Muslims.
B. Banu Qurayzah allied with the enemy army and violated the treaty of neutrality.
C. Banu Qurayzah secretly expelled Banu Nadīr.
D. Banu Qurayzah refused to accept Islam.
E. Banu Qurayzah killed Rasūlullāh's ﷺ companions during the Battle of the Trench.

2. Which of the following statements about Banu Qurayzah is correct?

A. They were one of the three prominent Jewish tribes in Madinah.
B. They signed a treaty of neutrality with Rasūlullāh ﷺ, after his migration to Madinah.
C. They were determined to destroy Rasūlullāh ﷺ and his followers.
D. During the Battle of the Trench, they sided with the Makkan army.
E. All of the above.

3. After the Battle of the Trench, Banu Qurayzah realized they had provoked the wrath of the Muslims for violaing the treaty of neutrality. At that point, what options did they consider to prevent Muslim retaliation?

A. They discussed accepting Islam.
B. They discussed launching a surprise attack on the Muslims on the day of the Sabbath.
C. They discussed killing their own women and children and then attacking the Muslims.
D. All of the above.
E. Only (a) and (b).

4. How long was the siege imposed on the Banu Qurayzah tribe by the Muslims?

A. Three days and three nights.
B. 25 days and nights.
C. Three months.
D. One year.
E. Three years.

5. After the siege on Banu Qurayzah, who was appointed to judge the case of Banu Qurayzah's betrayal?

A. Rasūlullāh ﷺ himself.
B. Abū Sufyan.
C. Sa'd Ibn Mu'adh.
D. Salman the Persian.
E. Banu Nadīr.

6. The person who judged the case of Banu Qurayzah's betrayal was appointed based on certain criteria. Which of the following criteria is correct?

A. The person was biased towards the Muslims.
B. The person was a former ally of the Banu Qurayzah, therefore, his appointment would eliminate any bias against the tribe.
C. Banu Qurayzah believed the person would remain neutral because he was a member of their tribe.
D. Only (a) and (c).
E. Only (b) and (c).

7. What type of punishment was imposed on Banu Qurayzah?

A. They were banished from Madīnah for six months.
B. The entire tribe was killed.
C. Some of the adult male members were killed, their women and children were taken captive, and their assets were distributed among the Muslims.
D. They were made slaves and their assets were distributed among the Muslims.
E. None of the above.

8. Banu Qurayzah was punished according to which law?

A. Jewish law as stated in the Torah.
B. Qur'ānic law.
C. The law set up by a tribunal.
D. Roman law.
E. They were not given a trial; they were simply killed.

9. What punishment does Jewish scripture, prescribe for the crime of violating peace or waging war against an ally?

A. Flog the guilty party with 100 stripes.
B. Banish the guilty party from society.
C. Imprison the guilty party and enslave them.
D. Kill the guilty party with the edge of a sword and destroy their property, livestock, and crops.
E. Kill only the male members of the guilty party with the edge of a sword and plunder their women, children, and wealth.

10. Read āyah 26 of the sūrah about Banu Qurayzah. Write the two things the Muslims did to the tribe.

____

____

Mission to Tabūk: *A Test of Steadfastness*

Objective of the Lesson:

The expedition to Tabūk challenged the Muslims to a severe test. Many of them failed the test and many others emerged successful. The Muslims did not have to fight the Byzantines, but the expedition proved to be a show of force to others. When the Muslims began conquering outlying areas at a later time, the experience of Tabūk helped them. This lesson discusses the expedition and the twists and turns of these historical events.

In 9 A.H./630 C.E., one year after Makkah was conquered, Nabi Muhammadﷺ undertook a mission to Tabūk to stop a possible attack by the Byzantines. Tabūk is northwest of Arabia in the border area of present-day Jordan. The mission is known as the Battle of Tabūk because Rasūlullāhﷺ halted here for ten days, waiting for the Roman army to show up for a battle. However, when the Byzantines did not appear, Rasūlullāhﷺ returned to Madīnah without engaging in a pre-emptive attack.

Even though there was no battle, the mission provides interesting details about the extensive preparations, participation, and battle strategy of the Muslims. There were trials and tribulations for the Muslims and the hypocrites before, during, and after the mission. This event also provided an impressive display of Muslim military power and command over the region. It is reported that the Muslim army was 30,000 strong. According to modern warfare terminology, the army was equivalent to three divisions, where each division consisted of 10,000 men. By any measure, a battle with three divisions would have been a massive one. It required an enormous amount of time, effort, and resources to mobilize such a large army. Rasūlullāh ﷺ had to keep the army motivated to fight a foreign enemy, known for its ferocity and superior capabilities.

The Roman Empire

During Rasūlullāh's ﷺ time, there were two major superpowers near Arabia—the Romans, or Byzantines, and the Persians. These superpowers were enemies and they fought fierce battles against each other. In the Qur'ān, sūrah Ar-Rūm begins with a reference to the Persian defeat of the Romans. Sūrah Ar-Rūm is a Makkan revelation. Between 610 C.E. and 619 C.E., the Romans were completely defeated by the Persians on all fronts—Jerusalem, Damascus, Alexandria, and large parts of Egypt and Libya. Āyah 3 of the sūrah contained a prophecy that the Romans would soon become victorious.

غُلِبَتِ ٱلرُّومُ ﴿٢﴾ فِىٓ أَدْنَى ٱلْأَرْضِ وَهُم مِّنۢ بَعْدِ غَلَبِهِمْ سَيَغْلِبُونَ ﴿٣﴾

The Romans have been defeated in the land nearby; and they, after their defeat, will conquer shortly. (30:2–3)

This prophecy began to be fulfilled shortly after the āyah was revealed. By 622 C.E., when Rasūlullāh ﷺ migrated to Madīnah, the Roman Emperor **Heraclius** defeated the Persians on many fronts and occupied Syria. For a long time, Syria was a colony of the Roman Empire. In 628 C.E., two years before the mission to Tabūk, the Romans completely defeated the mighty Persians. The Persian king, **Khosrow**, was captured and executed.

Roman and Persian interest in Arabia

During Rasūlullāh's ﷺ, Roman and Persian interest in Arabia was very low. These powers did not think the land had economic or political value. Politically, Arabia did not pose a threat to the Romans or the Persians. In the past, when Rasūlullāh ﷺ had sent the message of Islam to both empires, they rejected the message.

From the time the Muslims settled in Madīnah, they made several significant achievements that did not go unnoticed in the neighboring countries. Muslim victories in the Battle of The Trench and Khaybar, and the signing of the Hudaybiyah Treaty, were noted by the Byzantines. However, their first contact with the Muslims happened during the Battle of Mu'tah in 629 C.E., when a force of 3,000 Muslims successfully challenged the Ghassan tribe that was supported by the Byzantines. In this battle, the Ghassans had a 100,000-man army and another 100,000-man Byzantine army. Even then the Byzantine empire was not very interested in the politics of Arabia.

Barely 18 months after the Battle of Mu'tah, the political map of Arabia had changed. Shortly after the battle, the Muslims liberated

Interesting Facts

The Battle of Mu'tah was fought in 629 C.E. against the Ghassan Arabs, who lived near Jordan.

The battle began after the Ghassans killed a Muslim envoy who carried a letter to them, inviting them to accept Islam.

Rasūlullāh ﷺ sent an army of 3,000 men. Ghassans assembled 100,000 men, supported by another 100,000 men from Byzantine.

In the ensuing battle, three Muslim commanders died. Finally, Khālid Ibn Walīd became the army commander. His forces tactfully retreated, but they had demonstrated superior military strategy.

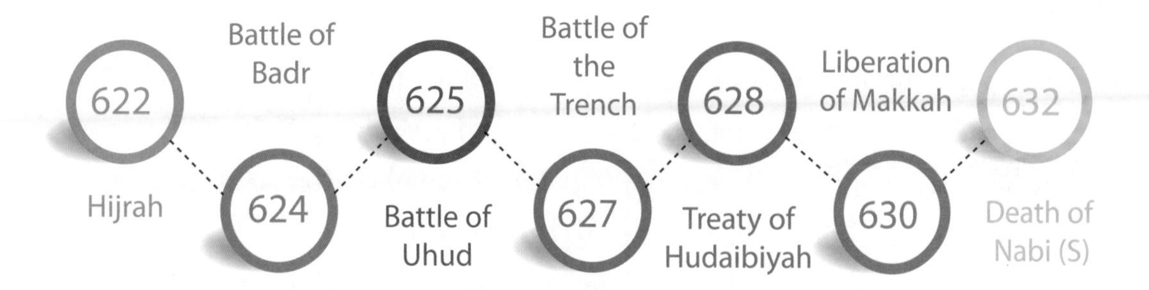

Makkah, defeated the Hawāzin tribe, and established Islam throughout the Hijāz region. Now the Byzantine empire began to show some interest in the developments in Arabia.

Possible Roman attack

Before the battles of Badr, Uhud, and Khandaq, Muslims were able to prepare for battle based on advance information received about enemy preparations. Before the mission to Tabūk, Rasūlullāh ﷺ received advance information. A rumor spread in Arabia that Heraclius had decided to attack Arabia. The rumor was circulated and magnified by some traders en-route from Syria to Madīnah. Abū 'Amir, a Christian man from Syria, also spread the rumor. War preparations may have already been underway as the Romans celebrated their recent victory over the Persians and possibly prepared for other crusades.

Muslim preparation for the battle

In the battles of Badr, Uhud, and Khandaq, the enemies advanced to Madīnah to attack the Muslims. This time, Rasūlullāh ﷺ decided that he could not allow the enemies to come close to Madīnah. He realized that if he delayed his war preparations, the Romans could attack the Muslim-controlled provinces or they might advance to Madīnah. He decided to march forward to Roman border to stop their advance to Madīnah.

Once the decision was made, Rasūlullāh ﷺ asked his companions to prepare for battle. He sent representatives to different Arab tribes, asking for their support against the Romans. All of the tribes sent men to participate in the battle. Thus, an army of about 30,000 men prepared to fight. It was not an easy task. This time, Rasūlullāh ﷺ did not allow 'Ali to participate in the mission. Instead, he appointed 'Ali to govern Madīnah in his absence.

Reluctance to participate

Even though thousands of Muslims readily came forward to join the army, many others made various excuses for not participating. **Sūrah at-Taubah** details this reluctance to participate in the mission.

These excuses included:

- It was a hot summer month, not a good time for a journey.
- Dates had ripened and people needed to stay to harvest them.
- Muslims were not powerful enough to defeat the mighty Roman army.
- Muslim men might become attracted to Roman women.
- Some men were already doing good deeds, therefore, they did not need to go.

Rasūlullāh ﷺ allowed many unwilling, hesitant men to decline participating in the mission. He knew that they would create problems during the mission instead of offer assistance. These unwilling, hesitant men became happy to learn that they could stay behind. Allāh ﷻ sent revelations to condemn them.[9:24; 9:39; 9:81]

If you do not set forth, He will chastise you with a painful chastisement, and He will exchange a people other than you, and you cannot harm Him in any way. For Allāh is Possessor of power over all things. (9:39)

Those who were left behind rejoiced at their sitting down behind the Rasūl of Allāh, and they hated to strive with their wealth and their lives in the cause of Allāh, and they said: "Do not go forth in this heat." You say: "The Fire of Hell is more intense in heat." Would that they understand!

Rasūlullāh ﷺ exempted the old, the sick, and minors. He also exempted some genuinely interested people who could not find weapons to fight with or camels to ride on.[9:91–92] These people cried because they could not participate in the mission. Allāh ﷻ sent revelations to applaud them.

Points to Ponder

Some men of Quraish in Makkah took upon themselves to providing drinking water to the pilgrims during Hajj. These men thought providing drinking water was more meritorious than participating in jihād. The Qur'ān says belief in Allāh ﷻ and struggle for the cause of Allāh ﷻ is much superior to any single commendable outward religious work. The outward display of religious piety has no value to Allāh ﷻ unless there is inner commitment to Allāh ﷻ in faith and in profession.

Conduct of the hypocrites

During the battle preparations and the actual journey, the Muslim army had to confront hypocrisy of many half-hearted Muslims. In addition to the general excuses given for not participating mentioned previously, two incidents deserve specific mention.

The first incident occurred about the time of the expedition, when the hypocrites built a false masjid near the Masjid of Qubā'. The purpose of the false masjid was twofold: (1) to give the impression that they were good Muslims, and (2) at a distance from Madīnah, the masjid would provide them cover to conspire against Islam. They even invited Rasūlullāh ﷺ to pray in the masjid. While Rasūlullāh ﷺ was returning from the expedition of Tabūk, Allāh ﷻ sent a revelation disclosing that the hypocrites built the masjid only to spread falsehood and create division among the Muslims.[9:107] Rasūlullāh ﷺ sent some of his companions to destroy the masjid built by the hypocrites.

The second incident occurred when 'Abdullāh ibn Ubayy deserted the Muslims during the actual journey. He took all the steps required to give the impression that he was ready to participate in the expedition. He encamped with all of his supporters at a certain location, apparently waiting to join the Muslim army. When the army marched toward Tabūk, 'Abdullāh ibn Ubayy and his followers cleverly stayed behind.

Camp at Tabūk

After traveling for nearly a month, the Muslims camped at Tabūk in the territory of Jordan. This territory was within Roman control. If the Romans had any intention of attacking Arabia or fighting the Muslims, this was the time to start the battle. However, there would be no battle. Muslim historians offer two reasons why no battle was fought.

According to one theory, the Romans were so afraid of the Muslim army that they avoided any clash with the Muslims. Not long before, the two sides had met at the Battle of Mu'tah, where 3,000 Muslims had successfully resisted 200,000 Romans. This time the Muslim forces were several times stronger than before. With the memory of the previous war still fresh in their minds, the Byzantines were not motivated enough to fight the Muslims. By withdrawing their army, they wished to give the impression that they had not mobilized any forces against the Muslims.

Another theory says the Romans had no intention of fighting the Muslims. Their main enemy was the Persians, and any war preparations were directed towards fighting their primary enemy on other fronts.

After waiting in Tabūk for about ten days, Rasūlullāh ﷺ decided to return to Madīnah. He ascertained that the Romans did not pose a threat, and they did not want to confront the Muslims. Rasūlullāh ﷺ could have plundered the Roman territory, but this was not his motive or mode of action. He made a pre-emptive march to Tabūk but did not launch a pre-emptive attack.

Positive outcome of the mission

Even though there was no battle and no war spoils to gain, there were several positive outcomes from the mission:

(a) The mission improved the prestige of the Muslim army, and Islam became known to the border regions. Rasūlullāh ﷺ impressed people on the frontier with his military strength. At the same time, he also impressed them with his kind-heartedness by not plundering their assets. People began to consider Islam a peaceful a religion.

(b) Rasūlullāh ﷺ made peace treaties with the leaders on the frontier. Some of the Arab tribes in the region agreed to not support the Romans against the Muslims. Muslim traders in Syria would be granted safety in the region.

(c) These peace treaties paved the way for many frontier tribes to accept Islam in the near future.

(d) Many Arab tribes that had not accepted Islam before began to accept Islam.

(e) The tiresome journey to the Jordan border helped the Muslim army learn the difficult terrain. The lengthy journey and the war preparations taught them methods of warfare against the superpowers of that time. Due to this experience, after Rasūlullāh ﷺ passed away, the Muslims were able to conquer Syria and expand to other territories north and east of Arabia.

The expedition to Tabūk provides interesting information about Muslim military power and command throughout the region. Although there was no battle, the mission offered many avenues for the spread Islam to other regions in the future. The mission demonstrated that Muslims were willing to respond to Rasūlullāh's ﷺ call and defend Islam with their wealth and lives.

Homework

1. During the mission to Tabūk, who was appointed governor of Madīnah to rule in the absence of Rasūlullāh ﷺ?

A. Abū Bakr.
B. ‘Ali.
C. ‘Uthman.
D. Salman al-Farsi.
E. Abū ‘Amir.

2. Why were the Romans not interested in attacking Arabia?

A. There were no sea routes to Arabia.
B. They were afraid of Rasūlullāh ﷺ.
C. There was no economic or political value in Arabia.
D. They were afraid of the summer months.
E. They needed to harvest the dates.

3. During which season was the mission to Tabūk undertaken?

A. Winter.
B. Summer.
C. Spring.
D. Hurricane.
E. Festival.

4. Who was the emperor of Persia at during Rasūlullāh's ﷺ time?

A. Heraclius.
B. Khosrow.
C. Alexander the Great.
D. Pharaoh.
E. Salman the Persian.

5. According to the lesson on the mission to Tabūk, who spread and magnified the rumor that the Romans were preparing to attack Arabia?

A. Heraclius.
B. Banu Nadir.
C. Abū Jahl.
D. Abū ‘Amir.
E. Khālid Ibn Walīd.

6. According to the lesson, many men expressed their unwillingness to participate in the mission. Why were they unwilling?

A. People were afraid of the mighty Romans.
B. It was summer and the heat was too oppressive for such a mission.
C. It was harvest season and the dates were ripe. Men wanted to harvest the fruit.
D. All of the above.
E. Only (a) and (c).

7. According to the lesson, Muslim historians provide two different reasons why the Romans did not show up to fight the Muslims. What are the two reasons?

1. ______________________________

2. ______________________________

8. What do you think was the greatest achievement for the Muslims as a result of the mission to Tabūk?

____

9. Read āyah 9:42. The āyah says the hypocrites would have participated in the expedition if they saw two advantages. What are the two advantages mentioned in the āyah?

1. ______________________________

2. ______________________________

10. Rasūlullāh ﷺ told some men, who were genuinely interested in participating in the mission to Tabūk, that they could not join because they did not have weapons or camels. How did they react?

A. They felt relief.
B. They were angry with Rasūlullāh ﷺ.
C. They cried because they were disappointed.
D. They secretly joined the mission.
E. They joined the Roman army.

Unit 4: Islamic Ethical Framework

The ethical framework prescribed in Islam is intimately connected to the teachings of the Qur'ān. This, in turn, forms the foundation of an ideal Islamic society. An Islamic ethical framework teaches Muslims to guard their behavior, actions, words, and thoughts. It guides followers to observe certain uniform moral and ethical codes when interacting with family, relatives, neighbors, or friends. It also teaches Muslims to engage in proper business practices, honorable financial transactions, and to respect for social affairs without bias and prejudice. Above all the ethical standard guides followers to be honest and forthright in private and public life.

Unit 4: Islamic Ethical Framework

Friends and Friendship: *Who is a Good Friend*

We should exercise caution about who we befriend. Good friends can help us become better people, but many "good" friends can actually be harmful. Students will learn what qualities to look in their friends and what types of friendships they should avoid.

Friendship With Non-Muslims

Most of us live in a predominantly non-Muslim environment. Many of our friends are non-Muslim. Can we have friendships with non-Muslims? The Qur'ān says that we can have friendships with non-Muslims, but only under certain conditions. This lesson discusses the topic of non-Muslim friendships.

Dating: *How Islam Views the Practice*

Dating is an acceptable social behavior in Western countries, but dating is prohibited in Islam. This lesson discusses dating issues for Muslim youths, and provides direction on how to avoid temptation and how to follow the proper guidance.

Hold Fast the Rope of Allāh ﷻ

This chapter discusses two āyāt from sūrah al-i 'Imrān—one that teaches us not to die unless we are Muslim, and one that teaches us not to split up but hold fast the rope of Allāh ﷻ. These messages are very pertinent today because many of us are at risk of dying as non-Muslim. Many of us are on the verge of splitting up because we have loosened our grip on the rope of Allāh ﷻ.

Elements of a Bad Life

Ideally, students should learn about the elements of a good life. However, it is also important to know the elements of a bad life because it is easy to get carried away by these elements. After all, these aspects often appear fun and attractive. Sometimes we do not understand the gravity of these bad aspects. Overindulgence in these elements can cause us to suffer in this life and in the Hereafter.

Friends and Friendship: *Who is a Good Friend?*

Objective of the Lesson:

We should exercise caution about who we befriend. Good friends can help us become better people, but many "good" friends can actually be harmful. Students will learn what qualities to look in their friends and what types of friendships they should avoid.

We live in a society where we interact with people from diverse backgrounds. We often have different ideologies, goals, beliefs, values, and interests. Despite the innumerable differences among us, we seek and enjoy companionship and association with our fellow human beings. We do this because we are social creatures. As human beings, we do not wish to live as isolated individuals.

Scientists study the social behavior of human beings in many different ways to understand our "social" tendencies. They have defined the social nature of human beings as a voluntary association of individuals for common interests. A society is an organized group working together or periodically meeting because of common interests, beliefs, or professions.

When we look for companionship and association with others, we develop friendships with people. So, what is meant by "friendship?" Friendship is a type of personal relationship that cannot be understood by simply reading a definition. But we can think of friendship as a relationship that we can choose. It is a relationship that occurs naturally in society; most of us do not have to go out into the world looking for a friend. There are other types of relationships that are simply acquaintances, but we might call them friendships. There are other types of relationships that we cannot choose, for example, family relationships. These are relationships we are born into, for example, our parents and siblings. No matter what happens, we cannot deny these relationships.

Some of our friendships are short-lived and some are long-lasting. Some friendships develop from our connections to school or work. Many of these relationships are actually acquaintances. Often, once we leave schools or jobs, the bonds of some of these friendships weaken and wear off.

Islam on friendship

In essence, friendship is a measure of the ties between two individuals. We live in societies where these ties always exist. We can even say human survival is based on friendship. The feeling of loneliness is enough to drive a person to near insanity. Wanting friendships is a natural instinct, and there is almost no escaping friendship in some form or another.

It might surprise you to know, the Qur'ān and the Sunnah of Rasūlullāh ﷺ deal extensively with the topic of friendship. Islam tells us what kind of person can be a friend, and should not be a friend, what to expect from a friend, and what to watch for from those who appear to be friends. There are benefits from certain friendships, but drawbacks result from other friendships.

Mistakes about "good friends"

Before we discuss the qualities of good friends, we should understand some common mistakes regarding friendship. Generally the following points are true:

- Good friends are those who share your happiness and sadness.
- Good friends are those who spend time with you.
- Good friends are those who share at least some of your interests.

However, these qualities alone are not sufficient for a good friend. To illustrate this point, let us consider an extreme example. Pretend you started using drugs at school. Soon your circle of friends would change—you would find new friends who share your common interests or beliefs. The commonality between you and them is using drugs. You would find these "friends" sharing your happiness and sadness, and spending time with you. You would find comfort and meaning in your life in their company and believe they are the ones who understand and love you. But within a few months or years, using drugs will destroy the lives of you and your friends. Even though you were "good friends" who shared each other's happiness, sadness, and time, the end result is devastating.

From this example, we can conclude that not all friends who appear to be "good friends" are truly the friends we want in our lives. How our friends affect our lives is very important.

What to look for in friendship

A good friend should share your happiness and sadness, spend time with you, and share some of your interests. However, the most important qualification for a friend is "righteousness." This is the primary criteria in a friend that is worthwhile in this life and in the afterlife. We cannot become friends with every righteous person, but we should try to find and befriend righteous people. People who are not righteous need not become our enemy; we can continue to be on good terms with them. These people might be acquaintances, whom we know from school or work. If our acquaintances are not righteous, it is advisable to keep some distance from them while showing noble and kind behavior. When making important life decisions, we should think twice about taking advice from non-righteous people. Their advice might be sincere, but we must weigh the advice in terms of our overall moral, ethical, and spiritual objectives in life.

The reason Islam requires us to make righteous friends is beautifully illustrated in Rasūlullāh's ﷺ advice: *"A person is likely to follow the faith of his friend, so look whom you befriend."*

If your friend is righteous, shares your happiness and sadness, remains loyal and trustworthy, and stands by you, this friendship is ideal. The Qur'ān says:

ٱلْأَخِلَّآءُ يَوْمَئِذٍۭ بَعْضُهُمْ لِبَعْضٍ عَدُوٌّ إِلَّا ٱلْمُتَّقِينَ ﴿٦٧﴾

The friends on that day—some of them will become enemies to some other, excepting the righteous. (Az-Zukhruf, 43:67)

Examples of good friends

A true friend is someone who supports you during hardship and encourages you to remain on the straight path. One of the finest friends that anyone ever had was Abū Bakr (R). When Rasulullāh ﷺ had to escape from Makkah, Abū Bakr risked his life and accompanied the Rasul ﷺ. If captured, both of them could have been killed. Abū Bakr could have easily avoided this risk by not going with Rasūlullāh ﷺ. As a true friend, he did not abandon Muhammad ﷺ during his time of need.

A similar example was the exemplary friendship of 'Umar and 'Uthmān. Both men supported Muhammad ﷺ during his hardship, because they knew Rasūlullāh ﷺ was on the right path.

Definition of a good friend

There are only a few important qualities of a good friend. The Qur'ān identifies a good friend as one who obeys Allāh ﷻ and His Rasul ﷺ. A good friend is also truthful, righteous, and testifies to the Oneness of Allāh ﷻ.[4:69] If someone possesses these five qualities, he or she would be the best kind of friend to have.

وَمَن يُطِعِ ٱللَّهَ وَٱلرَّسُولَ فَأُوْلَٰٓئِكَ مَعَ ٱلَّذِينَ أَنْعَمَ ٱللَّهُ عَلَيْهِم مِّنَ ٱلنَّبِيِّـۧنَ
وَٱلصِّدِّيقِينَ وَٱلشُّهَدَآءِ وَٱلصَّٰلِحِينَۚ وَحَسُنَ أُوْلَٰٓئِكَ رَفِيقًا ﴿٦٩﴾

And whoever obeys Allāh and the Rasul, then they are with those upon whom Allāh has bestowed favors—from among the prophets, and the truthful, and the witnesses, and the righteous. And what goodly friends are they! (4:69)

Friendship with Allāh ﷻ

The best friendship a person can have is friendship with Allāh ﷻ. It is true that it is a symbolic friendship, not an interpersonal relationship. You cannot see Allāh ﷻ but He can see you. It might surprise you, to know that friendship between a person and the "Unseen" is entirely possible. Allāh ﷻ is the Friend of the believers because He helps us to remain on the Right Path.[3:68] The Qur'ān says friendship with Allāh ﷻ is the best kind of friendship one can hope to develop.

أَلَآ إِنَّ أَوْلِيَآءَ ٱللَّهِ لَا خَوْفٌ عَلَيْهِمْ وَلَا هُمْ يَحْزَنُونَ ﴿٦٢﴾

Now surely for the friends of Allāh, there is no fear in them, nor will they grieve. (Yūnus 10:62)

أَمِ ٱتَّخَذُواْ مِن دُونِهِۦٓ أَوْلِيَآءَۖ فَٱللَّهُ هُوَ ٱلْوَلِيُّ وَهُوَ يُحْيِ ٱلْمَوْتَىٰ وَهُوَ عَلَىٰ كُلِّ شَيْءٍ قَدِيرٌ ﴿٩﴾

Or have they taken protecting-friends besides Him? But Allāh, He is the Protecting-Friend, and He quickens the dead, and He is Possessor of power over all things. (As-Shura 42:9)

Avoiding some friendships

Just as friendship with Allāh ﷻ is entirely possible, so is friendship with Shaitān. The worst type of friendship a person can have is with Shaitān.[2:257; 7:27] We must consciously avoid his friendship. He is our worst enemy, yet thousands of people treat him like a friend. Shaitān befriends innocent people, tempts them to believe in false things, and gives them false hope. You might remember that Shaitān took advantage of Ādam's (A) innocence and forgetfulness. He led Ādam (A) to believe that if he ate from the forbidden tree, he would become immortal or an angel.[7:20] But after Ādam (A) ate from the tree, he was expelled from the Garden and he became remorseful.[7:23-24]

Shaitān constantly tries to become friendly with us in order to cheat us.[4:120; 14:22; 17:64] He will try to ambush us. He will try to trap us whenever we are careless.[7:16] He will attack us in a planned way from all sides.[7:17] His attack will not appear rough or vicious. Instead, he will try to mislead us with sweet talk. He whispers temptations in order to pull us away the right path.[114:4]

After a person becomes friendly with Shaitān and listens to his temptations, Shaitān then misleads the person, causing his or her moral and spiritual destruction. After the damage is done, Shaitān will abandon him or her.[14:22; 37:30; 59:16] Therefore, we must avoid Shaitān's temptations. The Qur'ān says on the Judgment Day Shaitān will admit:

> *And when the matter will have been decided, Shaitān will say: "Surely Allāh promised you the promise of truth; I promised to you, but I broke it. And I had no authority over you, except that I called you and you responded to me; therefore do not blame me, but blame yourselves. I cannot be your rescuer, nor can you be my rescuer. I truly disclaim your making me partner before." Surely the wrong-doers—for them is a painful chastisement. (Ibrāhīm 14:22)*

Avoiding certain friendships

In addition to the invisible Shaitān, there are evil people among us—we must avoid them as well. Just as Shaitān tempts us with attractive promises and hope of rewards, people can also talk sweetly to us and make us believe they are our true friends. But in the end, they will cause our moral and spiritual downfall. These people might be a current friend or acquaintance. You should try to determine if they are truly a friend or if they might harm you. You should listen to Allāh ﷻ and His guidance. He will guide you in identifying the people to avoid.

In this lesson, we learned how to identify true friends in life and how to deal with friends who seem to be "good" friends. We also learned that the best friend we could ever have is Allāh ﷻ, even though we cannot see Him. If we become friends with Allāh ﷻ, we will have no fear or grief in life.[10:62] Allāh is our best protecting-friend.[42:9]

Shaitān is our worst enemy—he is constantly trying to tempt us to do the wrong things. There are evil people among us who behave a lot like Shaitān. They, too, can cause our spiritual downfall. We should try to identify and avoid these people as much as possible.

WEEKEND 16

Homework

1. Why do we need friendship?

____

____

____

____

2. According to the Qur'ān, what are the five requirements of a good friend?

1. ______________________________
2. ______________________________
3. ______________________________
4. ______________________________
5. ______________________________

3. Pretend you have started playing baseball. A player on your team is an excellent pitcher. He or she spends time with you after the game. Before you consider this person a friend, what is the primary quality that you should look for in him or her?

____

____

____

4. Based on Sūrah Yūnus, āyah 62 (mentioned in the lesson), what are the benefits for those who are friends with Allāh ﷻ?

____

____

5. What tactics does Shaitān use to mislead people? Select all answers that are correct.

A. He provides false hope.
B. He appears as a cruel, vicious monster.
C. He offers pleasant ideas and temptations.
D. Once a person is misled, Shaitān takes responsibility.

6. Why did Abū Bakr (R) accompany Rasūlullāh ﷺ to Madīnah?

A. Abū Bakr (R) had supplies to sell in Madīnah.
B. Abū Bakr (R) had already built a house in Madīnah.
C. His friend, Muhammad ﷺ was a righteous man and he was in danger.
D. Madīnah was a better town than Makkah.

7. What is the difference between a friend and an acquaintance?

____

____

____

Friendship With Non-Muslims

Objective of the Lesson:

Most of us live in a predominantly non-Muslim environment. Many of our friends are non-Muslim. Can we have friendships with non-Muslims? The Qur'ān says that we can have friendships with non-Muslims, but only under certain conditions. This lesson discusses the topic of non-Muslim friendships.

In the previous lesson, we discussed friends and friendship in general. However, we did not discuss what the Qur'ān says about friendships with non-Muslims. We all have non-Muslim friends at school and at work. We interact with them daily and spend time with them. Many of them come to our homes to visit, and we visit them in their homes. We live in a society where we interact with non-Muslims from every walk of life. Therefore, we must try to understand Qur'ānic instructions about interacting with non-Muslims. The Qur'ān does not tell Muslims to become hostile and unfriendly to other people in society.

The Qur'ān and the Sunnah of Rasūlullāh ﷺ did not discourage us from making ordinary friendships with people of other faiths. However, the Qur'ān has some āyāt that explain why we, as Muslims, should be cautious before befriending the People of the Book—particularly Jews and Christians. Many non-Muslim critics of Islam use these ayāt to claim that Islam is a violent religion, because these ayāt portray them in a negative way. Unless we have a thorough understanding of these ayāt, we will never appreciate the true message of the Qur'ān. Let us read a few āyāt in the Qur'ān that caution us about friendships with certain types of non-Muslims.[5:51; 5:57; 5:82; 60:13]

Christians and Jews

In a few āyāt, the Qur'ān discourages us from befriending Jews or Christians.

۞ يَٰٓأَيُّهَا ٱلَّذِينَ ءَامَنُوا۟ لَا تَتَّخِذُوا۟ ٱلْيَهُودَ وَٱلنَّصَٰرَىٰٓ أَوْلِيَآءَ ۘ بَعْضُهُمْ أَوْلِيَآءُ بَعْضٍ ۚ وَمَن يَتَوَلَّهُم مِّنكُمْ فَإِنَّهُۥ مِنْهُمْ ۗ إِنَّ ٱللَّهَ لَا يَهْدِى ٱلْقَوْمَ ٱلظَّٰلِمِينَ ﴿٥١﴾

O you who believe! do not take the Jews and Christians as allies. Some of them are allies of some other. And whoever from among you makes alliance with them, he is then one of them. Surely Allāh does not guide the unjust people. (5:51)

We should remember that these ayāt were revealed when the Muslims were in a state of war with Jews and Christians. These āyāt are not discussing normal conditions. Muslims are told they cannot become allies with Christians and Jews during times of war. Otherwise it is not a problem to befriend them. When the Qur'ān was revealed, Muslims were not involved in any wars with Persian sun-worshippers or Hindus. Therefore, the Qur'ān does not mention whether Muslims can be friends with them. The fact remains that those who fought a war against Muslims, cannot be friends of Muslims.

In the Qur'ān, ayāh 5:82 states the people closest to Muslims are Christians. This clearly indicates Islam respects them and considers them as good people. Therefore, if war-like conditions do not exist, then befriending them is not an issue.

Meaning of awliyā'

The primary meaning of the word **awliyā'** (singular, *wali*) is to place one's confidence in someone, to trust someone, or to do someone a favor. Allāh ﷻ is our *wali* because He is our protector. We trust Him, we rely upon Him, and we seek His help. A person can be a *wali* of another person. However, if a person is hostile to us, wants to harm us, or opposes us, then we cannot consider him or her a protector. We cannot trust or rely upon him or her. Once again, if we return to the ayāt about not being friends with Christians or Jews, it means the person cannot be our protector during times of war or similar situations.

In the English language, the word awliyā' is translated as "ally." An ally is different from personal friend. An ally indicates a formal cooperation between two individuals or groups for military or other purposes. In order to have an ally relationship, that is, to have an alliance, typically there is a treaty between the two parties. In personal friendships, we do not form such alliances.

Some Jews and Christians will go to Heaven

The Qur'ān recognizes that some Jews and Christians are good human beings and promises them paradise. This illustrates that some Jews and Christians are actually better in the sight of Allāh ﷻ than some Muslims. In light of this, it is not possible that Allāh ﷻ would tell us not to have personal friendships with Jews and Christians when He loves some of them so generously. The Qur'ān says:

۞ لَيۡسُواْ سَوَآءٗۗ مِّنۡ أَهۡلِ ٱلۡكِتَٰبِ أُمَّةٞ قَآئِمَةٞ يَتۡلُونَ ءَايَٰتِ ٱللَّهِ ءَانَآءَ ٱلَّيۡلِ وَهُمۡ يَسۡجُدُونَ ١١٣

They are not alike. Among the People of the Scripture, there is a community standing upright, they recite the Messages of Allāh by night-time, and they prostrate themselves. (3:113)

يُؤۡمِنُونَ بِٱللَّهِ وَٱلۡيَوۡمِ ٱلۡأٓخِرِ وَيَأۡمُرُونَ بِٱلۡمَعۡرُوفِ وَيَنۡهَوۡنَ عَنِ ٱلۡمُنكَرِ وَيُسَٰرِعُونَ فِي ٱلۡخَيۡرَٰتِۖ وَأُوْلَٰٓئِكَ مِنَ ٱلصَّٰلِحِينَ ١١٤

They believe in Allāh and the Future Day, and they bid doing good and forbid from doing wrong, and they vie with one another in good deeds; and these are among the righteous. (3:114)

It is clear that Allāh ﷻ is not asking us to end our friendships with people of other faiths. We should avoid friendships with people of other faiths only when they mock our religion, openly express hatred toward us, wage war against us, or want to cause harm to us. In such cases, we should not consider them awliyā, allies, or protecting friends. They cannot protect us.

Ordinary friendship is allowed

In the previous chapter, we mentioned that friends who are not righteous need not become our enemies. We can still continue to be on good terms with non-righteous people. Friends of other faiths might share some of our interests. They might play soccer or baseball with us, which a believing friend might not play. The Qur'ān does not prohibit us from making and maintaining good friendships with people who are not hostile towards us.

The greatest evidence in the Qur'ān that illustrates Muslims are allowed to maintain friendships with people of other faiths is provided in ayāh 60:8.

لَّا يَنْهَىٰكُمُ ٱللَّهُ عَنِ ٱلَّذِينَ لَمْ يُقَٰتِلُوكُمْ فِى ٱلدِّينِ وَلَمْ يُخْرِجُوكُم مِّن دِيَٰرِكُمْ أَن تَبَرُّوهُمْ وَتُقْسِطُوٓا۟ إِلَيْهِمْ ۚ إِنَّ ٱللَّهَ يُحِبُّ ٱلْمُقْسِطِينَ ﴿٨﴾

Allāh does not prohibit you from respecting those who have not fought you for the Religion, and who have not turned you out of your homes, that you show them kindness and act equitably towards them. Certainly Allāh loves the equitable ones. (60:8)

It is clear that the Qur'ān prohibits us from forming friendships with people who are openly hostile toward us. The fact is that no sensible person—whether a Jew, Hindu, Christian, or Buddhist—would form a friendship with someone who is determined to harm him or her. Even if the Qur'ān did not clarify this point, people from other faiths would behave similarly with their enemies. On the other hand, the Qur'ān clearly advises us to maintain good relations with people who are not at war with us and people who are not hostile toward us.

No violence

In this lesson, we learned that under some circumstances, we should not be friends with people of other faiths. However, we should remember that not being friends does not give us permission to fight them. We should not get involved in hatred or violence.

If Muslims are oppressed in one region, the people in that region will fight against their oppression. But Muslims around the world should not fight in their own neighborhoods, cities, and countries. Islam is a peace-loving religion. We should try to maintain peace during every stage in our lives.

Homework

1. Which of the following choices regarding friendships with people of other faiths is correct?

A. We can have friendships with others if they are not hostile toward us.
B. We can have friendships with others if there is no war between us.
C. We cannot have friendships if they mock our religion.
D. The Qur'ān does not discourage us from making general friendship with others.
E. All of the above.

2. What is the meaning of the Arabic term *awliyā*?

____

3. Which of the following choices about the Qur'ān telling us not to take Jews and Christians as awliya is correct?

A. The Qur'ān asks us not to trust them under any circumstance.
B. The Qur'ān asks us not to take them as good friends.
C. The Qur'ān asks us not to take them as protectors.
D. The Qur'ān asks us to hate them.
E. The Qur'ān asks us to stay away from their neighborhood.

4. When does the Qur'ān ask us not to take Jews and Christians as awliyā?

A. When there is war between Muslims and Jews or Christians.
B. When there is serious social hostility between Muslims and Jews or Christians.
C. When Jews or Christians want to harm Muslims.
D. When Jews or Christians ridicule Islam.
E. All of the above.

5. Under which of the following circumstances can we make or maintain friendships with Jews or Christians?

A. When our Jewish friend starts drinking and experimenting with drugs.
B. When our Jewish friend supports free speech, even if it relates to negative cartoons of Rasūlullāh ﷺ.
C. When our Christian friend repeatedly points out the bloody history of Islam.
D. When our Christian or Jewish friend never talks negatively about Islam.
E. When our Christian or Jewish friends openly disrespect Islam or the Qur'ān.

6. The Qur'ān says that as long as Jews and Christians do not show certain types of behavior, we can befriend them. What are the two behaviors mentioned in ayāh 60:8?

A. Fighting and friendship.
B. Jealousy and enmity.
C. Hostility and kindness.
D. Turning you out of your home and fighting against you.
E. Destroying a masjid and laughing about it.

7. Under which circumstances does the Qur'ān advise us not to take Jews and Christians as awliyā?

A. When we are at war with them.
B. When they visit our mosque.
C. When they compete with us.
D. When they preach their religion.

8. The Qur'ān does not say whether we can be friends with Hindus and Buddhists. Based on the lesson, what can you conclude about being friends with Hindus and Buddhists? Explain your answer.

____

____

____

Dating: *How Islam Looks at the Issue*

Objective of the Lesson:

Dating is an acceptable social behavior in Western countries, but dating is prohibited in Islam. This lesson discusses dating issues for Muslim youths, and provides direction on how to avoid temptation and how to follow the proper guidance.

Muslim students living in Western countries face many challenges in middle school and high school. These challenges actually begin much earlier—in elementary school—and increase dramatically in high school. In this lesson, we discuss the responsibilities of Muslim students, and how to follow Islamic manners and values without sacrificing Western identities.

One of the dominant aspects of life is the West is the interaction of men and women. In Western cultures, men and women socialize freely with each other, in one-on-one intimate relationships, for romantic reasons. Western societies does not consider this a bad moral example, and they encourage dating. Words such as boyfriend, girlfriend, dating, and so forth are not taboo words in Western societies.

In English usage, dating means "to go out with someone," such as for romantic reasons. Romance is an emotional, loving attraction between two people who are not biologically related. A brother's love for his sister is not romance, nor is a mother's love for her children. But a man and a woman who are not biologically related to each other can have a romantic relationship.

As Muslims, we must understand what our religion teaches about the interaction of men and women. We might say the answer is simple: Islam prohibits dating.

This is true. However, there is much more to know about this issue. Let us discuss what Islam says about dating.

Why we like each other

The reason men and women like each other is given in the Qur'ān. Sūrah 30, āyah 21, says that attraction between a man and a woman is a sign from Allāh ﷻ. He wants us to ponder this matter. He has created two emotions between men and women: love and mercy. Due to this love and mercy, men and women get married, have children, and continue the human race. Similar principles are also at work in nature as a whole.

وَمِنْ ءَايَـٰتِهِۦٓ أَنْ خَلَقَ لَكُم مِّنْ أَنفُسِكُمْ أَزْوَٰجًا لِّتَسْكُنُوٓا۟ إِلَيْهَا وَجَعَلَ بَيْنَكُم مَّوَدَّةً وَرَحْمَةً ۚ إِنَّ فِى ذَٰلِكَ لَـَٔايَـٰتٍ لِّقَوْمٍ يَتَفَكَّرُونَ ﴿٢١﴾

And of His Signs is that He creates for you mates out of yourselves, so that you may find tranquillity in them; and He has put love and mercy between you. Surely in this there are indeed signs for a people who reflect. (30:21)

Preserve species

One of the laws of nature is the "procreation of race." Procreation means to breed or reproduce. Whether we are discussing plants, animals, micro-organisms, or any other living being, every species reproduces. The urge to reproduce is common in all living organisms. In order for species to reproduce, Allāh ﷻ has devised a mechanism whereby the sexes of each species attract one another.

Imagine what would happen if there was no attraction or attachment within each species. There would be no urge among them to reproduce. If there was no reproduction, life on earth would perish. The population of each species would decline. The ecosystem would collapse and the food chain would break down. There would be major chaos in nature and the planet would eventually become deserted. In order to prevent such a disaster, Allāh ﷻ devised the process of reproduction to preserve all species.

Nature has a check-and-balance mechanism in place. For example, a fish lays thousands of eggs, but not all eggs hatch and not all hatchlings grow into adults. All species, including human beings, have a birth rate higher than replacement level. If the birth rate falls below the replacement level, the species will eventually perish. A replacement level is maintained through the God-given urge to reproduce and procreate race.

Human beings are different

Nature is preparing you so that you, too, can carry out Allāh's ﷻ wish—to continue the human race.

However, human beings are different. We are the best of creation. We have moral, ethical, and spiritual impulses that animals do not have. Animals eat, sleep, and reproduce without realizing the moral, ethical, and spiritual implications of their conduct. Animals do not have these obligations, so they will not be judged on the Day of Judgment. On the other hand, human beings are required to follow moral, ethical, and spiritual obligations because our conduct will be judged. We cannot behave like animals. We have certain principles to follow and certain codes of conduct to uphold.

Simple touching, hugging, kissing

While we are growing up—as teenagers, and young adults—we find that attraction to the opposite sex occupies a great deal of our time, emotions, and thoughts. This attraction can overtake our good senses and tempt us to follow the needs of our bodies. You might begin to think that simple touching, hugging or kissing is not harmful. You see many students are doing these things, so you might begin to believe it is acceptable behavior.

However, no matter how much we argue in favor of simple touching, hugging or kissing, the argument cannot defeat the Qur'ānic instruction about appropriate behavior:

قُل لِّلْمُؤْمِنِينَ يَغُضُّوا مِنْ أَبْصَٰرِهِمْ وَيَحْفَظُوا فُرُوجَهُمْ ذَٰلِكَ أَزْكَىٰ لَهُمْ إِنَّ ٱللَّهَ خَبِيرٌ بِمَا يَصْنَعُونَ ﴿٣٠﴾

Say to the believing men that they lower their eyes, and restrain their appetites. This is purer for them. Surely Allāh is Aware of what they do. (24:30)

وَقُل لِّلْمُؤْمِنَٰتِ يَغْضُضْنَ مِنْ أَبْصَٰرِهِنَّ وَيَحْفَظْنَ فُرُوجَهُنَّ وَلَا يُبْدِينَ زِينَتَهُنَّ

And say to the believing women that they should cast down their eyes, and guard their appetites, and do not display their ornaments.... (24:31)

We cannot justify holding someone's hand romantically, hugging the person, or kissing the person when the Qur'ān asks us to lower our gazes in the presence of the opposite sex. The Qur'ān also asks us to avoid meeting in secret unless we have something righteous to discuss.[2:235]

The Qur'ān or hadīth of Rasūlullāhﷺ do not give us permission to touch a person sexually if he or she is not already our spouse.

Strong condemnation

The Qur'ān uses very strong words to condemn pre-marital and extra-marital sex. The Qur'ān uses such words and phrases as "sinner" "transgressor", "rejecter of faith", "all your works will be in vain", and "you will be with losers in the Hereafter" to describe those who engage in pre-marital or extra-marital sex.[23:5–7]

فَمَنِ ٱبْتَغَىٰ وَرَآءَ ذَٰلِكَ فَأُولَٰٓئِكَ هُمُ ٱلْعَادُونَ ﴿٧﴾

But whoever seeks beyond that, they themselves are then the transgressors. (23:7)

When we read the Qur'ān about this issue, we realize that Allāh ﷻ is not describing a simple reproach or mild punishment. He is saying that all our good works will be in vain if we engage in pre-marital or extra-marital romance—whether it is touching, hugging, kissing or more. Our righteous works, salāt, fasting, and charity will be cancelled as a result of one act of romantic misconduct. This is a serious warning, and we must pay attention to it.

Dating without touching, kissing, hugging

We might think that it is possible to date someone without touching, kissing, or hugging. We might think we will remember Allāh ﷻ before doing anything. However, this is not possible.

We might not touch or hug someone in reality, but we will probably imagine it mentally. By engaging in these mental exercises, we weaken our souls. We weaken our resistance. We might find that dating without touching someone was possible for a day, week, or month, but some time down the road we will ignore the guidance.

Develop good moral values

When the whole world seems to be having fun, why should we develop good moral values and resist temptation? The answer is simple. Allāh ﷻ has given us the light of Islam and the promise of a rewarding Afterlife. Many of our friends are without guidance, without the light of Islam, and on the dangerous, slippery slope of moral and spiritual destruction.[9:109] A painful punishment awaits them in the Hereafter. When we reach the Hereafter, the time we spent on earth will seem like a tiny dot compared to eternal life. Therefore, their days of romantic relationships at the beach, parties, the mall, home, school, or elsewhere will seem like a fraction of a moment in the Hereafter.[23:112–114] We must ask ourselves: Am I willing to trade eternal, blissful life in the Hereafter for the temporary enjoyments of earthly life? Probably not. But how do we resist the temptation of passion?

The finest way to resist temptation is to remember our faith, patience, and commitment. We have to believe in and accept Allāh ﷻ as our friend rather than being friends with Shaitān. Shaitān makes false promises. He makes romantic objectives desirable and spiritual objectives burdensome and difficult. We should realize that the feeling of passion is really a test. We must pass the test by doing our best. This can be accomplished by avoiding dating and controlling our passions. This is simple to say but difficult to do in life. But all difficulties in life can be overcome through patience, hard work, and trust in Allāh ﷻ.

If we follow this guidance, Allāh ﷻ will make the situation easier for us. Initial passion will be difficult to control, but once we trust Allāh ﷻ and work hard to overcome these urges, we will find things become easier. Just as new diseases require new medicine, strong hormones and passions require us to submit to Allāh ﷻ with a stronger will and greater devotion. After all, Allāh ﷻ created us. He can make things easier for us. Allāh ﷻ says that with hardship comes ease.[94:6]

Best way to avoid dating

The best way to avoid the temptation of dating is to submit wholeheartedly to Allāh ﷻ and believe in His teachings without any hesitation or doubt. This must be done from the very beginning. Once we are committed to this belief, we will not only avoid dating, but we will also avoid all sins. There should not be any room in our minds to consider dating someone. There cannot be "gray area" in our minds about permissible dating. There is no such thing as permissible dating.

Dating your future life partner

Muslims often wonder: If someone intends to marry someone within a few months or a year, are they allowed to date? The answer lies in the Qur'ān. The Qur'ān does not allow romantic interaction between a man and a woman before their marriage.

The discussion above only reflects the basic moral teachings. We have to learn ways to avoid the temptation of dating. We should submit to Allāh ﷻ wholeheartedly and sincerely follow His guidance. We should not make excuses or establish faulty reasoning to justify dating.

Homework

1. Read ayāh 2:221 in the Qur'ān. This ayāh mentions who a Muslim cannot marry. Who is better for a Muslim to marry?

Cannot marry: ______________________________

Better to marry: ______________________________

2. The Qur'ān strictly forbids extra-marital affairs. In ayāh 17:32, two specific things are mentioned about sex outside of marriage. What two things are mentioned?

1. ______________________________

2. ______________________________

3. In ayāh 23:1, the Qur'ān says that success will come to those who follow certain criteria. The next few āyāt tell us some of the things needed to achieve success. One criterion applies to dating. Read ayāh 5 and write the criterion below.

____

4. How can you apply the message of 23:5 (in Q. 3 above) to your own life? Explain.

____

____

____

5. Read ayāh 24:30 in the Qur'ān and answer the following questions:

A. What two things are recommended for men to follow? ______________________________

____

B. How does the message of the ayāh apply to dating? ______________________________

____

6. Read ayāh 24:31 in the Qur'ān. What two things applicable to women are also applicable to men? Compare this ayāh to ayāh 24:30 to find the answer.

____

7. After reading ayāh 24:31, explain why a woman cannot date a man before marriage.

____

____

____

Hold Firmly the Rope of Allāh ﷻ

Objective of the Lesson:

This chapter discusses two āyāt from sūrah al-i 'Imrān—one that teaches us not to die unless we are Muslim, and one that teaches us not to split up but hold fast the rope of Allāh ﷻ. These messages are very pertinent today because many of us are at risk of dying as non-Muslim. Many of us are on the verge of splitting up because we have loosened our grip on the rope of Allāh ﷻ.

Sūrah Al-i 'Imrān contains a large number of fascinating āyāt that make us ponder. In this lesson, we describe two such āyāt that primarily address the early Muslims, who were very divided community, mired in idolatry and social chaos. There were many rifts among them. They had no unifying philosophy on which they could rest their allegiance. Different Arab tribes were enemies of each other. They were always on the verge of tribal warfare.

It appears that Muslims today are re-living many of these tribal conflicts. It seems like we are unable to unite under the umbrella of Islam. We have split up into distinct groups and sub-groups, each one complaining about the others. We are also like enemies to each other. Our love and respect for each other seems to have been diluted. Some of us are on the brink of a burning pit of fire because we cannot tolerate each other.

In view of the circumstances above, two āyāt from sūrah Al-i 'Imrān are especially pertinent for us. Let us analyze these two āyāt.

Al-i 'Imrān: Ayāh 3:102

Ayāh ayāh 102. This ayāh addresses the believers. This ayāh imposes obligations on new Muslims during Rasūlullāh's ﷺ time, and, in turn, on us today.

يَٰٓأَيُّهَا ٱلَّذِينَ ءَامَنُوا۟ ٱتَّقُوا۟ ٱللَّهَ حَقَّ تُقَاتِهِۦ وَلَا تَمُوتُنَّ إِلَّا وَأَنتُم مُّسْلِمُونَ ﴿١٠٢﴾

O you who believe! fear Allāh as He ought to be feared, and do not die unless you be Muslims.

The ayāh begins by drawing the attention of the believers, "*O you who believe!*" Therefore, the message that follows becomes obligatory for the believers. The point here is that belief in God is not enough; it must be substantiated by other necessary actions. In other words, belief must have an effect on one's life, and belief must encourage a set of actions approved and mandated by Allāh.

Fear Allāh as He ought to be feared. The word *taqwā* is often translated as "fear," or more precisely, "fear of God." However, the word does not mean fear in the sense of human feeling or emotion, for example, fear of falling or fear of darkness. *Taqwā* has a moral bearing—it points at one's character and conviction.

In a character-defining sense, *taqwā* requires people to cultivate a moral standard. It is a mental thing. In a conviction-defining sense, *taqwā* gives rise to the belief that the limits set by the Almighty cannot be overstepped, for this entails dire consequences. here it is a functional thing. Thus, a person who has *taqwā* is a *muttaqi.* He or she is a person who is fully aware of both mental and functional aspects of *taqwā*. The mental aspect keeps the person conscious of the limits set by Allāh, while the functional aspect restrains the person from overstepping those limits.

A verbal declaration of belief in Allāh is only part of the entire equation, belief must also be demonstrated by carrying out Allāh's commands in everyday life. The ayāh is asking believers to fear and revere Allāh as He ought to be feared and revered. In other words, He should be revered in an appropriate manner, and we should never compromise or dilute the nature of this reverence.

The command to fear Allāh also has a subtle indication of facing consequences if one does not fear Him the way He ought to be feared. Divine punishment for those who defy Him is extraordinarily severe. Keeping this in mind, one's fear of the divine must raise awareness of the consequences should one fail to fear Him.

Points to Ponder

Human fear is often connected to realistic danger in life. For example, the fear of driving on a busy highway, fear of poverty, fear of drowning, and so forth. Human fear is seldom connected to events that lie in the future. We know rampant destruction of the environment will hurt our children years from now. But we are not afraid. Similarly, people fully understand the consequences of defying Allāh, but they knowingly commit sins because at the moment of committing a sin, they are not afraid of divine punishment.

Do not die unless you be Muslims. The word *muslimūn* emphasizes the quality of submission to Allāh rather than the religious designation. It is commonly understood that at the time of death, one must say the Shahādah—the statement of faith. It is good to die with the statement of faith as one's last words. However, the command has much wider implications. It is a command for a person to die in state of complete and unqualified submission to Allāhﷻ—characterized by lifelong devotion and fulfilment of divine commands.

Al-i 'Imrān: Ayāh 3:103

Previously, in ayāh 102, the command not to die except in a state of complete submission to Allāhﷻ was addressed to the individual believer. In ayāh 103, the command applies to entire community. Let us read the ayāh.

وَٱعْتَصِمُوا۟ بِحَبْلِ ٱللَّهِ جَمِيعًا وَلَا تَفَرَّقُوا۟ ۚ وَٱذْكُرُوا۟ نِعْمَتَ ٱللَّهِ عَلَيْكُمْ إِذْ كُنتُمْ أَعْدَآءً
فَأَلَّفَ بَيْنَ قُلُوبِكُمْ فَأَصْبَحْتُم بِنِعْمَتِهِۦٓ إِخْوَٰنًا وَكُنتُمْ عَلَىٰ شَفَا حُفْرَةٍ مِّنَ
ٱلنَّارِ فَأَنقَذَكُم مِّنْهَا ۗ كَذَٰلِكَ يُبَيِّنُ ٱللَّهُ لَكُمْ ءَايَٰتِهِۦ لَعَلَّكُمْ تَهْتَدُونَ ﴿١٠٣﴾

And hold fast to the pact of Allāh all together, and do not split up; and remember the favor of Allāh on you: when you were enemies, then He put love into your hearts, then by His favor you became brethren. And you were on the brink of a pit of Fire, then He rescued you from it. Thus Allāh explains to you His Messages, that you may be guided. (3:103)

Hold fast to the pact of Allāh. The ayāh begins with the command to maintain unity in the community. In order to emphasize the point, the Qur'ān uses a metaphor for connectedness—the "Rope of Allāh." The word *habl* (lit. a rope, a cord; see usage in 111:5) if often translated using different shades of meaning to imply "covenant," "pact," "bond," "means to access Allāh" and so forth—all of which are ways by which a person makes a connection with God.

The Qur'ān uses the metaphor of a rope to reflect an Arab custom. In Arabian tradition, when two tribal chiefs made a pact with each other, each one held a rope and tied the ropes together. This symbolized two parties had entered into a pact.

For the early audience of the Qur'ān, the metaphor of *habl-Allāh* presented a novel concept. It signifies the covenant between Allāhﷻ and human beings. The covenant is stated in the form of guidance contained in the Qur'ān. By adhering to the guidance in the Qur'ān, believers hold fast to the "rope" of Allāhﷻ. The rope also provides a means of salvation—in this life and in the Hereafter. Imagine what would happen if a man is about to drown in the sea or slipped down a cliff, and then a rope is thrown to the man. He would grasp it firmly and be pulled to safety.

All together. The ayāh says the believers, all of them together, should grasp the rope of Allāhﷻ. Thus it is not only an individual duty but a duty upon all Muslims as a community to hold fast the covenant of Allāhﷻ.

And do not split up. This command, immediately after the command to hold fast to the rope of Allāh ﷻ, implies that abandoning or loosening the grip on the rope will give rise to divisions and schisms among the Muslims.

The implication of this command is now reinforced with regard to the history of Arabs before and after the advent of Islam. Prior to Islam, the Arab community was embroiled in tribal warfare threatening to devastate the nation. With the advent of Islam, these warring tribes realized they were being united by a bond of mutual love and respect, which soon deepened as they developed a feeling of brotherhood. The path to reach this level of communal feeling was not without perils, as frequent wars nearly destabilized them. But through Islam, Allāh ﷻ rescued them and established them as a great nation.

Allāh explains to you His Messages. The ayāh ends with an assurance that *Allāh explains to you His Messages, that you may be guided.* The basic purpose of sending divine guidance is to lead people to the path of righteousness. It worked during Rasūlullāh's ﷺ time, it works today, and it will work in the future. Whenever the Muslim community experiences conflict and disunity, it is possible we have loosened our grip on the covenant of Allāh ﷻ. In light of this, we should let go of petty disagreements among us and remain focused on uniting our community for greater benefit.

Homework

1. When the meaning of taqwā is interpreted as "fear of God," it has an effect on two aspects of a person. What are the two aspects?

A. A person's character and conviction.
B. A person's goal in life and upbringing.
C. A person's dedication and responsibility.
D. A person's drive and education.
E. A person's wealth and status.

2. Which of the following statement about how Allāh ﷻ should be feared is correct?

A. We should fear Him like we fear darkness.
B. We should fear overstepping the limits.
C. We should fear facing the consequences if we defy Him.
D. Only A and C are correct.
E. Only B and C are correct.

3. What is the significance of the word *muslimūn* in the phrase, "*Do not die unless you be muslimūn*"?

____

____

4. Which of the following statement about the significance of the phrase "Rope of Allāh" is correct?

A. It emphasizes the importance of remaining connected with Allāh ﷻ.
B. It is a covenant with Allāh ﷻ.
C. It is a bond with Allāh ﷻ.
D. It is a bridge connecting Paradise.
E. Only A, B, and C are correct.

5. According to the Qur'ān, how should we hold the "Rope of Allāh"?

A. As an individual.
B. As a collective unit.
C. By tying knots on threads found in Makkah and Madīnah.
D. All of the above.
E. Only A and B are correct.

6. In ayāh 3:103 in the Qur'ān, what does Allāh ﷻ tell us not to do?

A. Go near fire.
B. Split up.
C. Die unless we are Muslim.
D. Hold the Rope of Allāh.
E. Abandon the Qur'ān.

7. How did Allāh ﷻ change the enmity among the Arabs as mentioned in ayāh 3:103 in the Qur'ān?

A. By giving them education.
B. By giving them shelter.
C. By providing them food.
D. By curing diseases of the heart.
E. By putting love in their hearts.

8. There has to be a reason why some Muslims split up and form different groups. What specific reason is given for splitting up as indicated in ayāh 3:103 in the Qur'ān?

A. Muslims play with fire and hatred.
B. Muslims suffer from diseases in their hearts.
C. Muslims love the life of this world.
D. Muslims loosen the grip on the pact of Allāh ﷻ.
E. Muslims invent new teachings.

Elements of a Bad Life

Objective of the Lesson:

Ideally, students should learn about the elements of a good life. However, it is also important to know the elements of a bad life because it is easy to get carried away by these elements. After all, these aspects often appear fun and attractive. Sometimes we do not understand the gravity of these bad aspects. Overindulgence in these elements can cause us to suffer in this life and in the Hereafter.

The Qur'ān is a book of guidance. It guides us to the path of righteousness. The path to righteousness includes a large number of teachings that tell us what we need to do to stay on the path and what we should do to avoid deviating from the path. It is important that we learn the recommended actions. It is equally important that we learn the actions that are discouraged in Islam. Actions that are discouraged are not only disliked by the Almighty, but if committed, they also call for various forms of punishment.

We already know many of the prohibitions in the Qur'ān, but sometimes many of us knowingly and unknowingly indulge in these actions. The list of prohibited actions is long, however, we will discuss a few of them to learn more.

Jealousy

All of us experience jealousy in one form or another. Not all forms of jealousy are wrong. When jealousy is kept to a minimum, this helps motivate a person and brings a balance to a person's life. For example, if someone is very good at sports or academics, and another person feels jealous about it, then there is a possibility for the person to improve himself or herself. However, excessive or out-of-control jealousy is harmful and dangerous because it only destroys a person.

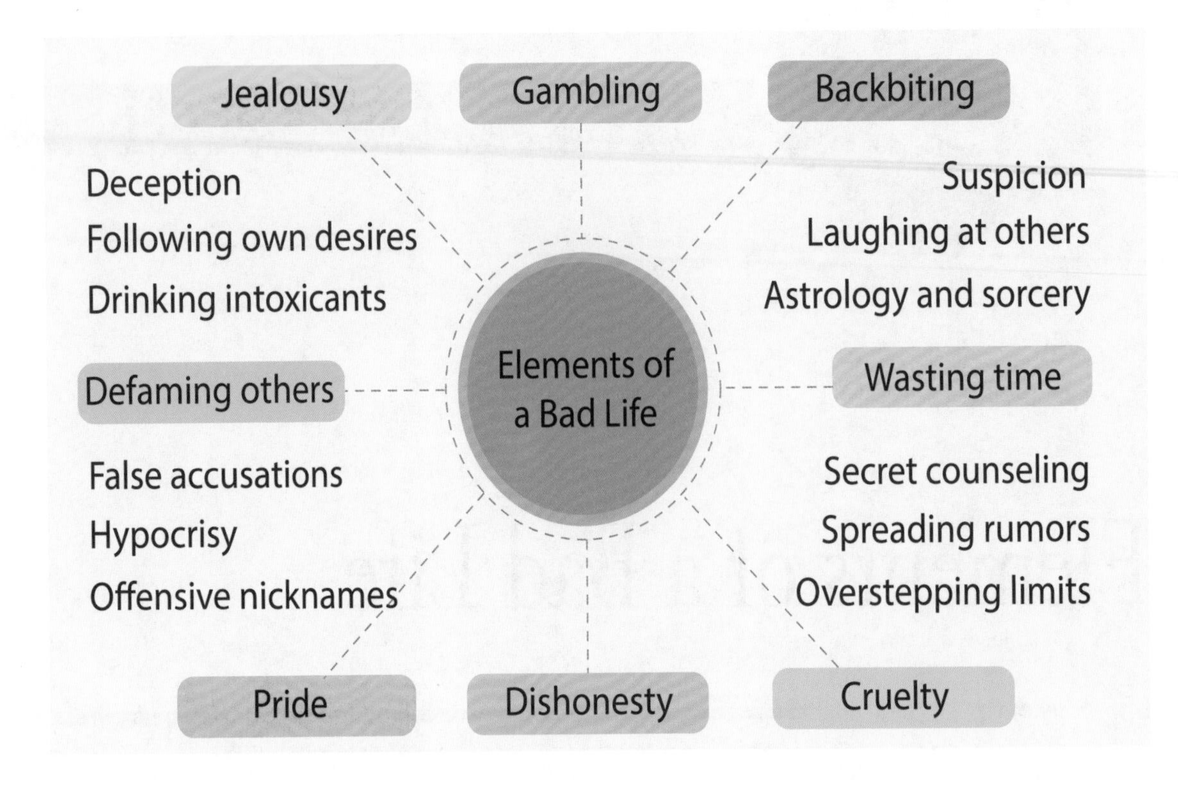

The Arabic word *hasad* (حسد) indicates envy and jealousy. Envy and jealousy seem to be the same thing, but there are differences between them. Envy occurs in reaction to lacking something, but jealousy occurs in reaction to the threat of losing something. Most people use envy and jealousy interchangeably.

The main reasons people feel jealous of others are insecurity, bitterness, envy, and obsession with something or someone. It occurs as a result of a real threat or an imaginary threat in our minds.

Allāh ﷻ created people with diverse levels of ability, merit, ownership, and other indicators. These might have been given to test people. Allāh ﷻ says He measures out everything according to divine wisdom. Some people receive more of one indicator and some receive a level amount or less. As a result, people become envious of others. Envy and jealousy are like diseases of the mind. If these diseases are not cured or restrained, they can cause profound moral and social damage. The irony is that seldom people want to cure themselves from being jealous of others. The force of jealousy only destroys, it never builds anything. For this reason, the Qur'ān teaches us to pray to Allāh ﷻ about the harm of peoples' jealousy.

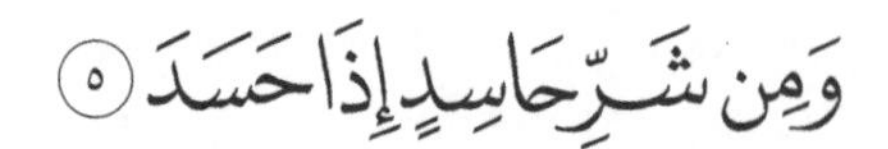

...and from the evil of the envier when he envies. (113:5)

Without using the word *hasad*, Allāh ﷻ advises us not to "strain our eyes," that is, not to envy others because He has given some people *splendor of the life of this world*, meaning affluence and comfort, because these are only a means to test certain people. We should always remember that the provisions He has reserved for us are immensely better and more lasting.

And do not strain your eyes towards that with which We have entertained different families out of them,—with the splendor of the life of this world, so that We may test them by that. And the provision of your Rabb is better and more lasting. (20:131)

Gambling

Gambling is risking money or anything of value on an uncertain event in hopes of winning something of greater value. Examples of gambling includes a lottery, bingo, card games, casinos, horse race, betting and so forth. In most Western societies, gambling is perceived as a low-risk fun activity. Sine legislative bodies and governments participate in organized gambling. There is also illegal gambling.

Just because Western societies approve of gambling as a form of entertainment, it does not become a permissible activity in the sight of God. The Qur'ān clearly discourages gambling:

They ask you about the intoxicants and games of chance. Say: "In both these there is a great sin and benefit for people; but the sin of it is more serious than their benefits." And they ask you as to what they should spend. Say: "What you can spare." Thus does Allāh make clear to you His Messages, that perhaps you may reflect. (2:219)

The ayāh highlights one important point about gambling—the sin outweighs the benefit. Gambling and lotteries benefit a select few. The odds of winning a major lottery are one in a million or more. Such huge odds against winning provides monetary gain to a few people, while thousands or millions lose money. Many lottery or gambling winners suffer as the easy gain is wasted within a few years.

Backbiting

Another element of a bad life is backbiting (*ghībah*), which simply means malicious talk about someone who is not present. Most of us, at one time or another, indulge in such talk thinking that it is harmless, simple talk that does not hurt anyone. The person being talked about is not present, therefore, we take the liberty of talking negatively about the person. Often we pretend that such talk is actually constructive criticism. But Allāh ﷻ knowsthese clever arguments. Therefore, He simply prohibits us from indulging in such talk. Sometimes talking behind someone's back might turn the conversation into *buhtān* (slander) and *namīm* (malicious gossip). The Qur'ān equates backbiting to eating the flesh of one's dead brother.

O you who believe! shun most of the suspicions, because some suspicions are sins indeed; and do not spy; and do not some of you backbite another. Does any one of you like to eat the flesh of his dead brother? Surely you loathe it! Therefore revere Allah. Certainly Allah is oft-Returning, most Rewarding. (49:12)

What is the best way to avoid backbiting? The best way is to stop ourselves immediately if we are about to say something bad about someone behind their back. If someone else initiates negative talk, tell them to stop or simply walk away. Do not contribute to the conversation. Remaining aware of this simple principle will help us avoid this bad habit.

Defaming others

To defame means to damage the good reputation of someone by making a false statement. Sometimes we indulge in such conduct, thinking it is constructive criticism, a means of venting our dislike for the person, or a way to gain an advantage over the person. If we only remember how much Allāh dislikes such conduct, we would think twice before defaming others. The Qur'ān says:

> *And whoever earns a mistake or a sin, then throws it upon an innocent, he then surely bears a slander and a flagrant crime. (4:112)*

Avoiding defaming or slandering someone requires us taking a few simple steps. These steps are similar to the ones taken to avoid backbiting. We should not initiate a false story about others, let alone spread it. Even if the story happens to be true, we should not abet it. If someone else spreads a defamation, tell them to stop it or simply walk away.

Wasting time

Time is priceless but it is also free to all. However, no one can buy or trade time. One can only make the best use of it or waste it. Sometimes people define the value of time in terms of money. Money can be spent or earned, but once time is spent, it cannot be earned back.

There is a common saying that "time and tide wait for no one". They come and go, but hey do not wait. One can only make the best use of time and tide. Time runs continuously without ever stopping. It never waits for anyone. A sprinter knows the importance of one-tenth of a second when the winner is decided in a 100-meter dash.

In our daily lives, we waste time without realizing it is priceless. The Qur'ān discusses the value of time in a large number of āyāt.

> *And nothing is the life of this world except a plaything and a vanity. And certainly the Home of the Hereafter is better for those who practice reverence. Do you not then understand? (6:32)*

Time is not clearly mentioned in this ayāh, but the message is not to waste time in idle activities or inaction, but to realize its value. Here the value of time is paired with life in the Hereafter. Having a better life in the Hereafter should be our ultimate goal. We can achieve this goal through the proper utilization of time.

Proper utilization of time does not mean we should spend all our waking hours in ritual worship. Islam does not endorse a life of extreme sacrifice and asceticism like that of monks and saints. Islam teaches us to worship Allāh ﷻ through ritual prayers and lead a good life. Total worship time in a day takes about 10 to 15 minutes, or about 1.5% of 16-hours of being awake.

Dishonesty

One of the worst elements of a bad life is dishonesty. Dishonesty means deceitfulness in one's character or behavior. We live in an age when societies consider some forms of dishonesty acceptable. especially to rise in one's career. Dishonesty probably helps some people achieve short-term goals in life. But at what cost? The cost far outweighs the benefits the person enjoys. Allāh ﷻ says:

> *...and whoever acts dishonestly, he will bring forth that dishonesty he has committed on the day of the Awakening; then each soul will be paid back fully what it has earned, and they will not be wronged. (3:161)*

As we grow older and enter the job market, we should remember not to earn a living in a dishonest manner. We should not be deceitful with our employer, our government or our country. A large number of people defraud their employer or government to gain certain benefits. Whatever we gain dishonesly—material or spiritual—will affect us in the Hereafter. The Qur'ān says "*these,—their refuge is the Fire because of that they have been earning.*"

Pride

Pride can be understood as a sense of personal dignity and values. How a person uses his or her pride can have positive or negative effects on the person and his or her surrounding. When used in a negative sense, pride means bragging about oneself, and act or habit of making undue claims in an overbearing manner. Pride gives rise to a feeling and attitude of superiority over, and contempt for, others. This type of pride is clearly an element of a bad life from which we should guard ourselves.

We all know the example of Iblīs—Shaitān. He had a negative attitude that prompted him to believe he was better than Adam (A). He presumed that being created from fire was superior to than Adam's (A) creation from clay. This undue claim and overbearing attitude led him to defy his Creator and suffer the consequences.

One's own desires

We should not follow our own desires in the matter of faith. What is meant by following our own desires? It is simply selfishness. It is about bypassing divine command and making up one's own methodologies and approaches to life. It is about making innovations in religion. If we think we are immune from following our own desires, then we need to think again and review many of our practices. We might be surprised to realize that many of us, in fact, follow our own desires. If we follow our own desires, not only are we moving away from religion, but -we are also earning divine wrath.

In the past, people received divine guidance. Then they began following their own desires, resulting in changing the religion to something quite different from the original. For example, fasting was prescribed to people in the past, but they changed this practice to follow their own desires. As a result, people fasted only on certain days and allowed eating fruits or drinking juices during fasting. In addition, people were told to worship one God, but they invented idols as a means of approaching God.

The list of elements of a bad life is long. We should take time to carefully review some of these elements and understand their seriousness. We should make an active effort to avoid these bad elements in our conduct and behavior.

Homework

1. What are the differences between envy and jealousy?

Envy: ____

Jealousy: ____

2. Read ayāh 20:131 in the Qur'ān. What does Allāh ﷻ not want us to do?

A. Differentiate between couples.
B. Enjoy the splendor of life.
C. Strain our eyes toward other peoples' affluence.
D. Use intoxicants at any time in life.
E. Entertain our eyes.

3. According to ayāh 20:131 in the Qur'ān, what is the reason behinds Allāh's ﷻ certain action mentioned in the ayāh?

A. To send splendor to people.
B. To entertain people.
C. To cause strain in our eyes.
D. To test people.
E. To give people provisions.

4. Read ayāh 2:219 in the Qur'ān. What two things are mentioned in the ayāh that contain more sins in them than benefits?

A. Idol worshipping and gambling.
B. Gambling and money laundering.
C. Alcohol and intoxicants.
D. Intoxicants and gambling.
E. Money and splendor.

5. Which elements of bad life compares an action with eating meat of one's dead brother?

A. Gambling.
B. Drinking.
C. Spreading rumor.
D. Defaming.
E. Backbiting.

6. Read ayāh 57:20 in the Qur'ān. How does the Qur'ān compare the life of this world to the life in the Hereafter?

A. Life in this world is a plaything and a competition.
B. Life in this world is a plaything and pastime.
C. Life in this world is vanity and gossip.
D. Life in this world is conflict and resolution.
E. Life in this world is bloodshed and peace.

7. Read ayāh 24:15 in the Qur'ān. Which element of a bad life is the Qur'ān prohibiting here?

A. Spreading rumors.
B. Spying.
C. Drinking intoxicants.
D. Telling lies.
E. Wasting resources.

8. Read ayāh 49:11 in the Qur'ān. Which element or elements of a bad life is the Qur'ān prohibiting here?

A. Laughing at others.
B. Defaming others.
C. Calling someone by a mean nickname.
D. All of the above.
E. Only A and C.

Unit 5: Islamic Values and Teachings

This unit focuses on some of the values and discipline involved in the process of self-reflection, which can shape and define a person. Duties towards one's parents are not only a moral responsibility; they are also a religious obligation. A person's psychological and emotional trauma is often the result of a lack of hope in life. Some of the causes of stress and depression lie in one's failure to realize that nobody is immune from trails in life. Enduring these trials can eventually help a person reach a new understanding of life. The chapter on permitted and prohibited food in Islam explains some of the prevalent myths about certain food and educates students about the types of meat Muslims are allowed to eat. The lesson on the performance of Hajj describes all the rituals associated with Hajj. The final chapter in this unit describes some of the parables in the Qur'ān.

Unit 5: Islamic Values and Teachings

Duties Towards Parents

Our duties towards our parents are clearly mentioned in the Qur'ān. What are the reasons for these obligations? This lesson discusses the topic and explains why duties towards our parents are the second-most important duty after our primary duty to worship Allāh ﷻ.

Hope, Hopefulness, Hopelessness

All believers are required to express hope when everything appears to fall apart. Hope provides strength and direction. On the other hand, a non-believer feels hopeless when disaster strikes. This chapter discusses the value of keeping hope and explains why people feel hopeless in life and provides solution to overcome hopelessness in life.

Trials in Life: *Everyone Will Experience Them*

All believers will experience trials in their lives. Even the messengers of Islam suffered trials. Experiencing difficulties make us better people. Those who do not have strong faith lose hope when they face difficulty. This lesson describes different types of trials, why Allāh ﷻ makes us experience them, and what we can do when we face difficulties in our lives.

Permitted and Prohibited Food

This chapter provides an overview of Muslim food laws as mentioned in the Qur'ān. Students will learn what types of animals are permissible to eat. However, the meat of some permissible animals cannot be eaten if they were not slaughtered in the prescribed manner. Students will also learn whether saying "Bismillah" before a meal makes it acceptable to eat the meat of an improperly slaughtered animal.

Performance of Hajj

The performance of Hajj requires a clear understanding of the ritual. Performing the ritual provides important spiritual benefits. Students will learn each step of Hajj, beginning with the first day and ending on the last day. Minor variations in the ritual are also discussed in the lesson.

Parables in the Qur'ān

The Qur'ān is not only a book of guidance, but it is also a book of high-quality literature. Just as literature uses metaphors, figures of speech and other techniques to tell a story, the Qur'ān also uses many of these techniques. The parable is a literary style used frequently in the Qur'ān. In this chapter, students will learn some of the parables in the Qur'ān.

WEEKEND 21

Classwork

Duties Towards Parents

Objective of the Lesson:

Our duties towards our parents are clearly mentioned in the Qur'ān. What are the reasons for these obligations? This lesson discusses the topic and explains why duties towards our parents are the second-most important duty after our primary duty to worship Allāh ﷻ.

As human beings, we all have different duties. Some duties are to ourselves—for example, taking a shower, clipping nails, wearing clean clothes, and so forth. Some obligations are to others. We live in a social environment and we are social beings. We have responsibilities to our families, our relatives, our friends, and our neighbors. We also have obligations to our environment, our country, and our world. Above all, we have duties to Allāh ﷻ—these are part of our spiritual duty.

Our responsibilities to Allāh ﷻ are the most important ones. Worshipping Allah is the number-one duty for all human beings, particularly Muslims.[51:56]

Doing good deeds for our parents is also an important duty. In fact, this duty is the most important one after worshipping Allāh ﷻ. If Allāh ﷻ had allowed us to worship multiple things, He would have allowed us to worship our parents! Why does the Qur'ān emphasize honoring our parents so much? Let us try to understand.

Our priorities change as we grow

Our duties to our parents are beautifully narrated in the Qur'ān in many places. More ayāt discuss duties to our parents than parents duties to their children. The reason is clear. It is natural for all parents to love their children. No matter how young or how old children are, parents love their children unconditionally. It never decreases. However, sometimes children's dedication for their parents decreases when they grow up. When a child becomes an adult, his or her priorities in life change. After living on his or her own, an adult's dependence on his or her parents decreases. An adult no longer needs parental help with bathing, clothing, or feeding. They no longer want parental help in their lives. Their love for their parents remains the same, but they tend to drift away from them. They spend more time with friends, go to college, find jobs, get married, and have children. They discover new loves in life—love for their husbands, wives, and children. This is normal and natural. This instinct is actually a God-given instinct.

When these adults were younger, they loved their parents dearly and cried when they missed their parents. They ran to them for comfort and love. To children, their parents are their entire world. But this changes when those same children grow up and become adults. It is natural that their priorities in life change. The Qur'ān reminds us that some priorities should never change. This priority is our dedication and obligation to our parents.

Status of parents in Islam

The status of a person is based on his or her position, dedication, and obligation in society and how others treat the person. The status of a teacher is a result of his or her appointment as a teacher and the respect shown by students. Similarly, the status of a governor is a result of his or her appointment as the governor and the trust shown by constituents. The same analogy applies to the status of parents in Islam.

In Islam, parents are given a very high status, and children are expected to show them proper respect. They can show respect by doing good deeds for their parents. The Qur'ān explains this point in verses 4:36, 6:151, and 17:23. Allāh says what we should not do, and then He tells us what we should do.

Not to do: Do not associate anyone or anything with Allāh.

To do: Do good to our parents.

And worship Allāh and do not associate with Him anything, ***and goodness towards the parents****, and to the close relatives, and the orphans, and the poor, and the neighbor who is related, and the neighbor who is alien, and the companion by the side, and the traveler, and what your right hands possess. Surely Allāh does not love him who is proud, boastful. (4:36)*

قُلْ تَعَالَوْا أَتْلُ مَا حَرَّمَ رَبُّكُمْ عَلَيْكُمْ ۖ أَلَّا تُشْرِكُوا بِهِ شَيْئًا ۖ وَبِالْوَالِدَيْنِ إِحْسَانًا ۖ
وَلَا تَقْتُلُوا أَوْلَادَكُم مِّنْ إِمْلَاقٍ

Say: "Come, I shall recite what your Lord has forbidden to you, that you do not associate with Him anything. And ***doing good to parents****, and that you do not kill your children for poverty..." (6:151)*

Significance of ihsān

The Qur'ān does not explain the meaning of the phrase "doing good to the parents." The entire concept of "good" is summed up in the word *ihsān*. The word *ihsān* denotes doing what is right, good, and beautiful. In other words, we should show our parents kindness, compassion, gratitude, obedience, and respect. We should pray for them and support them financially if they are in need. The list of possible good deeds is endless. We should simply remember not to do anything that would harm or disrespect for our parents.

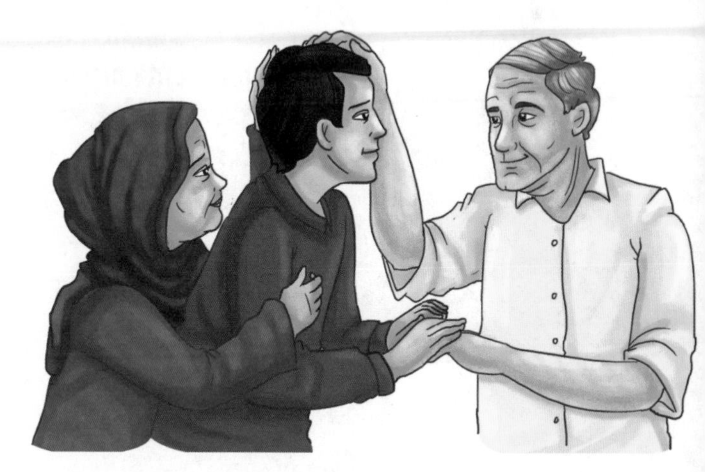

Patience with parents

It is easy to lose our patience when situations do not go our way. Our parents might do many things that cause us to lose our patience. Our parents might not understand the generation gap—the differences in outlook or opinion between people of different generations. We might think their ideas and approach to life are old-fashioned.

During our parents youth, many of the technologies that we have today did not exist. For example, computers and cell phones were new inventions. They used cassette tapes, CD-ROM discs, and land-line phones. MP3, Smartphone, wi-fi, gaming systems and so forth did not exist. With the progress of time, people and their opinions change.

We should remember that even though newer technology and new gadgets become available, some value systems remain relevant forever. They are timeless. One of these value systems is the parent-child relationship. If our parents do not understand us, we have to remain patient with them. The Qur'ān tells us not to lose patience with our parents and not to speak the smallest word of disrespect or displeasure to them.

وَقَضَىٰ رَبُّكَ أَلَّا تَعْبُدُوٓا۟ إِلَّآ إِيَّاهُ وَبِٱلْوَٰلِدَيْنِ إِحْسَٰنًا ۚ إِمَّا يَبْلُغَنَّ عِندَكَ ٱلْكِبَرَ أَحَدُ
هُمَآ أَوْ كِلَاهُمَا فَلَا تَقُل لَّهُمَآ أُفٍّ وَلَا تَنْهَرْهُمَا وَقُل لَّهُمَا قَوْلًا كَرِيمًا ﴿٢٣﴾

And your Lord has commanded that you do not worship anyone except Him alone, and ***doing good to the parents****. If one of them or both of them reach old age in your presence, even then do not say to them, "Ugh," and do not scold them, and speak to them a generous speech. (17:23)*

And lower to them the wings of humility out of tenderness; and say: "My Rabb! have mercy on them as they brought me up when I was small." (17:24)

Praying for parents

We are forbidden from speaking harshly to our parents. We are also encouraged to pray for them. Ayāh 17:24, contains a beautiful du'ā. We should make a point of memorizing this du'ā and praying to Allāh ﷻ every day. Even after our parents die, we should continue to pray for them.

رَّبِّ ٱرۡحَمۡهُمَا كَمَا رَبَّيَانِي صَغِيرٗا ﴿٢٤﴾

When parents are non-Muslims

It is possible that one or both of our parents are non-Muslims. Allāh ﷻ teaches us that regardless of their faith, we must treat them well and show courtesy to them. But if they ask us to obey other gods, or observe rituals not approved of in Islam, we should refuse to obey them. However, such a refusal should be gentle and polite. The Qur'ān says:

We have enjoined on man kindness to parents: but if they strive [to force] you to associate [others] with Me [in worship] anything of which you have no knowledge, then do not obey them. Towards Me is your return, and I shall inform you of all that you used to do. (29:8)

Hadīth on the status of parents

There are several ahādīth where Rasūlullāh ﷺ stresses the importance and status of our parents. Here is one of the most famous ahādīth:

A man once asked Rasūlullāh ﷺ: "Who is the most entitled to be treated with the best companionship by me?"

Rasūlullāh ﷺ replied, "Your mother." The man asked, "Who is next?" Rasūlullāh ﷺ said, "Your mother." The man asked again, "Who is next?" Rasūlullāh ﷺ said, "Your mother." The man asked for the fourth time, "Who is next?" Rasūlullāh ﷺ said, "Your father." (reported by Bukhārī and Muslim).

Another hadīth reports that one day, the mother of Asma bint Abū Bakr went from Makkah to Madīnah to meet her daughter. Her mother was not a Muslim. Asma asked Rasūlullāh ﷺ how she should treat her. Rasūlullāh ﷺ told her to be kind and considerate, and to behave as a daughter should behave towards her mother.

Why we should love our parents

Allāh ﷻ reminds us of the pain and suffering our mothers had to endure while giving birth. This is the single-most important reason we should thank her. In the āyah below, notice that Allāh ﷻ says: "*Give thanks to Me and to your parents.*"

And We have enjoined on people concerning his parents—his mother carries him with suffering upon suffering, and his weaning is in two years—saying: "Give thanks to Me and to your parents. Towards Me is the return. (31:14)

*And We have enjoined on man the doing of good to his parents. His mother bears him with pain, and with pain does she give birth to him. And his bearing and his weaning takes thirty months. When he attains his maturity and reaches forty years, he says: "**My Lord! Grant me that I may give thanks for your favors with which you have favored upon me and upon my parents, and that I may do good which may please You, and do good to me with regard to my offspring. Surely I turn to You, and I am indeed among the Muslims.**" (46:15)*

This āyah contains a beautiful du'ā. We should make a point of memorizing this du'ā and praying to Allāhﷻ every day. This du'ā not only seeks good things for us and for our parents, but also for our future children. Here is the āyah in Arabic:

رَبِّ أَوْزِعْنِيٓ أَنْ أَشْكُرَ نِعْمَتَكَ ٱلَّتِيٓ أَنْعَمْتَ عَلَيَّ وَعَلَىٰ وَٰلِدَيَّ وَأَنْ أَعْمَلَ صَٰلِحًا تَرْضَىٰهُ وَأَصْلِحْ لِي
فِي ذُرِّيَّتِيٓ ۖ إِنِّي تُبْتُ إِلَيْكَ وَإِنِّي مِنَ ٱلْمُسْلِمِينَ ﴿١٥﴾

Rights of parents

After analyzing the entire lesson, we can easily summarize the rights of parents. All parents deserve following rights from their children.

1. The right to kind words
2. The right to kind behavior
3. The right to be looked after and helped
4. The right to be treated well
5. The right to be respected

We should always remember these rights, and continue carrying out our duties towards our parents. Allāhﷻ will love us and reward us if we follow His commands.

WEEKEND 21

Homework

1. Memorize the du'ā in āyah 17:24 about our parents from the lesson. Be ready to recite it in front of the class next week.

2. Based on the lesson, parents have certain rights with respect to their children. Write down these rights and indicate whether you are willing to respect them.

	Are you willing to respect these rights? Yes / No
A. ______________________	________
B. ______________________	________
C. ______________________	________
D. ______________________	________
E. ______________________	________

3. Read āyah 14 from sūrah Luqmān. What is the one thing we should give to both Allāh ﷻ and our parents?

____

4. One hadīth mentions we should provide our mothers the best companionship. How many times do we have to provide the best companionship to our mothers before we provide it to our fathers?

____

5. In āyah 17:23, Allāh ﷻ tells us not to do two things to our parents, particularly when they become old. What are the two things we should not do?

1. ______________________________________

2. ______________________________________

6. The beautiful du'ā in āyah 46:15 says we should seek good things for three different people. Who are the three people?

A. ______________________________

B. ______________________________

C. ______________________________

7. Which of the following statements is correct about the status of parents in Islam?

A. Their status is equal to that of God.
B. Their status is similar to worshipping God.
C. Their status is second to worshipping God.
D. Their status is very high only when they become old.
E. Their status is similar to the prophets.

8. When our parents become old, how should we speak with them?

A. Only over the phone.
B. With a generous speech.
C. Say nothing at all.
D. Say "ugh" if they make a serious mistake.
E. Scold them mildly but not too harshly.

9. Based on the lesson, write down five rights of parents.

A. The rights to: ______________________________

B. The rights to: ______________________________

C. The rights to: ______________________________

D. The rights to: ______________________________

E. The rights to: ______________________________

10. Read ayāh 31:14 in the Qur'ān. This ayāh describe giving thanks. To whom should we give thanks?

A. To Allāh ﷻ and to our parents.
B. Only to Allāh ﷻ, not to anybody else.
C. To our parents, but nobody else.
D. Only to Allāh ﷻ and to our mother.
E. None of the above.

WEEKEND 22

Classwork

Hope, Hopefulness, Hopelessness

Objective of the Lesson:

All believers are required to express hope when everything appears to fall apart. Hope provides strength and direction. On the other hand, a non-believer feels hopeless when disaster strikes. This chapter discusses the value of keeping hope and explains why people feel hopeless in life and provides solution to overcome hopelessness in life.

We all hope for different goals in life. We might hope for success, for good grades on exams, for money, for children, and for a happy life. Everyone must have hope in life. Even after a person receives everything he or she desires in life, he or she can still hope to achieve more. A person can hope for material things, non-material things or both. Non-material goals include good happiness, health, fame, and peace of mind.

With certain hopes, there is not much we can do to make them happen. With others, we can do something to make them happen. For example, when winter arrives, one can hope for spring to arrive a few months later. But no matter what a person does, spring will not arrive any earlier. In another example, we can hope to do well on a math exam. However, in order to do well on the exam, we must study. If we do not study enough, our hopes of doing well on the exam might remain unfulfilled. When we are required to work hard, we need to show some degree of perseverance.

Keeping these examples in mind, we can now define hope as an emotional belief in a positive outcome, often as a result of having faith in the outcome and requiring a certain amount of perseverance and divine inspiration.

Hope from an Islamic standpoint

From an Islamic standpoint, hope is not simply an emotional belief, but a **faith-based expectation**. It is a belief that something is going to happen—in this life and in the Afterlife.

Such hope about the future will become a reality when we fulfill some of our required duties. The Qur'ān says:

إِنَّ ٱلَّذِينَ ءَامَنُوا۟ وَٱلَّذِينَ هَاجَرُوا۟ وَجَـٰهَدُوا۟ فِى سَبِيلِ ٱللَّهِ أُو۟لَـٰٓئِكَ يَرْجُونَ رَحْمَتَ ٱللَّهِ ۚ وَٱللَّهُ غَفُورٌ رَّحِيمٌ ﴿٢١٨﴾

Surely as to those who believed, and those who migrated and struggled hard in Allāh's way—these do hope for Allāh's mercy. And Allāh is Protector, most-Rewarding. (2:218)

In this āyah, a person hopes to receive mercy from Allāh ﷻ. But the person has to believe, struggle on the path of Allāh ﷻ, and to migrate, if necessary.

In another āyah, the Qur'ān tells us to perform certain duties—for example, recite the Qur'ān, establish salāt, and spend money on righteous causes. Only when these requirements are met, can we hope for a good result.[35:29]

Hope and wishful thinking

Hope is different from wishful thinking. The word for wishful thinking is **tamanna**. Simply speaking, wishful thinking is a delusion, a fantasy, a dream, or a desire for something. A person might have a fantasy about something, but the possibility of the fantasy happening in real life may be remote. Therefore, *tamanna* is false hope. It is different from hope in the sense that the fulfillment of many hopes is assured by Allāh ﷻ, but the fulfillment of a fantasy is not assured by Allāh ﷻ. On the contrary, Allāh ﷻ has condemned idle fantasies. Furthermore, wishful thinking is characterized by some degree of laziness. One who engages in wishful thinking does not take any action—no struggle and no labor are required. However, when one hopes for something, he or she is required to take action. Hope requires action, struggle, and labor.

This does not mean that all wishful thinking is negative and all hopes are approved by Allāh ﷻ. Some hopes are as negative as idle wishful thinking. In fact, if we hope for something that is not positive, such hopes are invalid. In the Qur'ān, Allāh ﷻ says:

ذَرْهُمْ يَأْكُلُوا۟ وَيَتَمَتَّعُوا۟ وَيُلْهِهِمُ ٱلْأَمَلُ ۖ فَسَوْفَ يَعْلَمُونَ ٣

Leave them to eat and enjoy, and let the hopes distract them. But soon they will know. (15:3)

Here, the sinners hope for something. However, their hopes are not backed by righteous deeds, and these hopes will only distract them from the true objective of life—to follow Allāh's command. Eventually, they will suffer.

Hope and optimism

Hope and optimism are not the same. Optimism is one step ahead of hope. When one hopes for something, he or she simply wants something to happen. But in order to make that hope a reality, the person is required to do something—believe in Allāh, perform salāt, migrate if necessary, spend money on righteous causes, and so forth. Only when a person does one or all of these things will hope gradually turn into optimism. Then he or she has a strong conviction that Allāh will fulfill these hopes. If we truly love Allāh, our hopes turn into optimism and we believe our hopes will be fulfilled. Allāh says:

ٱلَّذِينَ صَبَرُوا۟ وَعَمِلُوا۟ ٱلصَّـٰلِحَـٰتِ أُو۟لَـٰٓئِكَ لَهُم مَّغْفِرَةٌ وَأَجْرٌ كَبِيرٌ ١١

those who persevere and do good; these,—for them there is protection and a great reward. (11:11)

Hope and despair

The meaning of despair is to feel hopeless or to lose all hope.

What happens to those who do not love Allāh and do not have hope? Many people live lives that do not include God. Godless people are not necessarily those who do not believe in Islam; a Muslim person can also be godless. You might notice that many Muslims do not truly love Allāh. They can be nice people, but they do not obey Allāh, do not perform salāt, do not give to charity, do not fast, and so on. Or they might do things that Allāh has clearly prohibited. Such people also hope for various things in life. When their hopes are fulfilled, they feel happy. However, when bad things happen to them, they lose hope.

وَإِذَآ أَذَقْنَا ٱلنَّاسَ رَحْمَةً فَرِحُوا۟ بِهَا ۖ وَإِن تُصِبْهُمْ سَيِّئَةٌۢ بِمَا قَدَّمَتْ أَيْدِيهِمْ إِذَا هُمْ يَقْنَطُونَ ٣٦

And when We cause mankind to taste mercy, they rejoice in it; but if an evil afflicts them due to what their hands have sent forward, lo! they do despair. (30:36)

Many people move further away from God when bad things happen to them. Hopelessness grips their lives. This is because they do not take any positive action or they hope for negative things. Sometimes they hope for something, but their hope is

not backed by righteous deeds. Their hopes are more like fantasies or wishful thinking. Therefore, when they experience bad times, they lament and curse the situation. They think it is the result of to "fate." They blame events on fate, and they blame Allāh ﷻ.

Hope and despair are opposites. Faith gives us hope for a positive outcome, as well as a way to attain that positive outcome. Despair is a result of not using the tools to achieve a positive outcome. Thus, despair is a state of mind indicating a crisis of faith or an ignorance of faith. If these people had faith, they would not have felt despair. Rather, they would have prayed to Allāh ﷻ and persevered.

Examples from messengers' lives

All of the messengers of Islam were tortured by their followers. However, none of them ever gave up hope. Their hope was backed by strong belief, righteous deeds, and perseverance.

When Ayyūb (A) lost his good health, wealth, and children, he never gave up hope and trust in Allāh ﷻ. Later Allāh ﷻ gave him good health, wealth and children. When Zakariyyāh (A) hoped for a child, his hope was not a fantasy but backed by utmost trust in Allāh ﷻ. Eventually Allāh ﷻ gave him a child. When our Nabi Muhammad ﷺ was persecuted in Makkah and Madīnah, he did not give up hope.

No matter what happened in their lives, the messengers trusted Allāh ﷻ, hoped for better days, struggled hard, and persevered. They knew that hope alone would not yield the desired result. All the messengers prayed to Allāh ﷻ to make their hope fruitful. Prayer has a strong, positive effect on people's lives. Like the messengers, we must pray to Allāh ﷻ to make our hopes a reality.

Hope is a necessity for those who seek Allāh ﷻ and walk on His path. A seeker of God will perish if he or she loses hope. In order to make our hopes fruitful, we must work hard, walk on the right path, persevere, and obey Allāh ﷻ.

حَسْبِيَ ٱللَّهُ لَآ إِلَٰهَ إِلَّا هُوَ ۖ عَلَيْهِ تَوَكَّلْتُ ۖ وَهُوَ رَبُّ ٱلْعَرْشِ ٱلْعَظِيمِ ﴿١٢٩﴾

Allāh is sufficient for me; there is no deity but Him. Upon Him I do rely; and He is the Rabb of the mighty Throne. (9:129)

WEEKEND 22 Homework

1. According to the lesson on hope, which of the following concepts must be included in the definition of hope?

A. All hopes must have faith to back them up.
B. All hopes require some perseverance.
C. All hopes require some divine inspiration.
D. All hopes must have belief in a positive outcome.
E. All of the above.

2. According to the lesson, which of the following statements about wishful thinking is correct?

A. Wishful thinking is a good pastime.
B. Wishful thinking is recommended in the Qur'ān.
C. Wishful thinking is a fantasy or false hope.
D. Wishful thinking results in optimism.
E. Wishful thinking leads one to Hell.

3. Which of the following choices about hope and optimism is correct?

A. Hope follows optimism.
B. Optimism follows hope.
C. Hope and optimism are parts of the Five Pillars of Islam.
D. Hope and optimism contradict each other.
E. Hope is good; optimism is a sin.

4. According to the lesson, what happens when you hope for something but do not take action?

A. Such hopes are the best hopes one can make.
B. Such hopes are invalid.
C. Such hopes are fulfilled only in the hereafter.
D. Such hopes are the tools of the messengers.
E. None of the above.

5. Read āyah 7:56 in the Qur'ān. When believers call upon Allāh ﷻ, what two things are they required to do?

1. ______________________________

2. ______________________________

6. Read āyah 30:36 in the Qur'ān. When a calamity afflicts a godless person, how does he or she respond?

A. He or she becomes God-conscious.
B. He or she loses hope.
C. He or she commits more sin.
D. He or she perseveres.
E. He or she turns to false gods.

7. Which of the following is characterized by laziness?

A. Wishful thinking.
B. Hope.
C. Optimism.
D. Faith.
E. Prayer.

8. According to the lesson, what is one of the characteristics of despair?

A. Having strong faith.
B. Ignorance of faith.
C. Being closer to hope.
D. Having a supplement to faith.
E. Hanging on to hope.

9. According to the lesson, what could happen to a seeker of God if he or she loses hope?

A. He or she will perish.
B. He or she will be rewarded.
C. He or she will enter Heaven.
D. He or she will be turned into an ape.
E. He or she will achieve Taqwā.

10. According to the lesson, what did the messengers of Allāh عَزَّ وَجَلَّ do when they were persecuted?

A. They trusted Allāh ﷻ.
B. They hoped for good things.
C. They struggled hard.
D. They persevered.
E. All of the above.

Trials in Life: *Everyone Will Experience Them*

Objective of the Lesson:

All believers will experience trials in their lives. Even the messengers of Islam suffered trials. Experiencing difficulties make us better people. Those who do not have strong faith lose hope when they face difficulty. This lesson describes different types of trials, why Allāh makes us experience them, and what we can do when we face difficulties in our lives.

The basic meaning of the word "trial" is assessment, test, or review. The word "trial" also means suffering, distress, hardship, and pain. The Miriam Webster dictionary provides other definitions of the word—one states that a trial is "a test of faith, patience, or stamina through subjection to suffering or temptation." This idea is beautifully expressed in the Qur'ān regarding the trials of human beings. The Qur'ān uses two different words that both mean a "trial." One is **balā**, and the other is **fitna**.

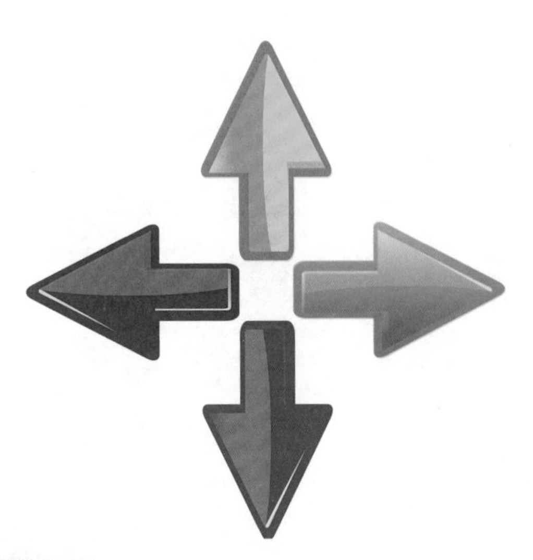

The word *fitna* typically means hardship, suffering, temptation or affliction, whereby one is "tried" with respect to good or evil. In contrast, the word *balā* does not signify an ordinary trial, but a harsh and severe trial, conducted openly and publicly so that it becomes an example for others. It can happen on an individual level and a community level.

A common misconception is that if we are true believers and good Muslims, nothing bad will happen to us. The truth is hardship happens to even the best people. Bad things also happen as a direct result of sin. Sometimes bad things happen to us as a result of unwise choices in life. Other times hardships occur for no apparent reason.

Enduring trials in life gives us an opportunity to show ourselves and God that we will be faithful. When we are afflicted with hardship, we might blame God saying, "Why me?" Or we can experience the trial, increase our faith in God, and strive to remain steadfast in our faith. We can allow hardship to make us lose our faith and become distrustful of God, or we can allow it to make us better Muslims with stronger faith. One of the divine plans is to let us achieve spiritual growth in life so that we become successful in the Hereafter. Spiritual growth can often be achieved when we endure trials in life, not by experiencing comfort and ease in life.

When Allāh tests someone, it is to determine who is a better person or the level of the person's faith. But because Allāh already knows it. Allāh tests a person so that he or she learns his or her own nature. Also, these tests occur throughout a person's life so that when he or she reaches the Hereafter, he or she will understand the value of judgment. These trials make us better people.

Everything is created to test us

Allāh has created everything on this earth so that human beings experience trials. He uses some of these difficulties to test us.

إِنَّا جَعَلْنَا مَا عَلَى ٱلْأَرْضِ زِينَةً لَّهَا لِنَبْلُوَهُمْ أَيُّهُمْ أَحْسَنُ عَمَلًا ٧

We have certainly made whatever is on the earth as an ornament for it, in order that We may try them as to which of them is the most excellent in deeds. (18:7)

ٱلَّذِى خَلَقَ ٱلْمَوْتَ وَٱلْحَيَوٰةَ لِيَبْلُوَكُمْ أَيُّكُمْ أَحْسَنُ عَمَلًا ۚ وَهُوَ ٱلْعَزِيزُ ٱلْغَفُورُ ٢

[Allāh is the one] Who created Death and Life that He may test you—which of you is the best in deeds? And He is the Exalted in Might, the Forgiving. (67: 2)

We might wonder: Can anyone escape from trials? Are good Muslims exempt from facing trials? Did the messengers escape from trials? The answer to these questions is "no." All the messengers faced trails. The fact that they were not excluded from trials is beautifully illustrated in the following ayāh. This ayāh shows that nobody is excused from facing hardship.

أَحَسِبَ ٱلنَّاسُ أَن يُتْرَكُوٓا۟ أَن يَقُولُوٓا۟ ءَامَنَّا وَهُمْ لَا يُفْتَنُونَ ٢

Do men think that they will be left alone on saying: "We believe," and that they will not be tested? (29:2)

Types of trials

Trials can be divided into several different types. Broadly speaking, there are two categories of trials—positive and negative. The Qur'ān says:

كُلُّ نَفْسٍ ذَآئِقَةُ ٱلْمَوْتِ ۗ وَنَبْلُوكُم بِٱلشَّرِّ وَٱلْخَيْرِ فِتْنَةً ۖ وَإِلَيْنَا تُرْجَعُونَ ٣٥

*Every individual must have to taste death. And We discipline you with **evil** and **good** by way of trying. And towards Us you will be returned. (21:35)*

Trials can involve prosperity or poverty. Sometimes we forget that wealth can be a trial. However, the Qur'ān describes loss and suffering as major types of trials, as noted in the following ayāh:

وَلَنَبْلُوَنَّكُم بِشَىْءٍ مِّنَ ٱلْخَوْفِ وَٱلْجُوعِ وَنَقْصٍ مِّنَ ٱلْأَمْوَٰلِ وَٱلْأَنفُسِ وَٱلثَّمَرَٰتِ ۗ وَبَشِّرِ ٱلصَّٰبِرِينَ ١٥٥

And We shall certainly test you with something of fear, and hunger, and loss of property and lives, and of fruits. And give glad tidings to those who persevere. (2:155)

The Qur'ān also speaks of positive situations as trials.[89:15–16]

فَأَمَّا ٱلْإِنسَٰنُ إِذَا مَا ٱبْتَلَىٰهُ رَبُّهُۥ فَأَكْرَمَهُۥ وَنَعَّمَهُۥ فَيَقُولُ رَبِّىٓ أَكْرَمَنِ ١٥

Moreover as for man, when his Rabb disciplines him, thus honors him and favors him, then he says: "My Rabb has honored me." (89:15)

Sometimes we personally face difficulties, sometimes our family faces difficulties, and sometimes an entire community or nation faces difficulties.

Purpose of trials

Previously we learned that one of the objectives of trials is to teach a person about his or her own nature. The Qur'ān says that human beings are placed on earth to prove ourselves. We have to demonstrate our character, integrity, morals, values, and piety.[3:140; 5:94] After all these trials are completed on earth, our final resting place is in the Hereafter. Many times, there is no healing from the trials we face on earth. There is no healing from the sickness and pain we suffer. But what matters most is how we demonstrate our patience, how we bear our burdens, and how we keep our faith in God. The Qur'ān says:

أَمْ حَسِبْتُمْ أَن تَدْخُلُوا۟ ٱلْجَنَّةَ وَلَمَّا يَعْلَمِ ٱللَّهُ ٱلَّذِينَ جَٰهَدُوا۟ مِنكُمْ وَيَعْلَمَ ٱلصَّٰبِرِينَ ١٤٢

Do you calculate on entering the Garden, while Allah has not yet learned those among you who strive hard and distinguished the persevering ones? (3:142)

Allāh provides in a calculated way

Sometimes we wonder why Allāh ﷻ makes us endure a trial. We have already noted the reasons previously. But we might also need to understand there is a purpose for each trials. In other words, why is one person given wealth as his or her trial, while another person is given poverty as his or her trial? This is how Allāhﷻ measures things:

أَوَلَمْ يَعْلَمُوٓا۟ أَنَّ ٱللَّهَ يَبْسُطُ ٱلرِّزْقَ لِمَن يَشَآءُ وَيَقْدِرُ ۚ إِنَّ فِى ذَٰلِكَ لَـَٔايَٰتٍ لِّقَوْمٍ يُؤْمِنُونَ ﴿٥٢﴾

Do they not know that Allāh extends provision for whom He pleases, and He measures out? Surely there are indeed Signs in this for a people who believe. (39:52)

We must have faith in the way Allāhﷻ measures things—both good and bad.[13:26; 29:62; 39:52] We must remember that Allāhﷻ is making these decisions for a reason, and He knows the best.

We should not envy others because they have more money or material things than we do.

And do not envy that by which Allāh has made some of you excel above the others. For men there is a share out of what they earn, and for women there is a share of what they earn. And ask Allāh for His grace. Surely Allāh is ever Knower of everything. (4:32)

A true believer should always show gratitude to Allāhﷻ when He provides blessings and he or she should exercise perseverance when He does not provide them. On the other hand, those who have weak faith will behave differently in good times and bad times. During good times, these people are forgetful of Allāhﷻ, but when bad times occur, they feel hopeless.[11:9; 17:83; 41:49]

لَّا يَسْـَٔمُ ٱلْإِنسَٰنُ مِن دُعَآءِ ٱلْخَيْرِ وَإِن مَّسَّهُ ٱلشَّرُّ فَيَـُٔوسٌ قَنُوطٌ ﴿٤٩﴾

Man is not tired of praying for good; but if evil touches him, then he is disappointed, despairing. (41:49)

Failure in trials

Now that we understand that everyone has to face trials in life, how do we successfully endure these trials? The real question is: What causes people to fail a trial?

In order to be successful, we must first recognize that trials are always occuring. Once we recognize this reality, we can respond to the trial and emerge successful. Even small things, such as a friend cheating us, someone laughing at us, or our brother not sharing something with us can be a trial. Any type of hardship is a trial we have to overcome.

Sometimes a good thing happens in our lives. This is a trial. Sometimes a bad thing happens. This is a trial, too. Sometimes when a bad thing happens, we are disappointed and do not realize that Allāhﷻ has a plan for us. The plan might be a simple test or it might bring us something better after we experience the trial.

People fail to endure trials because they do not have enough faith in Allāhﷻ. By not trusting Allāhﷻ, people only harm themselves.

Prayer to avoid difficult trials

Although Allāh ﷻ said that all of us will have to face trials, Allāh ﷻ also wants us to pray to Him to not face difficult trials.

The prayer is not about eliminating trials altogether, as this would contradict Allāh's ﷻ policy of testing all human beings. The prayer is about not suffering through a trial that we cannot withstand.

رَبَّنَا لَا تُؤَاخِذۡنَآ إِن نَّسِينَآ أَوۡ أَخۡطَأۡنَاۚ رَبَّنَا وَلَا تَحۡمِلۡ عَلَيۡنَآ إِصۡرٗا كَمَا
حَمَلۡتَهُۥ عَلَى ٱلَّذِينَ مِن قَبۡلِنَاۚ رَبَّنَا وَلَا تُحَمِّلۡنَا مَا لَا طَاقَةَ لَنَا بِهِۦۖ وَٱعۡفُ
عَنَّا وَٱغۡفِرۡ لَنَا وَٱرۡحَمۡنَآۚ أَنتَ مَوۡلَىٰنَا فَٱنصُرۡنَا عَلَى ٱلۡقَوۡمِ ٱلۡكَٰفِرِينَ ٢٨٦

"Our Rabb! do not take us to task if we forget, or we make a mistake; our Rabb! and do not lay upon us a burden as you had lain on those before us; our Rabb! and do not impose upon us that for which we have no strength. Therefore, pardon us; and grant us protection; and be kind to us. You are our Patron; therefore, help us over the Unbelieving people." (2:286)

Trials of the messengers

All messengers, including our beloved Nabi Muhammad ﷺ, experienced difficult trials and tribulations throughout their lives. Name any nabi and messenger, and you will see that he suffered persecution during his life. The messengers did not have good times throughout their lives. Some of the messengers were poor and some were rich. The messengers who were poor did not complain about their poverty. The messengers who were rich did not boast about their riches. Allāh ﷻ could have easily made them not suffer in life. But He chose to put them trough trials.

In this lesson, we learned that all human beings are subject to trials. We also learned that through trials, we can realize our true nature and true worth. We should understand that trials are always occuring. Our objective should be to emerge successful. We must respond in a morally, ethically, and spiritually correct manner so that we emerge successful in this life and in the Afterlife.

Homework

1. From your knowledge, mention an incident or situation in any messenger's life that you think was a trial for him. Briefly explain how the incident or situation was a trial.

____

____

____

2. From your knowledge, mention an incident or situation from Nabi Muhammad's ﷺ life that you think was a trial for him. Briefly explain how the incident or situation was a trial.

____

____

____

3. People who do not believe in Allāh ﷻ react in a certain way when good things happen to them. Read āyah 17:83. How do they behave when good things happen to them?

____

4. People who do not believe in Allāh ﷻ react in a certain way when something bad happen to them. How do most of them behave when bad things happen to them?

A. They become Muslims.
B. They lose all hope.
C. They just ignore the bad days.
D. They shift their attention to sports.
E. They go to sleep.

5. According to the Qur'ān, what is the main purpose of trials?

A. So that we can be successful.
B. So that some of us can fail.
C. So that we can prove ourselves.
D. So that the Awakening can take place.
E. So that people realize that suffering is part of life.

6. Read āyah 2:155, which discusses about trials. The ways to succeed in these types of trials are described in the next few ayāt. What are the ways to succeed?

7. Pretned a very bad thing happens to your family. Everybody is sad and upset. You realize it is a trial for your family. What is the best way to respond to such a trial?

A. Ask an Imam to pray for you.
B. Cry in prayer and ask Allāhﷻ: "Why me, why us?"
C. Become angry because you have been doing your prayers, yet you suffered.
D. Blame it on your father.
E. Tell everybody to persevere and trust Allāhﷻ.

8. God has blessed your family with good times and lots of wealth. Realizing that this could be a trial for you, what should you do?

A. Wait a few more years and then do some charity work.
B. Do nothing because you still need to pay for college.
C. Give it all away to charity.
D. Relax, because your family deserves it after years of hard work.
E. Express thanks to Allāhﷻ and spend part of it on righteous causes.

9. Read āyah 29:65. In bad times, these people prayed to Allāhﷻ. But when a bad time was over, they did something different. Based on the āyah, which of the following choices shows what they might have done after the bad time was over?

A. They tried to forget the storm and move ahead.
B. They laughed, knowing that they were alive.
C. They knew the storm was part of life. So they kept sailing.
D. They knocked on wood and were glad the sun was shining again.
E. All of the above.

10. Now you understnad that trials are a part of life. What should be your response to trials?

A. Get over it, a trial is just a part of life.
B. Donate some money for a good cause.
C. Persevere and maintain faith in Allāhﷻ.
D. Recite sūrah Fātihah ten times.
E. Copy Qur'ān recitations to your MP3 player or mobile phone.

Permitted and Prohibited Food

Objective of the Lesson:

This chapter provides an overview of Muslim food laws as mentioned in the Qur'ān. Students will learn what types of animals are permissible to eat. However, the meat of some permissible animals cannot be eaten if they were not slaughtered in the prescribed manner. Students will also learn whether saying "Bismillah" before a meal makes it acceptable to eat the meat of an improperly slaughtered animal.

The Qur'ān and hadīth clearly explain the permitted and prohibited foods for Muslims. Based on these teachings, we know the types of foods that are allowed and the types of foods that are not allowed in Islam. However, with such a large variety of fast-food items available today, many Muslims are often confused about what is permitted and what is prohibited.

In this lesson, we will read the Qur'ānic rulings on prohibited food. The issue of prohibited food is a serious matter. Allāh ﷻ described the food laws very clearly in the Qur'ān. As responsible students of Islam, we need to clearly understand the subject. Due to the complexity of the subject, we will study this topic again in the Level 9 with additional details and emphases.

Understanding prohibition āyāt

The Qur'ān describes two broad categories of consumables on its list of prohibited items. One category covers intoxicants and the other covers meat. In this lesson, we will briefly discuss alcohol and intoxicants, but in Level 9, we will explore the subject in more detail.

The laws regarding intoxicants and meat are discussed separately in the Qur'ān. It is important to understand that āyāt about meat-related issues do not mention alcohol. Similarly, āyāt about alcohol-related prohibitions do not mention meat-related prohibitions.

If an ayāh states a certain food is prohibited, but it does not mention other already prohibited foods, the foods that are not mentioned in the ayāh do not become permitted food. For example, pork is prohibited in ayāh 2:173, but in ayāh 5:90, pork is not mentioned. If we read only ayāh 5:90, this does not make pork a permitted food. When understand this concept, prohibited and permitted food will be much easier to understand.

Prohibition of intoxicants

Sūrah Baqarah, Mā'idah, An'ām, and an-Nahl offer the most decisive commands about prohibited food—meat and intoxicants. In this lesson, we will analyze all the āyāt so that the issue can be fully understood. The following two āyāt tell us to avoid intoxicants because they are harmful to us.

يَٰٓأَيُّهَا ٱلَّذِينَ ءَامَنُوٓا۟ إِنَّمَا ٱلْخَمْرُ وَٱلْمَيْسِرُ وَٱلْأَنصَابُ وَٱلْأَزْلَٰمُ رِجْسٌ مِّنْ عَمَلِ ٱلشَّيْطَٰنِ
فَٱجْتَنِبُوهُ لَعَلَّكُمْ تُفْلِحُونَ ﴿٩٠﴾

O you who believe! surely the intoxicants and gambling, and setting up of stones, and divining by arrows are unclean things—among the handiwork of Shaitān; therefore, avoid this that you may attain success. (5:90)

Shaitān only desires to create enmity and hatred among you by means of intoxicants and gambling, and to divert you from the remembrance of Allāh and from salāt. Will you not then abstain? (5:91)

Prohibitions about meat

Many cultures and societies in the world consume various types of mammal and fish products. Most societies do not eat certain products, for example, dog or snake meat, but there are cultures that do not consider it taboo to eat these meats. The Qur'ān clearly states the types of meat that are harām, or forbidden. The first ayāh that mentions the prohibited food is in sūrah Baqarah:

إِنَّمَا حَرَّمَ عَلَيْكُمُ ٱلْمَيْتَةَ وَٱلدَّمَ وَلَحْمَ ٱلْخِنزِيرِ وَمَآ أُهِلَّ بِهِۦ لِغَيْرِ ٱللَّهِ ۖ فَمَنِ ٱضْطُرَّ
غَيْرَ بَاغٍ وَلَا عَادٍ فَلَآ إِثْمَ عَلَيْهِ ۚ إِنَّ ٱللَّهَ غَفُورٌ رَّحِيمٌ ﴿١٧٣﴾

He has forbidden you only what dies of itself, and the blood, and the flesh of swine, and that over which any other than Allāh has been invoked. But whoever is constrained, without being disobedient nor exceeding the limit, no sin be upon him then. Allāh is certainly most Forgiving, most Rewarding. (2:173)

In this ayāh, four categories of food are clearly mentioned as harām:

1. Meat of an animal that is already dead, called "carrion"
2. Blood
3. Meat of swine or pig
4. Meat of any animal in which, at the time of slaughtering, the name of a person, deity, or anything else is invoked instead of Allāh's ﷻ name.

The same message is repeated in the Qur'ān in other places.

قُل لَّآ أَجِدُ فِي مَآ أُوحِيَ إِلَيَّ مُحَرَّمًا عَلَىٰ طَاعِمٖ يَطۡعَمُهُۥٓ إِلَّآ أَن يَكُونَ مَيۡتَةً أَوۡ دَمٗا
مَّسۡفُوحًا أَوۡ لَحۡمَ خِنزِيرٖ فَإِنَّهُۥ رِجۡسٌ أَوۡ فِسۡقًا أُهِلَّ لِغَيۡرِ ٱللَّهِ بِهِۦۚ فَمَنِ ٱضۡطُرَّ
غَيۡرَ بَاغٖ وَلَا عَادٖ فَإِنَّ رَبَّكَ غَفُورٞ رَّحِيمٞ ١٤٥

*Say: "I do not find in what has been revealed to me anything forbidden to an eater to eat it except that it be dead by itself, or blood poured forth, or flesh of pig—for that is impure indeed, or what is a disobedience—**being slaughtered over other than that of Allāh on it**; but whoever is compelled, without rebellion nor exceeding limits, then surely your Lord is most Forgiving, most Rewarding. (6:145)*

إِنَّمَا حَرَّمَ عَلَيۡكُمُ ٱلۡمَيۡتَةَ وَٱلدَّمَ وَلَحۡمَ ٱلۡخِنزِيرِ وَمَآ أُهِلَّ لِغَيۡرِ ٱللَّهِ بِهِۦۖ فَمَنِ
ٱضۡطُرَّ غَيۡرَ بَاغٖ وَلَا عَادٖ فَإِنَّ ٱللَّهَ غَفُورٞ رَّحِيمٞ ١١٥

*He has forbidden you only what dies of itself, and the blood, and the flesh of swine, and what **is slaughtered with other than Allāh upon it**; but whoever is compelled by necessity, without being rebellious and not exceeding the limit, then Allāh is indeed most Forgiving, most Rewarding. (16:115)*

Cause of death makes an animal harām

Regarding the permitted animals to eat, the manner in which they were killed or slaughtered determines whether the meat can be eaten. For example, cow meat is permissible for Muslims, but the nature of the cow's death might prohibit consumption. The Qur'ān describes **seven types** of death that would make a particular animal harām, even if the animal was otherwise permitted.

Forbidden to you are—that which died of itself, and the blood and the flesh of swine, and whatever has been slaughtered for other than Allāh upon it; and the strangled, and stunned to death, and dead through falling, and killed by horns, and what wild beasts have eaten, except what you have slaughtered; and what has been sacrificed on stones set up, and that you seek to divide by drawing arrows—all that is transgression. (5:3)

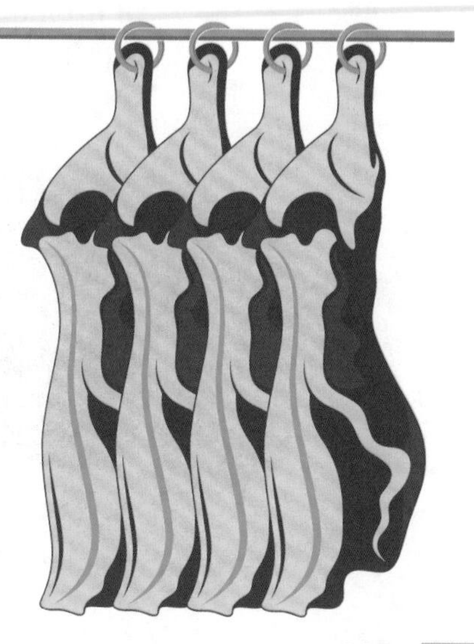

The methods of slaughter described in this ayāh can be summarized as follows:

1. Killing by strangling,
2. Killing by any type of violent blow,
3. Killing by a head-long fall,
4. Killing by stabbing or piercing to death,
5. Killing by another animal that ate part of the flesh,
6. Killing by sacrificing on an altar as part of an idolatrous practice,
7. Dividing meat by drawing lots, with arrows and so forth as done in the past.

If no name is pronounced

Allāhﷻ has clearly instructed Muslims to mention His name when an animal is slaughtered. If Allāh'sﷻ name is not mentioned when an animal is slaughtered, the meat cannot be eaten.

وَلَا تَأْكُلُوا مِمَّا لَمْ يُذْكَرِ اسْمُ اللَّهِ عَلَيْهِ وَإِنَّهُ لَفِسْقٌ ۗ وَإِنَّ الشَّيَاطِينَ لَيُوحُونَ
إِلَىٰ أَوْلِيَائِهِمْ لِيُجَادِلُوكُمْ ۖ وَإِنْ أَطَعْتُمُوهُمْ إِنَّكُمْ لَمُشْرِكُونَ ﴿١٢١﴾

*And **do not eat** of that upon which **Allāh's name has not been mentioned**, for it is surely disobedience. And certainly shaitān will inspire their allies to dispute with you; and if you obey them, you will surely become polytheists. (6:121)*

There is a difference of opinion among many Muslims when Allāh'sﷻ name is not pronounced at the time of slaughter. This happens in automated slaughterhouses in many Western countries, including the United States, Europe, and Australia. Muslim opinion differs whether such meat purchased from supermarkets, or meat products purchased at many fast-food restaurants, can be consumed if Allāh'sﷻ name is pronounced at the time of eating.

Muslim scholars and imāms offer differing opinions on the subject. This difference of opinion can be settled by studying the Qur'ānic instructions on this matter. In ayāh 6:118, the Qur'ān permits to eat meat on which Allāh'sﷻ name has been pronounced. Ayāh 6:121 (quoted previously) clearly states not to eat any meat on which Allāh'sﷻ name has not been pronounced.

Āyāt 6:121 and 6:118 use the past tense and the passive voice regarding Allāh'sﷻname: *has not been mentioned*. This indicates the requirement to declare Allāh'sﷻ name arises well before the food is cooked or served—at the time of slaughter. The passive voice indicates the name shpuld have been pronounced by someone else, evidently the slaughterer at the time of slaughtering. It is important to realize that declaring Allāh'sﷻ name at the time of eating does not make unlawful food lawful. No hadīth or Qur'ānic ayāh states that

saying "Bismillāh" can render unlawful food lawful. If food is unlawful, then it remains unlawful.

Misinterpretation of ayāh 5:5

Sometimes many Muslims misinterpret ayāh 5:5 to conclude that the Qur'ān allows us to eat the food of the People of the Book without any qualification. At a glance, it appears that meat available in Western supermarkets and fast-food restaurants are halāl for Muslims because the meat might have been prepared by the People of the Book.

> *This day the good things have been made lawful for you. And the food of those who have been given the Book is lawful for you, and your food is lawful for them ... (5:5)*

Many Christians and some Jews consume pork and wine. If they offer us pork or wine, such foods do not become permissible for us. Pork and wine are not lawful for us, therefore, such foods offered by the People of the Book remain unlawful. According to the Bible and the Talmud, the People of the Book are required to slaughter an animal in a specific manner, particularly by invoking God's name. If this is not done, then such meat is not permissible—even for them. If a certain meat is not permissible for them, it cannot be permissible for us. We should remember that if their food meets our Islamic standards, only then is it lawful. If their food does not meet our standards, then it remains unlawful.

What is halāl food?

The Qur'ān explains that we should not only eat lawful food but also "good" food. Other than intoxicants and meat, there are no specific food laws given about other foods, for example grains, vegetables, fruits, and so forth. The Qur'ān simply provides a broad standard about harām and halāl foods.

> *O you mankind! eat of what is on the earth, **lawful, pure**; and do not follow in the footsteps of Shaitān. Surely he is to you an open enemy. (2:168)*

> *O you who believe! eat of **the good things** that We have provided you with; and give thanks to Allāh, if it is Him alone Whom you worship. (2:172)*

> *And **do not say**—because your tongues are given to telling lies: "**This is lawful and that is unlawful**"—so that you forge a lie against Allāh. Surely those who forge a lie against Allāh do not prosper. (16:116)*

These āyāt remind us not to follow in Shaitān's footsteps. They also tell us to be grateful to Allāh ﷻ for the food He provides. An equally important message is not to make lawful food unlawful.

Based on these āyāt, we see that in order for a food to be halāl, it must be "lawful" and "good." On the other hand, harām food includes all foods that are "unlawful" and bad.

Homework

1. In order for food to be halāl, what primary criteria must be met?

A. The food must be good; nothing else matters.
B. The food must be lawful; nothing else matters.
C. The food must be lawful and pure.
D. Allāh's name must be pronounced at the time of eating.
E. All of the above.

2. How many different causes of death of an animal are mentioned in āyah 5:3 that would make the meat of the animal harām?

A. 5 types.
B. 6 types.
C. 7 types.
D. 8 types.
E. 10 types.

3. Cow meat and goat meat are permitted, yet their meat can be unlawful. Which of the following would make the meat of the animal unlawful?

A. Slaughtering the cow on a stone altar.
B. Killing the cow or goat with a violent blow.
C. Killing the cow or goat by strangling.
D. Killing the cow or goat with a head-long fall.
E. All of the above.

4. If Allāh's name is not mentioned at the time of slaughtering, as in an automated slaughterhouse, what should a person respond?

A. The person can eat the meat if he or she says Allāh's name before eating.
B. The person cannot eat the meat because Allāh's name was not pronounced at the time of slaughter.
C. The person must seek a fatwā from a scholar and follow the scholar.
D. The person must take extra care to cook the food to get rid of all the germs.
E. A name was not mentioned, so there is no problem; the person can eat the meat.

5. The Qur'ān says not to eat food upon which Allāh's name has not been mentioned. This ruling applies to fruits and vegetables. True / False

6. Read āyah 6:121. How does the Qur'ān view the conduct of a person who eats the meat of an animal and Allāh's ﷻ name was not pronounced?

A. The Qur'ān says Allāh ﷻ will forgive the person.
B. The Qur'ān the person to say Bismillah at the time of eating; therefore, it overlooks this conduct.
C. The Qur'an says the person will be punished severely in this life and in the Hereafter.
D. The Qur'ān views it as serious disobedience.
E. The Qur'ān views it as a matter of dispute among scholars.

7. In āyah 5:90, intoxicants are prohibited, but in āyah 2:173, intoxicants are not mentioned. Based on this information, which of the following conclusions can be made?

A. Intoxicants can be consumed in small quantities.
B. Intoxicants were made permissible at a later time.
C. No conclusion can be made.
D. Both intoxicants and prohibited types of meat are unlawful.
E. The ayāt cancel each other out.

8. Āyah 6:145 prohibits certain types of meat. But it does allow eating the meat under one condition. Which of the following choices about the meat is correct?

A. It can be eaten in small quantities at a public gathering.
B. It can be eaten in small quantities in school.
C. It can be eaten only when a person is traveling.
D. It can be eaten if the exceeding the limits are not exceeded.
E. It can be eaten only if a person is compelled, if a person does not become rebellious, or if a person does not exceed the limits.

9. You are stranded on an island without food, water, or shelter. After five days of starvation, you are exhausted. The natives of the island find you and bring you cooked meat. You do not know what type of meat it is or how the animal was killed. What should you do?

A. Refuse to eat and die a slow death.
B. Eat the meat to save your life.
C. Ask the natives to slaughter permitted animal and cook its meat.
D. Wait two more days before deciding whether to eat the meat.
E. Speak to them about Islam and try to make them accept Islam.

10. In order for the meat of an unspecified animal to be halāl for Muslims, what three criteria must be met?

1. ____

2. ____

3. ____

WEEKEND 25 Classwork

Performance of Hajj

Objective of the Lesson:

The performance of Hajj requires a clear understanding of the ritual. Performing the ritual provides important spiritual benefits. Students will learn each step of Hajj, beginning with the first day and ending on the last day. Minor variations in the ritual are also discussed in the lesson.

Hajj is the annual pilgrimage of Muslims to Makkah and a pillar of Islam. Every adult Muslim who has the physical and financial ability, as well as safe passage, is required to perform Hajj. While Hajj can only occur at the appointed time during the month of Dhul Hajj, the 'Umrah pilgrimage can be performed any time of year.

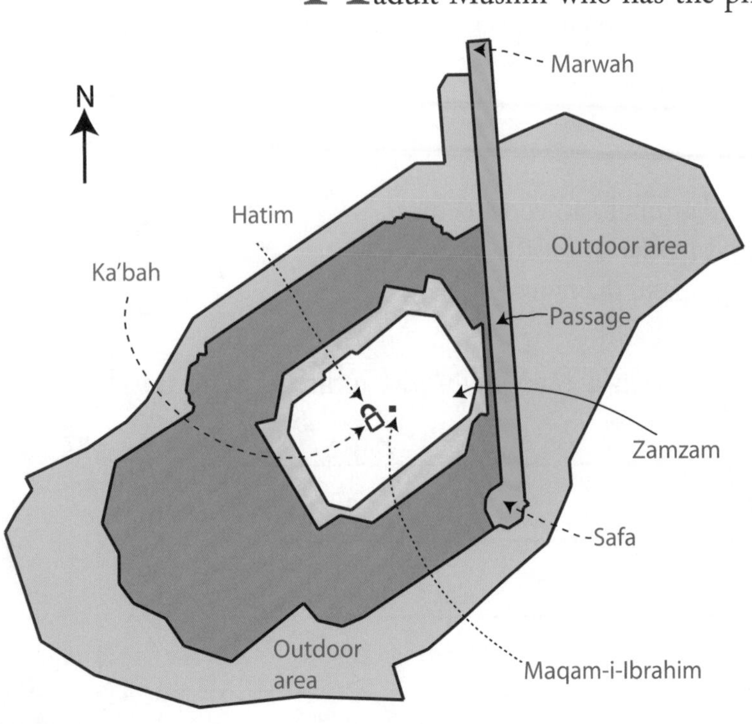

Types of Hajj

Hajj can be performed in three different ways. The residents of Makkah perform **Hajj-e-Ifrad**. People who reach Makkah before Hajj perform **Hajj-e-Tamattu'**. People who reach Makkah at the time of Hajj perform **Hajj-e-Qiran**. The pilgrims who perform Tamattu' or Qiran Hajj must perform the 'Umrah prior to Hajj.

Benefits of Hajj

It is narrated that Rasūlullāh ﷺ stated that an accepted Hajj (Hajj-e-Mabroor) offers the reward of entry to Jannah. It is also narrated that an accepted Hajj erases all previous sins, as if the person is a newborn baby.

Mīqāt and Ihrām

Hajj requires pilgrims to maintain a state of physical and spiritual purity. To maintain purity, pilgrims wear ihrām. For women, ihrām is any clean clothing that covers the body except the hands and face. For men, ihrām is two unstitched, white pieces of cloth. These two simple white cloths erase class boundaries between the rich and the poor. All are equal in front of our Lord except those who have more taqwa. The ihrām cloth must be worn before the pilgrims cross the geographical boundaries known as **Mīqāts**. The five mīqāts are located at specific distances from Makkah. Most airlines alert pilgrims when they cross a mīqāt. Once a mīqāt is crossed, the pilgrims continuously recite the **talbiyah**. The translation of the talbiyah is "Here I am, O Allāh, here I am. You have no partners, here I am. Surely all the praise and the riches and the Kingdom belong to You. You have no partners with You."

لَبَّيكَ اللّٰهُمَّ لَبَّيك ،
لَبَّيكَ لا شَرِيكَ لَكَ لَبَّيك ،
إنَّ الحَمدَ وَ النِّعمَةَ لَكَ وَ المُلك
لا شَرِيكَ لَكَ

Labbaik Allāhumma labbaik. Labbaika la sharīka laka labbaik. Innal hamda wa na'mata laka wal mulk la sharika laka.

'Umrah

Once the pilgrims reach Masjid al-Harām in Makkah, they perform the minor Hajj, or 'Umrah. The rituals of 'Umrah can be completed within a few hours. To begin 'Umrah, first the pilgrims have to be in the state of ihrām and wear ihrām clothing. They enter the state of ihrām at one of the Mīqāt stations. Then pilgrims arrive in Masjid al-Harām and begin tawāf. Tawāf is walking around the Ka'bah. They walk around the Ka'bah in a counter-clockwise direction. The tawāf involves completing seven circles around the Ka'bah. During these ritual, the pilgrims recite many du'ā. The tawāf is followed by two ra'akat salāt behind the **Maqam-e-Ibrāhīm**. It

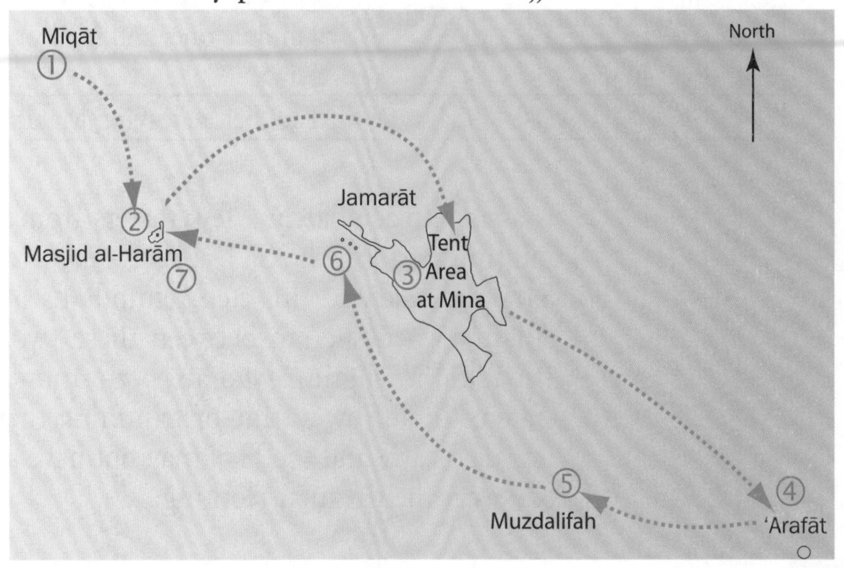

Days of Dul Hajj	State of Ihrām	Fajr Salāh	Actions	Night
8 Dhul Hajj	In Ihrām	In Makkah	• Ihrām for Hajj • Depart Makkah for Mina • Dhuhr, 'Asr, Maghrib, and Isha salāt at Mina	Spend the night at Mina
9 Dhul Hajj	In Ihrām	At Mina	• Arrive at 'Arafāt • Dhuhr and 'Asr Salāt at Arafat • Listen to Hajj Khutbha • Spend time in prayer • Leave 'Arafāt after sunset	• Arrive at Muzdalifah • Maghrib and Isha salāt • Collect 49–70 small pebbles. • Spend the night at Muzdalifah
10 Dhul Hajj	In Ihrām until hair cut	At Muzdalifah	• Arrive at Mina • Throw 7 rocks at Big Jamarāt • Sacrifice at Mina • Cut hair, then come out of Ihrām • Arrive at Masjid Al-Harām for Tawāf-e-Ifadah	Spend the night at Mina
11 Dhul Hajj	No Ihrām	At Mina	• Throw 7 rocks at each Jamarāt: first at the small one, then the middle one, and finally the large one. • If Tawāf-e- Ifadah is not performed, then go to Masjid Al-Harām for the Tawāf	Spend the night at Mina
12 Dhul Hajj	No Ihrām	At Mina	Throw 7 rocks at each Jamarāt: first at the small one, then the middle one, and finally the large one.	• If possible before Maghrib, go to Makkah for departure after Tawāf-e-Wida • If unable to go to Makkah, spend the night at Mina
13 Dhul Hajj	No Ihrām	At Mina	Throw 7 rocks at each Jamarāt: first the small one, then the middle one, and finally the large one.	Go to Makkah for departure after Tawāf-e-Wida
Tawāf-e-Wida is the final act before leaving Makkah. (Tawāf-e Wida has no Sa'i.)				

is a small place barely a few meters from the Ka'bah. After drinking zamzam water, pilgrims perform the **Sa'i**. This is seven rounds of brisk walking between the hills of Safā and Marwa. This step reminds us of Mother Hajar's perseverance and trust in Allāh ﷻ when she ran between these two hills in search of water for her infant son Ismā'īl. The pilgrims who are performing Hajj-e-Tamattu' can now come out of the state of Ihrām by cutting or trimming their hair. This is because the pilgrims arrived few days early and the Hajj may not have started yet. After finishing 'Umrah, pilgrims can wear their regular clothing.

Dhul Hajj 8

This is the first day of Hajj. Pilgrims take a shower, wear ihrām cloth, make an intention for Hajj, and start reciting the talbiyah. Note that 'Umrah was already completed by those who arrived before Hajj. Next they proceed to Mina, which is a valley near Makkah. Mina has hundreds of thousands of tents to house the pilgrims. Then the pilgrims spend the day in prayer and spend the night in Mina.

Dhul Hajj 9

The pilgrims now proceed to 'Arafāt. The day of 'Arafāt is the most important day of Hajj. The importance of 'Arafāt is emphasized in the phrase, "Hajj is 'Arafāt." Pilgrims spend the day in earnest prayer and ask Allāh ﷻ for forgiveness. After sunset, the pilgrims proceed to a nearby place named Muzdalifah. The Maghrib and Isha salāt are performed together in Muzdalifah, but not in 'Arafāt. Muzdalifah does not have tents or housing. Therefore, the pilgrims spend the night under the open sky. Here the pilgrims collect 49–70 small pebbles to throw at Jamarāt during the next three to four days.

Dhul Hajj 10

The Fajr salāt is performed at Muzdalifah. Next the pilgrims proceed to their tents in Mina. From here they proceed to Jamarāt to throw pebbles to renounce the satanic tendencies of their souls. The Jamarāt is located within walking distance across from the tents. On this day, the pilgrims throw seven pebbles at only the big Jamarāt. Not long ago, the Jamarāt were shaped like pillars, and they were too small for the large crowd. Now the Jamarāt are rebuilt as wide walls, so the pilgrims can avoid stampedes. Then the pilgrims sacrifice an animal or arrange to make a sacrifice. This is the day of Eid al-Adha. The pilgrims shave or trim their hair. Once their hair is cut, the pilgrims

Three Types of Hajj			
	Tamattu'	**Qiran**	**Ifrad**
Perform 'Umrah first	Yes	Yes	No
Remove Ihrām after 'Umrah	Yes	No	Does not apply
New Ihrām for Hajj	Yes	Same Ihrām for 'Umrah and Hajj	Yes
Animal Sacrifice	Yes	Yes	Optional
Intention (Niyyah)	Separately for 'Umrah and Hajj	Together for 'Umrah and Hajj	For Hajj only
Tawāf-e- Ifadah	Yes	Yes	Yes
Tawāf-e-Wida	Yes	Yes	No

can come out of the state of Ihrām. The next step is to perform **Tawāf-e-Ifadah**. The pilgrims travel from Mina to Masjid al-Harām. Tawāf-e-Ifadah involves steps similar to the 'Umrah, that is, seven rounds of tawāf around the Ka'bah and two rakat salāt at Maqam-e-Ibrāhīm and Sa'i. Then the pilgrims return to Mina to spend the night.

Dhul Hajj 11

Since the previous day, the pilgrims are not wearing ihrām cloths anymore. If Tawāf-e-Ifadah was not performed the previous day, then it can be completed today. The pilgrims throw seven pebbles at each of the three Jamarāt. The total number of pebbles thrown today is 21. The day and night is spent in Mina.

Dhul Hajj 12 and 13

Some pilgrims may decide to depart Makkah on Dhul Hajj 12. Before they depart Mina, they must throw seven pebbles at each of the three Jamarāt (a total of 21 pebbles). Before they leave Makkah, they must complete **Tawāf-e-Wida**. By today, these pilgrims will have thrown a total of 49 pebbles (7+21+21).

The pilgrims who do not leave Makkah on Dhul Hajj 12, remain in Mina. On Dhul Hajj 13, they throw seven pebbles at each of the three Jamarāt. These pilgrims will have thrown 21 more pebbles, making the total count 70. Next they return to Makkah to depart for home. The last ritual in Makkah is Tawāf-e-Wida, or the Farewell Tawāf. This completes the rituals of Hajj.

Performing the Hajj is not just a ritual, but an intense physical and spiritual exercise. It allows us to show our love for Allāhﷻ, submit to Him totally, prepare for death and the Hereafter, and avoid Shaitān. Hajj teaches us how short this life is and how the grand reward awaits all believers in the Hereafter. Every adult Muslim—if he or she is healthy and can afford it—must perform Hajj.

Madīnah

Most pilgrims visit Madīnah either before or after Hajj. Performing salāt in the Masjid al-Nabawi provides tremendous rewards and blessings. However, visiting Madīnah is not an official step in performing the Hajj.

WEEKEND 25

Homework

1. What are the three types of Hajj?

   1. ______________________________

   2. ______________________________

   3. ______________________________

2. What is the most important day of Hajj?

   A. Dhul Hajj 8, pilgrims in Mina.
   B. Dhul Hajj 9, pilgrims in 'Arafāt.
   C. Dhul Hajj 10, pilgrims throw pebbles at the Jamarāt in Mina.
   D. Dhul Hajj 11, Tawāf-e-Ifadah at Masjid al-Harām.

3. When do the pilgrims reach Muzdalifah, and where do they arrive from?

   A. Dhul Hajj 8, directly from Mina.
   B. Dhul Hajj 9, directly from Mina.
   C. Dhul Hajj 9, directly from 'Arafāt.
   D. Dhul Hajj 8, directly from Makkah.

4. What is the last ritual of Hajj in Makkah?

   ____

5. What is the reward for an accepted Hajj (Hajj-e-Mabroor)?

   ____

6. Arrange the four rituals of 'Umrah in the order they are performed.

   Drinking Zamzam water ________

   Sa'i (the brisk walks between Safā and Marwa) ________

   Salāt behind Maqam-e-Ibrāhīm ________

   Tawāf (the seven circular walks around the Ka'bah) ________

7. Memorize the Talbiyah. Be ready to recite it in front of the class next week.

8. In which direction must the tawāf of Ka'bah be performed?

A. Counter-clockwise direction.
B. Clockwise direction.
C. North-south direction.
D. Longitudinal direction.
E. South-west direction.

9. At the end of tawāf, the pilgrims perform two rak'at salāt at a specific place. What is that place?

A. Behind Maqam-e Ibrāhīm.
B. Behind Baitul Muqaddas.
C. Behind Safa and Marwah.
D. Behind the outer walls of Makkah.
E. Behind the Jamarat.

10. Which day is considered to be the first day of Hajj?

A. The 10th day of Dhul Hajj.
B. The 8th day of Dhul Hajj.
C. The Day of Arafat.
D. The 13th day of Dhul Hajj.
E. The 1st Day of Dhul Hajj.

11. What is the term for the type of Hajj where the pilgrim performs only the Hajj, and does not do 'Umrah. Animal sacrifice may or may not have been performed.

A. Hajj Tamattu.
B. Hajj Ifrad.
C. Hajj Qiran.
D. Hijjat-al Widah.
E. Tawaf e-Ifada.

12. When a person intends to perform Hajj and 'Umrah together, and the person completes them wearing the same Ihrām, he or she has performed a specific type of Hajj. What is the term for this type of Hajj?

A. Hajj Tamattu'.
B. Hajj Ifrad.
C. Hajj Qiran.
D. Hijjat-al Widah.
E. Tawaf e-Ifada.

WEEKEND

26

Classwork

Parables in the Qur'ān

Objective of the Lesson:

The Qur'ān is not only a book of guidance, but it is also a book of high-quality literature. Just as literature uses metaphors, figures of speech and other techniques to tell a story, the Qur'ān also uses many of these techniques. The parable is a literary style used frequently in the Qur'ān. In this chapter, students will learn some of the parables in the Qur'ān.

Thought is an idea or opinion that occurs in the mind. Thought is expressed to others through words. The more refined a thought is, the more refined is the expression of the thought in words. A word is a sound that carries a meaning and harmonizes with the thought. This is how early human beings developed language—they expressed their thoughts in words and the words carried a meaning that harmonized with the thought.

As language evolved, people learned how to combine words to provide a meaningful expression of an idea. With the progression of civilization, human language also evolved. Language added beauty, structure, figures of speech, metaphors, and other techniques to human expression..

Good literature uses a variety of figures of speech and techniques to communicate. The Qur'ān is not only a book of guidance, but it is also a book of literature. Its meaning can be fully understood if we understand its literary styles. It uses effective, forceful, concise, and beautiful language so successfully that with a few thousand words and 6,236 āyāt, the Qur'ān is the complete and perfect book of guidance for mankind for all time periods.

Parable

One of the techniques of language is a parable. A parable is a figure of speech that presents a short narrative, typically with a moral lesson at the end. A common feature of a parable is the use of a picturesque figure of speech where one familiar thing is expressed, but something else is meant.

'Isā (A) used parables

Among all the messengers, 'Isā (A) is known to have made extensive use of parables in his teachings. He used parables when he spoke to common people publicly, but when he spoke to them privately, he explained the meaning of the parables. He used terms such as "Kingdom of God," "Heavenly Father," "Lamp on a stand," and many other parables in his teachings. Students of the Bible study these parables and their intended meanings in detail.

Parables in the Qur'ān

The parables in the Qur'ān are called as **'amthāl** (ٱلْأَمْثَال). They are used to convey knowledge and wisdom to inspire readers. The Qur'ānic parables work the same way as any other parables—they convey a basic truth and then offer a moral.

وَلَقَدْ ضَرَبْنَا لِلنَّاسِ فِي هَٰذَا ٱلْقُرْءَانِ مِن كُلِّ مَثَلٍ لَّعَلَّهُمْ يَتَذَكَّرُونَ ﴿٢٧﴾

And certainly We have set forth for mankind in this Qur'ān all kinds of parables, that perhaps they might think. (39:27)

وَتِلْكَ ٱلْأَمْثَٰلُ نَضْرِبُهَا لِلنَّاسِ لَعَلَّهُمْ يَتَفَكَّرُونَ ﴿٢١﴾

...And these parables—We set them forth for mankind that they may reflect. (59:21)

The parables in the Qur'ān were first addressed to the contemporaries of the Messenger ﷺ. But the intended beneficiaries of the parables are the people who are born after the Messenger ﷺ. They are the ones who need to understand the meaning of the parables and reflect on the message. These parables should be understood in light of the totality of the message of the Qur'ān.

Parable in ayāh 7:176

A good example of a parable can be found in ayāh 7:126 of the Qur'ān. Here, earthly minded people are compared to a dog.

And had We wished, We would invariably have exalted him thereby; but he inclined towards the earth, and he followed his low desires. So his parable is like the parable of the dog; if you drive him, he lolls out his tongue, or if you leave him alone, he lolls out his tongue. Such is the parable of the people who belie Our Messages. So you relate the tales in order that they may reflect. (7:176)

It is normal for a dog to let its tongue hang out as a means of cooling off through evaporation, and as an indicator of happiness. These are a dog's habitual response. The Qur'ān compares the habitual response of a dog to the habitual reaction of a person who disregards the divine message due to his or her low desires or low earthly motives. Earthly motives are comparable to a person's bad habits. Bad habits cling to a person like rust clings toon an iron. Both are hard to remove.

Earthly motives and spiritual goals are opposite to one another. Regardless of whether earthly minded people are warned about their behavior or left alone, they continue their customary bad habits—dwelling on low desires. The Qur'ān says, "*Surely those who disbelieve—it being alike to them whether you warn them, or do not warn them—they will not believe.*"[2:6] For this reason, the parable compares the response of such a person to the habitual response of a dog.

Parable in ayāh 2:265

A beautiful example of a parable can be found in ayāh 2:265 of the Qur'ān. Here, the reward of charity is illustrated through a parable.

> *And the likeness of those who spend their wealth seeking the pleasure of Allāh, and for the strengthening of their souls, is like the parable of a garden on a hill upon which heavy rain falls, so it brings forth its fruit twofold; but if heavy rain does not fall on it, then dew. And Allāh is Watchful of what you do. (2:265)*

The spiritual objective of charity is to seek the pleasure of Allāhﷻ and strengthen the soul of the donor. Obtaining the pleasure of Allāhﷻ is the single most-important achievement that leads to success in the Hereafter (5:119; 9:72,100; 89:28; 92:19–21).

The Qur'ān also promises that people will see some results in this life as well. However, the rewards will vary according to divine wisdom—some will receive more than others. The parable compares this life to a garden. The garden is on high land. Therefore, by analogy, flood water will not damage it. This garden might receive abundant rainfall or very little rainfall. The reason is explained in the Qur'ān—Allāhﷻ measures out everything for a reason.

If the garden receives abundant rainfall, the garden will provide dense and luxuriant yield. The ayāh says the yield will be twofold, which is an enormous amount by any standard. If heavy rain does not fall,then dew will be sufficient. Therefore, a true believer will not complain about the amount of rainfall, for he or she realizes that whatever Allāhﷻ sends will be enough. The ayāh indicates that dew will also yield enough crops due to blessings from Allāhﷻ. Thus, based on the degree and sincerity of charity, Allāhﷻ will invariably reward the donor, but the reward might vary.

Parable in ayāh 14:18

Another meaningful parable is mentioned in ayāh 14:18, where the deeds of nonbelievers are compared to ashes. Here the deeds are considered good actions. These deeds have produced a result—ironically, only ashes. Ashes are powdery residue left over after something is burnt. The ashes still have some organic or combustible residue left in them, but in all probability, the value of the ashes is very little.

On a stormy day, wind will blow away the ashes. A person has no control over protecting the ashes from blowing away. First, life-long righteous deed was rendered into ashes. Second, wind scattered the ashes, leaving nothing behind. The point is that good deeds of nonbelievers will be rendered null and void because the gravity of not beleiving in God will outweigh their bona fide righteous deeds.

Parable in ayāh 2:171

Sūrah Baqarah, ayāh 171 offers another illustrative parable.

> *And the parable of those who disbelieved is like the parable of one who shouts to that which does not hear anything except a call and a cry. Deafness, dumbness blindness—so that they do not exercise wisdom. (2:171)*

Who is that to whom one "shouts" at? Is it an idol or a cow? The ayāh intentionally leaves the subject unspecified, however, the audience at that time fully understood the implied meaning. A person shouts at a cow (7:179; 25:44), which only understands the yell as a sound and does not understand the meaning. Had the subject been a deity, instead of the word "shout," a word similar to "prayer" or "appeal" would have been used. Besides, if the subject was a deity, the intended force of the parable would have been lost.

In the parable, the person is calling his or her idol god, who has no capacity to decipher the call of the worshipper. The call is a meaningless yell. The worshipper is described as afflicted with deafness, dumbness, and blindness, because the person has no ability to realize the idols cannot and do not hear the call of the worshippers.

Homework

1. What is the meaning of parables?

____

____

2. Which nabi used parables extensively in his teachings?

A. Yūnus (A).
B. Mūsā (A).
C. 'Isā (A).
D. Muhammad ﷺ.
E. None of the above.

3. Which of the following is not the purpose of using parables in the Qur'ān?

A. To summarize a history.
B. To communicate a message through picturesque figure of speech.
C. To say something in place of something else.
D. To make people think or reflect.
E. To make the message easier to understand.

4. Read ayāh 22:31 in the Qur'ān. In a parable, what two things are mentioned about those who associate with Allāh ﷻ?

A. Birds prey upon him, and he falls from a tree.
B. Animals prey upon him as he falls from a high place.
C. Birds prey upon him, and winds blow him to a far-off place.
D. Ashes are scattered, and winds blow him to a far-off place.
E. Wind blows and ashes are scattered all over.

5. In ayāh 62:5 in the Qur'ān, the scholars who studied the Tawrāt but never attempted to understand or implement its teachings are compared to an animal. What is the animal?

A. Donkey.
B. Camel.
C. Sheep.
D. Cow.
E. Horse.

6. In ayāh 22:73 in the Qur'ān, the uselessness of idols is illustrated with the use of a parable. What is that parable?

A. The inability of the idols to create a fly.
B. The inability of the idols to listen to prayer.
C. The inability of the idols to take back an item from a fly if it snatched it.
D. Only A and B.
E. Only A and C.

7. In a parable in ayāh 2:265 in the Qur'ān, why is dew said to be sufficient for a garden on a hill?

A. Dew will also help the twofold growth of crop.
B. Dew will help keep the garden alive for next year.
C. Dew will cause heavy rain to fall.
D. Dew will help a smaller growth of crops.
E. Dew will cause the crops to die.

8. In a parable in ayāh 14:18 in the Qur'ān, what do the life-long righteous deeds of a nonbeliever turns into?

A. Garbage.
B. Mud.
C. Cotton.
D. Dry leaves.
E. Ashes.

*Unit 6: Islam After Rasūlullāh*ﷺ

The history of Islam after Rasūlullāhﷺ includes a series of disturbances and political rivalries at the same time the empire expanded to almost all of north Africa, parts of Europe, and Persia. This unit focuses on some of the majore developments. The chapter on the early history of Shī'ah Muslims discusses on why some Muslims disagreed with the majority and how they emerged as an offshoot of mainstream Islam. The next two lessons explain how notable Muslim dynasties emerged, one after another, and capitalized on the series of disturbances that followed the Messenger'sﷺ death. These two dynasties contributed volumes to the cause of Islam. Their rise was as illustrious, as their downfall was shameful. These dynasties collapsed due to corruption, the failure to follow the Islamic ethical framework, and the failure to abide by Islamic values and teachings.

Unit 6: Islam After Rasūlullāh ﷺ

Early History of Shī'ah Muslims

In this lesson, students will be introduced to the origin and early history of Shī'ah Muslims. Students will also learn what led to the division of among Muslims and what prompted the early Shī'ah to disagree with the majority of Muslims at that time.

Umayyad Dynasty

The short-lived Umayyad Dynasty helped shape the early history of Islam. The dynasty was embroiled in bloody battles during its entire rule, but it also contributed to expanding the territories of the Muslim empire. However, the Umayyad Dynasty's downfall was accelerated by several factors. Students will read an overview of the dynasty beginning with its foundation and ending with its collapse.

Abbasid Dynasty

The long-lasting Abbasid Dynasty shifted its focus from mainland Arabia to Iraq. The success of the dynasty was rooted in its efficient administrative system. The dynasty also significantly expanded learning and achieved the highest level of Islamic advancement. Students will learn how the dynasty was formed and the cause of its downfall.

Early History of Shī'ah Muslims

Objective of the Lesson:

In this lesson, students will be introduced to the origin and early history of Shī'ah Muslims. Students will also learn what led to the division of among Muslims and what prompted the early Shī'ah to disagree with the majority of Muslims at that time.

Every now and then we hear a reference to Shī'ah Muslims. These Muslims are called Shī'ites and the principles they follow are called Shī'ism. We also hear about the tension and clashes between Sunni and Shī'ah Muslims in different parts of the world. Our non-Muslim friends might ask us who the Sunnis and Shī'ites are, and whether they are similar or dissimilar. In the world today, about 180 million people are Shī'ah Muslims, representing roughly 15% of the Muslim population. We should know about the Shī'ah Muslims, who are our close brethren in Islam.

The singular form or adjectival form of Shī'ah refers to an individual who follows Nabi Muhammad ﷺ as Rasūlullāh and 'Ali Ibn Abi Talib (R) as an Imam. He or she follows the Qur'ān, the teachings of Rasūlullāh ﷺ and the religious guidance of Rasūlullāh's ﷺ family, referred to as **Ahl-al Bayt,** or the "people of the [Prophet's] house."

The word Shī'ah is the short form of the original term **Shī'at 'Ali**, which means "the followers of 'Ali." The term was coined during the early years of Islam after Nabi Muhammad ﷺ passed away. At that time, a group of companions wanted 'Ali to be the successor, or Khalīfah, of the Muslim community. As we know, Abū Bakr (R) was appointed as the first Khalīfah

of the Muslim community. People who did not like his appointment as Khalīfah began to identify themselves as Shī'at 'Ali, or the followers of 'Ali.

Appointment of khalīfah

The Muslim community was united under Rasūlullāhﷺ during his lifetime. After he passed away, the prominent companions felt they should formally appoint a leader. This person would not be a prophet or a king, but simply an official representative to uphold the teachings of the Qur'ān and Rasūlullāhﷺ. People would look to this person as their leader, judge, and guide. He would command respect and attention from the various tribes. He would have the necessary skills and authority to keep the community united and solve its crises.

When Rasūlullāhﷺ passed away, Abū Bakr was one of the most senior companions, well respected and admired by all. He was also one of Rasūlullāh'sﷺ closest companions and a partner to him during many difficult times. When the companions chose to formally appoint a successor, the key people involved in making the decision unanimously agreed to make Abū Bakr the Khalīfah. He was 59 years old at that time; 'Ali was only 32 years old. 'Ali was not present when the decision was made. The decision was not made by an "election," but by a process called **ijma,** or a consensus of a group of important people.

Within two years of his appointment, Abū Bakr died in the year 634 C.E. Once again, using the same ijma process of an advisory council, 'Umar (R) was appointed the Khalīfah. He was assassinated by a Persian slave in 644 C.E. Again, another advisory council discussed who should be the next Khalīfah. The consensus was 'Uthmān (R), a prominent senior member of the Umayya clan. When 'Uthmān was assassinated in 656 C.E., the next Khalīfah chosen was 'Ali (R). After the appointment of 'Ali, a rift occurred among the Muslims that persists to this day in the Sunni and Shī'ah forms of Islam.

'Ali's appointment questioned

Just as the first three appointments of Khalīfahs cannot be questioned, the appointment of 'Ali also cannot be questioned. These appointments were made by an advisory council and agreed upon by all the members. However, the governor of Syria, Mu'awiyah, questioned the validity of 'Ali's appointment.

Mu'awiyah was appointed the governor of Syria by 'Umar. He was the son of Abū Sufyān, a prominent member of the Umayya clan. As governor of Syria, Mu'awiyah developed a large naval force and fought several naval wars against the Byzantine empire. He believed that the assassination of 'Uthmān, also an Umayyah member, could have been prevented if 'Ali had responded in a more careful manner. He believed 'Ali would not take the necessary steps to punish the culprits because 'Ali's own followers were involved in the conspiracy. As a result, Mu'awiyah refused to recognize 'Ali as a Khalīfah. This tension between 'Ali and Mu'awiyah escalated into the **Battle of Siffin,** which was fought in 657 C.E. near the Euphrates river in Iraq. ‘Ali did not want to shed the blood of his fellow Muslims, so he agreed to settle their differences. The committee overseeing the dispute decided against ‘Ali and chose Mu’awiyah as the next Khalīfah.

Viewpoint of ‘Ali’s camp

The supporters of ‘Ali not only rejected the committee’s decision, but they also believed that he should have been Khalīfah immediately after the death of Nabi Muhammad ﷺ. They believed ‘Ali was unfairly ignored three times as the rightful Khalīfah. Also, they did not believe in the institution of khalīfah. They preferred to use the term Imam. According to them, the Imam cannot be elected, but must be chosen from the family of Nabi Muhammad ﷺ. ‘Ali was not a descendent of Rasūlullāh ﷺ, but he was Rasūlullāh’s ﷺ first cousin and son-in-law.

> **Interesting Facts**
>
> According to Shī‘ah Muslims, the People of the House include: Muhammad ﷺ, ‘Ali Ibn Abū Talib, Fātimah, Hasan, and Husayn.
>
> Different sects among the Shī‘ah dispute about the number of Imams and the path of their succession. The majority of them are the Twelvers. They believe in 12 Imams.
>
> Among the Twelvers, each Imam of the past was the son of the previous Imam except for Husayn, who was the brother of Hasan.
>
> The last Imam—the 12th one—is Imam Muhammad Al-Mahdi. It is claimed that he is hidden. According to the Shī‘ah Muslims, he will reappear during the last days of the world.

Early Shī‘ism

The Shī‘ites do not recognize the first three Khalīfahs. They also do not believe in the caliphate, but an imamate. The imamate is the institution of Imams. According to the Shī‘ah, ‘Ali Ibn Abū Talib was the first Imam. His son, Hasan, was the second Imam, and his second son, Husayn, was the third Imam. Husayn’s son, Zainul Abideen, was the fourth Imam. Most Shī‘ahs believe in a total of twelve Imams, and they are called the **Twelvers.**

Denominations among Shī‘ites

Over time, several denominations, or sects, emerged from the original Shī‘ah Muslims. Some sects are based on who their Imam was and how many Imams were recognized. Other sects focus on principles and ideologies. Some of the Shī‘ah denominations are Ismaili Shī‘ah, Naziri Ismaili, Dawoodi Bohras, Seveners, and Zaidis. The Seveners believe there were only seven Imams.

Differences between the Shī‘ites and Sunnis

Both the Shī‘ites and the Sunnis follow Qur’ānic teachings and believe Muhammad ﷺ was the last prophet. Both pray five daily prayers, fast, and pay zakāt. But they disagree on the interpretation of law. Many Islamic laws are based on hadīth. The Shī‘ites reject some of the Sunni hadīth, and the Sunnis reject most of the Shī‘ah hadīth. The Shī‘ahs particularly reject hadīth that were not narrated by Alh-al Bayt. However, both Muslim groups celebrate Eid ul-Fitr and Eid ul-Adha, and perform pilgrimages.

The Shī‘ahs also believe the burial site of Imam ‘Ali is sacred and visit this site (in Kufa, but some believe it is in Najaf, Iraq). They celebrate the **Festival of Muharram** and **‘Ashūrā** to commemorate the martyrdom of Husayn. The Sunnis have no problem with ‘Ashūrā, but they consider its celebration less important. Other key events include **Arab’een**, which occurs 40 days after ‘Ashūrā to commemorate the suffering of the women and children of Husayn's household. **Eid Al-Ghadeer** is celebrated to commemorate Rasūlullāh'sﷺ speech that is believed to endorse the Imamate of 'Ali. **Milad un-Nabi** celebrates the birth of Rasūlullāhﷺ. The Shī'ahs do not have a high regard for 'Ā'ishah because she led an army against 'Ali in the **Battle of the Camel.**

What should our position be?

The division between the Shī'ahs and the Sunnis began soon after Rasūlullāhﷺ passed away. In the long history of Islam, Shī'ahs and Sunnis have expressed hate and anger towards each other. In many countries, Shī'ahs and Sunnis have even killed each other due to religious intolerance. However, Islam teaches us to tolerate every religion and every opinion.[2:193, 256; 3:64; 6:104; 10:99; 17:7; 18:29]

Shī'ahs and Sunnis do not follow different religions—all of them are Muslim. Although there are some differences between them, we should learn to respect everyone despite these differences. Religious differences are often a matter of interpretation. We should remember that Allāhﷻ will ultimately judge a person's faith. He will reward or punish the person accordingly. We should not declare another person a non-Muslim when he or she has declared faith in the Oneness of Allāhﷻ and believes in Rasūlullāhﷺ.

Homework

1. According to the lesson, when did the first rift occur between the mainstream Muslims and the Shīʿah Muslims?

A. After Imam Husayn was murdered.
B. Soon after the death of Rasūlullāh ﷺ.
C. Soon after the Shīʿahs settled down in Iran.
D. Long before the birth of Rasūlullāh ﷺ.
E. When the Umayyad dynasty was formed.

2. According to Shīʿah belief, who was their first Imam?

A. ʿAli Ibn Abū Talib (R).
B. Imam Hasan.
C. Imam Husayn.
D. Nabi Muhammad ﷺ.
E. Abū Bakr (R).

3. From the Shīʿah perspective, which of the following choices about ʿĀ'ishah (ra) is correct?

A. Shīʿahs recognize her as one of the Imams.
B. Shīʿahs recognize her as a prophet.
C. Shīʿahs do not have much respect for her.
D. Shīʿahs love her as much as they love ʿAli (R).
E. None of the above.

4. Which of the following statements about how the Shīʿah recognize the Khalīfahs is correct?

A. They do not believe in Abū Bakr (R), but they accept ʿUthmān (R).
B. They do not believe in any of the three Khalīfahs.
C. They do not believe in the institution of Khalīfahs.
D. Only (b) and (c).
E. Only (a) and (c).

5. Most Shīʿahs believe in how many Imams?

A. Only 1 Imam—Ali (R).
B. 5 Imams.
C. 12 Imams.
D. 21 Imams.
E. 25 Imams.

6. According to Shīʿah belief, who has the right to be appointed as Imam?

A. Anyone appointed by consensus or ijma.
B. Anyone appointed by Rasūlullāhﷺ.
C. A person belonging to Ahl-al Bayt.
D. A person belonging to Arabia.
E. A person belonging to the Umayyad Dynasty.

7. According to Shīʿah belief, which of the following statements about the appointment of an Imam is correct?

A. Appointment of an Imam cannot be done through an election.
B. An Imam can be appointed through an election.
C. An Imam can be appointed only through the process of ijma.
D. An Imam can be appointed only by Allāhﷻ.
E. An Imam can be appointed by a king.

8. Which of the following choices about the Battle of Siffin is correct?

A. ʿAli and ʿĀʾishah fought the battle.
B. ʿAli and Mu'awiyah fought the battle.
C. Mu'awiyah and Yazid fought the battle.
D. ʿUmar and Mu'awiyah fought the battle.
E. The battle was fought soon after the battle of Uhud.

9. According to Shīʿah belief, which of the following statements about the appointment of Khalīfas is correct?

A. ʿAli was chosen to be the first Khalīfa, but he declined.
B. ʿAli was chosen to be the first Khalīfa, but Abū Bakr intervened.
C. ʿAli's followers whole-heartedly accepted all three Khalīfas.
D. ʿAli was overlooked during the first three appointments of Khalīfas.
E. ʿAli never wanted to be a Khalīfa, but he was forced to become one.

10. What is the meaning of the term Shīʿat ʿAli?

A. The sword of ʿAli.
B. The birthplace of ʿAli.
C. The followers of ʿAli.
D. The rejection of ʿAli.
E. The capital formed by ʿAli.

WEEKEND 28 Classwork

Umayyad Dynasty

Objective of the Lesson:

The short-lived Umayyad Dynasty helped shape the early history of Islam. The dynasty was embroiled in bloody battles during its entire rule, but it also contributed to expanding the territories of the Muslim empire. However, the Umayyad Dynasty's downfall was accelerated by several factors. Students will read an overview of the dynasty beginning with its foundation and ending with its collapse.

After Rasūl Muhammad ﷺ passed away, the four Rightly Guided Khalīfahs continued to propagate Islam. When the last of the four Khalīfahs died, Muslims witnessed the emergence of two dynasties—the Umayyad and the Abbasid. These two dynasties dominated early Islamic history for 600 years. They occupied and ruled large parts of Arabia, parts of Europe and central Asia, and Africa.

In this lesson, we will briefly study the Umayyad dynasty. We will learn how it formed, its primary achievements, and how it met its downfall. This history provides interesting insight into the spread of Islam. The Umayyad Dynasty was the first Arab dynasty and lasted for nearly 90 years. During this time, many of the companions (*Sahābah*) and followers of the companions (*Taba Tābi'īn*) were still alive. The Abbasid Dynasty, formed by the followers of the companions, rose to power after the fall of the Umayyad Dynasty. This dynasty lasted about 509 years.

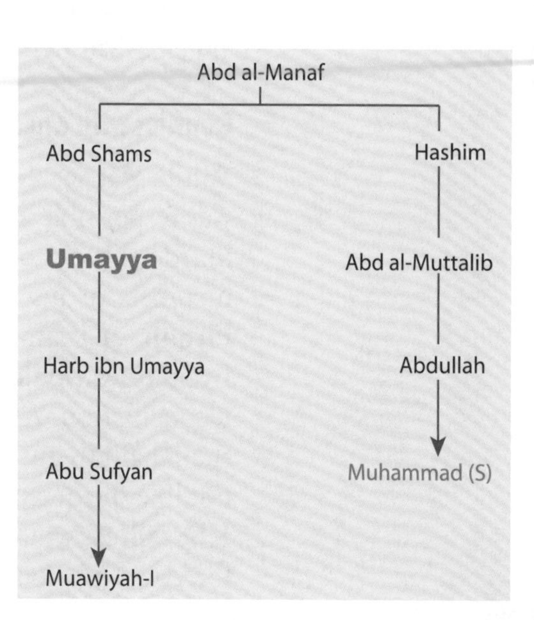

Origin of Umayyad Dynasty

The first Islamic dynasty was named after **Umayya Ibn Abd Shams**, the great-grandfather of Mu'awiyah. One of Umayya's ancestors was Abd al-Munaf, who was also an ancestor of Nabi Muhammad ﷺ.

Islamic Dynasties

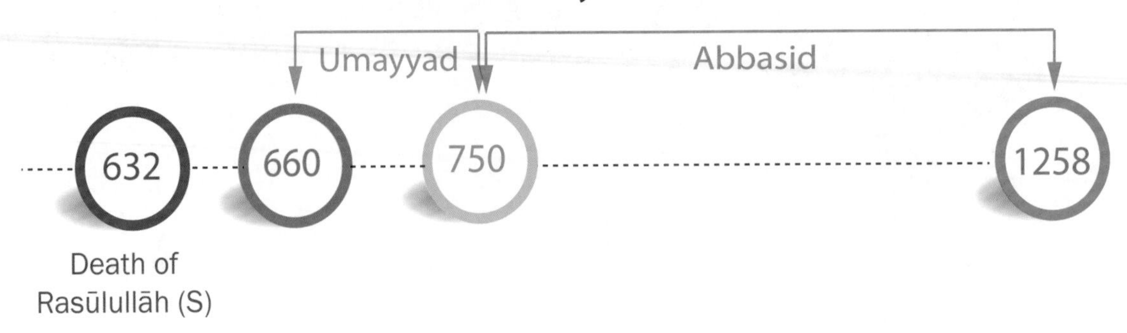

The forerunners of the Umayyad Dynasty, the Umayyads, were merchants by profession. The Hashim and Umayya clans belonged to the Quraish tribe. The forerunners of the Umayyads initially resisted Islam, and many of their leaders fought wars against the Muslims. It was not until the fall of Makkah that most of the Umayyads accepted Islam.

Khalīfah ʻUthmān was a descendant of Umayya. Although ʻUthmān was one of the four Rightly Guided Khalīfahs, he is not credited with the formation of the Umayyad dynasty. This is because ʻUthmān did not appoint or declare a successor to assume power after his death. The names of the dynasties are based on the ethnicity of the person who established the dynasty and appointed his successors.

All historians credit Mu'awiyah (602 C.E.–680 C.E.), a member of the Umayya clan, as the founder of the dynasty. He was the son of Abū Sufyān, who, originally opposed to Muhammadﷺ but later accepted Islam and became a companion. During ʻUmar's time, he appointed Mu'awiyah governor of Syria. After ʻUmar died, ʻUthmān became the Khalīfah of the Muslim nation. He continued to expand the Muslim territories. In many of the newly conquered territories, ʻUthmān appointed people from the Umayyad clan. He retained his cousin, Mu'awiyah, the governor of Syria. After ʻUthmān was assassinated, Mu'awiyah wanted to become the next Khalīfah. But a group of senior companions decided to appoint ʻAli as the next Khalīfah. This decision angered Mu'awiyah.

Conflict with Mu'awiyah

While ʻAli served as Khalīfah, a dispute arose between he and Mu'awiyah over who was responsible for killing ʻUthmān. Mu'awiyah believed ʻAli was protecting ʻUthmān's murderers. In order to capture the murderers, Mu'awiyah marched with 70,000 members of his army against ʻAli in 657 C.E. This was the beginning of the **First Fitnah,** or Islamic Civil War. Both parties realized that if they fought each other, the Byzantines would use the opportunity to attack the Muslims. Both parties agreed to a reconciliation. After negotiating, the committee decided that ʻAli would no longer be the Khalīfah anymore and declared Mu'awiyah the Khalīfah. The followers of ʻAli did not like the decision. Within three years, ʻAli was assassinated in 661 C.E. by a group of **Kharajites**, which means "those who withdrew." The group had withdrawn its support for ʻAli. The group also wanted to assassinate Mu'awiyah but failed.

The senior companions who normally appointed the Khalīfah could not decide who should be the next Khalīfah. There was widespread disagreement among the Muslims about whether the Khalīfah could be "appointed" or chosen from the immediate descendants of 'Ali. No decision could be reached, so 'Ali's elder son, Hasan, declared himself Khalīfah. However, he resigned from his duties within six months. In the meantime, Mu'awiyah, who had already been declared the Khalīfah by certain groups, declared himself Khalīfah of the entire Muslim community.

End of Rightly Guided Khalīfahs

Later historians refused to accept Mu'awiyah as the rightful Khalīfah because he did not receive formal approval from the companions, who originally appointed the Khalīfah. Thus, the institution of Rightly Guided Khalīfahs ended with 'Ali. All rulers after 'Ali were simply called Khalīfahs, not Rightly Guided Khalīfahs. Besides, the Shī'ahs refused to believe in the Khalīfah system—they believed in the Imam system. According to them, the first Imam was 'Ali, the second was Hasan, the third was Husayn, and so forth.

Damascus becomes the capital

In order to strengthen his claim to the office of Khalīfah, Mu'awiyah moved the capital of the Muslim empire from Madīnah to Damascus. Mu'awiyah wanted to strengthen his political power and weaken the Shī'ah influence that had begun to increase since 'Ali's time. With the transfer of the capital, formal Umayyad rule was established. Mu'awiyah was recognized as the first Khalīfah, or king of the Umayyad Dynasty. Mu'awiyah maintained the unity of the empire, but he could not prevent the rise of Shī'ah influence or the threat from the growing numbers of non-Arab Muslims. These new Muslims felt deprived of the privileges enjoyed by Arab Muslims.

Appointment of Yazid

Mu'awiyah died in 680 C.E. Before his death, he obtained the advisory council's approval to appoint Yazid as the next Khalīfah of the dynasty. The Shī'ahs rejected Yazid as Khalīfah and demanded that 'Ali's second son, Husayn, be the Khalīfah. Yazid viewed this as a rebellion by the Shī'ahs against his authority. In order to suppress the Shī'ah rebellion, Yazid's army met Husayn and his small army at Karbala near the banks of the Euphrates River. Yazid's army easily defeated Husayn and killed him. In order to suppress any further claims on the Calīphate, Yazid's army invaded Arabia and ransacked Madīnah and Makkah. During the battle, the Ka'bah caught fire. Makkah would have been destroyed, but the death of Yazid spared the city.

Khalīfah 'Abd Al-Malik

Within two years of Yazid's death, 'Abd al-Malik rose to power. He ruled for 20 years. During his rule, the dynasty reached its peak in terms of administrative reforms, innovative systems, and territorial expansion. He developed an administrative system based on the Byzantine model. This model was adapted by other Muslim rulers in later years and continued to serve as the standard for all future administrations. 'Abd al-Malik made Arabic the official state language, issued the first Islamic coinage,

Points to Remember

The Umayyad Dynasty was formed by Mu'awiyah—the son of Abū Sufyān.

The dynasty was formed shortly after the First Islamic Civil War over the struggle for caliphate following the murder of 'Uthmān.

In order to minimize Shi'ah influence, Mu'awiyah moved the capital of the dynasty from Madīnah to Damascus.

Yazid, the second Khalifah of the dynasty killed Husayn, the grandson of Rasūlullāh ﷺ.

Yazid attacked Madīnah and Makkah.

The power of the dynasty began to decline when the rulers began to enjoy luxurious lifestyle. They mistreated non-Arab converts to Islam—the Mawalis. Ultimately the descendants of al-'Abbas defeated the Umayyads and established the Abbasid Dynasty.

introduced a postal system, and developed irrigation systems and canals in the Tigris-Euphrates valley in Iraq. During his rule, the borders of Muslim territory expanded all the way to China in the east and the Atlantic Ocean in the west.

Mistreatment of the Mawalis

The **Mawalis** were non-Arab converts to Islam. The Mawalis were treated as second-class citizens and deprived of the privileges enjoyed by the Muslims of Arab descent. Even though they had accepted Islam, they were forced to pay the jizya tax imposed on non-Muslims. One of the Umayyad rulers, **'Umar II,** tried to solve this problem. He ordered that all non-Arab Muslims should be treated as equals to the Arabs. The Mawali army was granted a state pension. But these reforms came a little too late. The Mawalis rebelled against the ruling class. 'Umar II died shortly before all the social improvements could be enacted.

Downfall of the dynasty

Mistreatment of the mawalis and the luxurious lifestyle of the rulers eventually caused the downfall of the Umayyad Dynasty. Enemies of the Umayyad Dynasty continued to challenge the army in Syria. Skirmishes with the Byzantine empire and the Turkish kingdoms further weakened the Umayyad army. Internal conflict weakened the empire. Secret organizations rallied to make many internal groups powerful enough to weaken the administration. Many Shī'ahs and non-Arab Muslims became hostile towards the rulers. Eventually, the descendants of Al-'Abbās staged a massive counter-attack and overthrew the Umayyad rulers. Soon the descendants of Al-'Abbās established the Abbasid Empire. They massacred almost all of the remaining Umayyad clan members. A few members were able to escape to Spain and formed a Second Umayyad Dynasty there. However, on the Arabian Peninsula, Umayyad rule ended in 750 C.E.

Although it only lasted about 90 years, the Umayyad Dynasty was significant in many ways. The dynasty expanded the boundaries of the Muslim empire across North Africa, Iran, west of present-day Pakistan and Afghanistan to Sindh in Northern India, and across Gibraltar in Europe and central Asia. More and more people in the conquered regions accepted Islam. Amid all these successes, the rulers failed to give the new Muslims equal human rights and justice. Such unfair treatment violates Qur'ānic principles. Eventually Allāh ﷻ caused the downfall of the Umayyads.

Homework

1. Which city was the capital of the Umayyad Dynasty?

A. Syria.
B. Madīnah.
C. Damascus.
D. Baghdad.
E. Karbala.

2. Who was the founder of the Umayyad Dynasty?

A. Umayya.
B. 'Uthmān.
C. Mu'awiyah.
D. Abū Sufyān.
E. Yazid.

3. Which of the following Umayyad rulers made significant improvements in the administration of the empire?

A. Yazid.
B. 'Abd al-Malik.
C. Sulayman.
D. 'Umar II.
E. Yazid II.

4. Which of the following statements about the Mawalis during Umayyad rule is correct?

A. They were treated unfairly.
B. They were treated as equals to the people of Arab descent.
C. They were made slaves.
D. They were imprisoned and tortured.
E. They were respected and given good administrative jobs.

5. Who was responsible for killing 'Ali?

A. The Umayyad rulers.
B. The Kharajites.
C. The Mawalis.
D. The Byzantines.
E. The Mongols.

6. Which Umayyad ruler tried to bring social justice to the empire by treating everyone equally?

A. Yazid.
B. Mu'awiyah.
C. 'Abd al-Malik.
D. 'Umar II.
E. Yazid II.

7. According to the lesson, what caused the downfall of the Umayyad dynasty?

A. Too much power and wealth.
B. Luxury and the mistreatment of the Mawalis.
C. Lethargy and excessive love of Islam.
D. Favoring the Mawalis and Shī'ahs.
E. All of the above.

8. Which Umayyad ruler established Arabic as the official state language, issued the first Islamic coinage, and developed a postal system?

A. Yazid.
B. Yazid II.
C. Umar II.
D. Sulayman.
E. 'Abd al-Malik.

9. Which of the following statements about territorial expansion during Umayyad rule is correct?

A. Territory expanded only in Africa.
B. Territory expanded only in Europe.
C. Territory remained within the Arabian Peninsula.
D. Territory expanded only in Spain and Turkey.
E. Territory expanded to North Africa, across Gibraltar, and to central Asia.

10. Who overthrew Umayyad rule?

A. The Byzantines.
B. The Mamluks.
C. Rasūlullāh's ﷺ uncle Al-'Abbās.
D. The descendants of Al-'Abbās.
E. Hindus from the East.

WEEKEND 29 Classwork

Abbasid Dynasty

Objective of the Lesson:

The long-lasting Abbasid Dynasty shifted its focus from mainland Arabia to Iraq. The success of the dynasty was rooted in its efficient administrative system. The dynasty also significantly expanded learning and achieved the highest level of Islamic advancement. Students will learn how the dynasty was formed and the cause of its downfall.

The Abbasid dynasty was one of the most notable dynasties in the history of Islam. It came into prominence after it overthrew the Umayyad dynasty, and it collapsed after the Mongol invasion in 1258 C.E. Although it lasted about 509 years, it flourished during the first two hundred years and then started to decline. The pinnacle of the dynasty is considered the Golden Age of Islam.

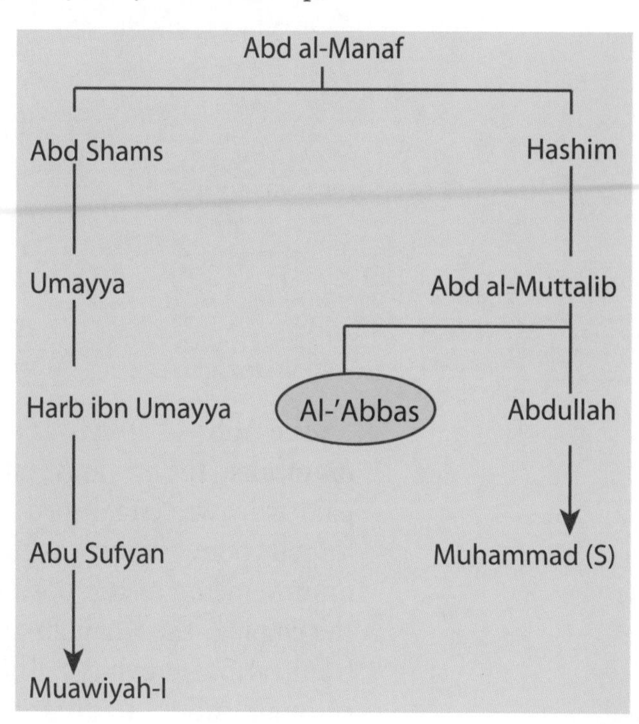

In this lesson, we will learn about the Abbasid dynasty and attempt to understand how it began, its primary achievements, and the cause of its downfall. The dynasty's capital was Baghdad. Unlike the Umayyad Dynasty, the Abbasid was a **multi-ethnic** Muslim empire. The rulers were of Arab origin, but the society largely comprised non-Arab Muslims, particularly Persians. The entire empire embraced Islam as the official state religion and the Qur'ān and the Sunnah as its guiding principles. All the authentic books of hadīth were collected and compiled during this dynasty's rule. The six compilers of hadīth lived and died during the reign of this dynasty.

Origin of the Abbasid Dynasty

The dynasty derived its name from Al-'Abbās, who was Rasūlullāh'sﷺ uncle. The descendants of Al-'Abbās claimed that they were the rightful successors of Rasūlullāhﷺ as opposed to the Umayyads, who were the descendents of Umayya, a clan separate from the Hashimite clan of Rasūlullāhﷺ.

In 750 C.E., the descendants of Al-'Abbās and other non-Umayyad Arabs mobilized forces to overthrow the Umayyad rulers. All but one of the Umayyad rulers, their families, and their supporters were killed. Then non-Umayyad Arabs formed a dynasty in the name of Al-'Abbās.

Baghdad becomes the capital

One of the first strategic moves by the first Abbasid Khalīfah was to shift the state capital from Damascus to a newly formed city called Baghdad. The second Abbasid Khalīfah, **al-Mansur**, moved the capital. This move signaled a new era under a new government. As you may remember, the Umayyad Khalīfa Mu'awiyah changed the capital when he came to power—from Madīnah to Damascus. Changing the capital to Baghdad was necessary for several reasons. First, the Abbasids needed the support of the **mawalis** (non-Arab converts to Islam). Second, most of the loyal mawalis lived in the Persian belt. Third, the Abbasids wanted to reduce Arab dominance in the empire. Baghdad had been a small village, but in 762 C.E., the Abbasids made it a prolific city and the new capital of its empire.

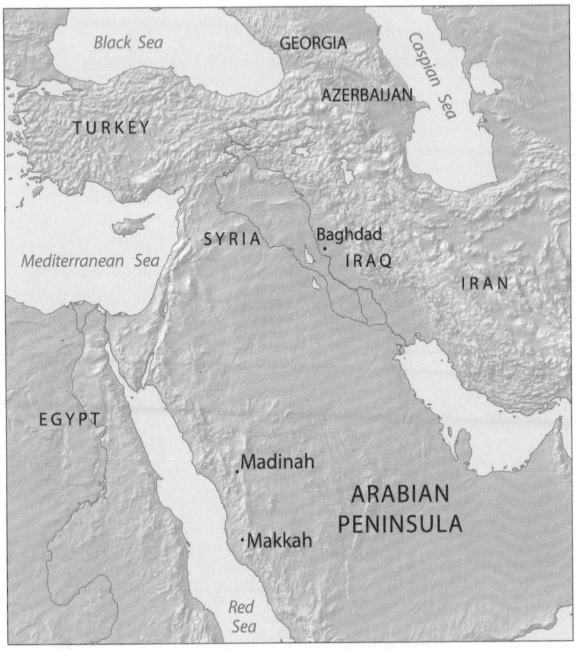

Method of administration

The method of administration in the Abbasid Empire was very different from the previous one. Unlike the Umayyad Khalīfahs, who acted like tribal leaders, and who consulted a council of tribal and military leaders, the Abbasid Khalīfas acted like absolute monarchs. They had supreme power. They also distanced themselves from the public, appearing only during ceremonial occasions. In order to carry out day-to-day operations, the Khalīfahs created two positions called **wazir** and **amir**. A wazir was the head of civilian administration. The main function of a wazir was to collect tax money and oversee the administration. During the early years of the Abbasid period, a wazir was always a non-Arab mawali. An amir was a military person.

The Abbasid army was composed of Persian and non-Arab Turkish slaves known as **mamluks**. The previous system of voluntary tribal armies was abolished and a systematic paid army was established. The postal system was improved with the introduction of a formal "pony express" using horses to carry military and official communications. The improvements to the postal system significantly enhanced the intelligence service of the empire. The Khalīfah and his wazirs were able to receive quick timely information from various provinces. The empire also introduced the use of pigeons to carry secret communications to distant places.

Advancement of learning

One of the most significant developments during the Abbasid period was the introduction of the Chinese technique of paper-making. The use of cheap, readily available paper revolutionized the field of learning. Not only the government needed enormous volumes of paper, but educated people also required volumes of paper to promote knowledge. Literacy among Muslim people increased. People began translating Greek, Latin, and old Sanskrit books into Arabic and Persian. Libraries were well-stocked with books. Many new authors appeared. Many scholars emerged and enjoyed recognition from the government and the public. During the Abbasid period, Imam Bukhārī collected his famous books of hadīth. During this collection process, Bukhārī noted large numbers of spurious hadīth were in circulation. The goal of these false hadīth was to undermine Islam.

Points to Remember

The Abbasid Dynasty is named after Rasūlullāh's ﷺ uncle, Al-'Abbās.

The dynasty shifted its focus from North Africa and the Arabian belt to Persia.

The capital of the dynasty was moved from Damascus to the new city of Baghdad.

The dynasty adopted a large amount of the Persian culture and values.

Harun al-Rashid was the most prominent Khalifah of the dynasty. During his rule, the dynasty reached its Golden Age.

The power of the dynasty began to decline during the caliphate of al-Musta'sim. The key reason for the decline was the a shift away from Islam and Islamic values.

Prosperity of Baghdad

Although Baghdad was not located near any sea port, the city prospered under the patronage of the Abbasid Khalīfas. During this period, Baghdad was one of the main centers of the global trading network, only paralleled by **Constantinople** (present-day Istanbul) in Europe and distant cities in China. The nearest sea was the Mediterranean Sea in the northwest and the Persian Gulf in the south. Both seas opened up widely traveled sea routes for merchants. They traveled by sea to India, East Africa, Sri Lanka, Indonesia, China, Spain, and the Byzantine Empire. Over several decades, trade continued to fuel the local economy, bringing prosperity to the empire.

The Caliphate reached its Golden Age during the time of **Harun al-Rashid** (786–809). New ideas and technologies transformed the caliphate. Science and literature flourished during this time. Harun and his son, **al-Ma'mun**, funded the translation of a large number of Greek texts into Arabic. The influx of Greek thought and philosophy greatly stimulated Islamic science and medicine.

Decline of the caliphate

The rise and prosperity of the caliphate also created some problems. The first sign of trouble began during the glory of the Golden Age. Decline does not happen overnight, and in the case of the Abbasids, their decline happened over time. Several factors contributed to their downfall—the main one was the gradual shift away from Islam and Islamic values. Over several years, decreasing power and glory, together with increasing revolts, precipitated its collapse.

Shī'a revolt

When the capital of the empire moved from Damascus to Baghdad, this helped to gain the confidence of non-Arab Muslim. However, it also alienated the Arabs and reduced

Arab support. Originally, Shī'ahs supported the Abbasids in toppling the Umayyad empire, but after the Abbasids established the empire, the Shī'ahs were abandoned. The Abbasids adopted the Sunni philosophy. This led to a number of revolts by the Shī'ahs in different parts of the empire at different periods.

Mamluk revolt

In the beginning, the caliphate had hired Turkish slaves as soldiers in place of Arabs in order to minimize Arab influence. These Turks, known as mamluks, became very powerful and violent. Many of them became gangsters and created widespread disturbances in Baghdad. One of the Abbasid Khalīfas, **Mu'tasim,** moved the capital from Baghdad to Samarra to avoid the gangsters. This move further weakened the caliphate and created a rift between the rulers and the people. Along with a weakening administration, the infrastructure of the caliphate began to show serious signs of decline. Irrigation and agriculture, the backbone of Abbasid affluence, began to deteriorate.

Decline in spiritual values

Along with these problems, there was also a notable decrease in the spiritual character of the caliphate. As soon as the caliphate reached the pinnacle of glory, it began to ethically and morally relax. Reflecting a principle of Allāh ﷻ, the decline of the nation began when it neglected its spiritual righteousness.

Within 150 years of gaining power, the empire began to delegate excessive powers to local amirs. Mamluks continued to become more powerful. Shortly after Harun al-Rashid's rule, many of the rulers of the autonomous provinces began to rule their territories with minimal supervision from the caliphate. Thus, the provinces became virtually independent nations. The Khalīfahs did not challenge the independent authorities. They had given these rulers too much authority well before these problems started.

Halagu Khan and the caliphate's end

A much-weakened Abbasid Dynasty continued to rule from Baghdad. In 1258 C.E., Halagu Khan attacked Baghdad. He was a Mongol king and a grandson of Genghis Khan. Halagu Khan was afraid to spill the blood of **al-Musta'sim**, the last Khalīfah of the Abbasids. He thought there would be a large-scale uprising among the Muslims if al-Musta'sim, a descendant of Rasūlullāh ﷺ, was killed. The Shī'ah Muslims convinced Halagu Khan that nothing would happen. The Shī'ahs were oppressed by the Abbasids, and they wanted to topple the caliphate. The Shī'ahs explained that there was no large-scale bloodshed when the Jews killed John the Baptist, when the Romans tried to crucify Jesus, or when Yazid killed Husayn. Finally Halagu Khan captured al-Musta'sim and brutally killed him by using horses to trample him. With the exception of a few members, his entire family was executed. The death of al-Musta'sim brought an end to the glorious caliphate.

Homework

1. All of the following choices refer to the descendants of Al-'Abbās. Which of the following choices about the Abbasid Caliphate is correct?

A. Descendants of Al-'Abbās formed the caliphate and they were the Umayyads.
B. Descendants of Al-'Abbās formed the caliphate and they were the Shī'ites.
C. Descendants of Al-'Abbās formed the caliphate and they claimed that they were the rightful successors of Rasūlullāh ﷺ.
D. Descendants of Al-'Abbās toppled Halagu Khan to occupy Baghdad.
E. Descendants of Al-'Abbās moved the capital from Baghdad to Damascus.

2. Which of the following choices about the Abbasid Caliphate is NOT correct?

A. It was a multi-ethnic Muslim empire.
B. The Shī'ahs enjoyed much recognition by the Caliphate.
C. It advanced learning at all levels.
D. Science and technology greatly advanced during the caliphate.
E. Merchants often traveled by sea routes to various countries.

3. Which Abbasid Khalīfah was largely responsible for the translation of a large number of Greek texts into Arabic?

A. Yazid.
B. Al-Ma'mun.
C. Al-'Abbās.
D. Al- Musta'sim.
E. Abdur Rahman.

4. Which of the following statements about the mamluks during the Abbasid Caliphate is correct?

A. They were the religious leaders.
B. They were the wazirs.
C. They were the Greek soldiers employed by the caliphate.
D. They were the Persian slaves.
E. They were the Turkish slaves employed by the army.

5. Which of the following statements about the postal system during the Abbasid Caliphate is correct?

A. A horse-riding mail system was introduced.
B. Pigeon mail was introduced.
C. A railway system improved mail delivery.
D. Only (a) and (b)
E. Only (b) and (c)

6. What was the main function of the wazir during the Abbasid Caliphate?

A. To collect and compile hadīth.
B. To establish schools and translate Greek literature.
C. To collect taxes and oversee administrative duties.
D. To write romantic tales of *Arabian Nights*.
E. To serve as reserve soldiers.

7. Which of the following statements is NOT a reason for the decline of the Abbasid Caliphate?

A. The Abbasids advanced learning.
B. Isolation of the Arabs and reduced Arab support.
C. The Shī'ahs were mistreated and deprived.
D. The mamluks became too powerful and began to revolt.
E. Too much power was delegated to local authorities

8. Which of the following statements about the Abbasid Khalīfah al-Musta'sim is true?

A. He moved the capital from Damascus to Baghdad.
B. He was the founder of the Abbasid Caliphate.
C. He was killed by Halagu Khan.
D. He was the architect behind the glory of the caliphate.
E. He was the son of Al-'Abbās, an uncle of Rasūlullāhﷺ.

9. Which of the following choices is NOT a reason for shifting the capital from Damascus to Baghdad?

A. Baghdad was a sea port.
B. To seek the support of the mawalis.
C. Most of the mawalis lived in Persia.
D. To reduce Arab influence.
E. None of the above.

10. Approximately how many years did the Abbasid Caliphate last?

A. 90 years.
B. 150 years.
C. 200 years.
D. 500 years.
E. 750 years.

Appendix - 1

Steps of Salāt

For the Teacher

The description provided in these pages is the commonly accepted way of performing salāt in Hanafi madhhab. There may be minor variations, which are allowed. All the variations should have supporting proof that Rasūlullāh ﷺ had occasionally practiced that variation. The teacher/parents are requested to show the ideal practice according to their madhhab. The salāt has to be made in Arabic language only.

Physical preparation for salāh:

Physical cleanliness: Before performing salāh, make sure your body is clean. You must complete *wudu*, and be in the state of *wudu*. During the salāh, do not look sideways, do not look at others, and do not talk to others. Do not make unnecessary movements. Do not scratch, yawn, laugh, or smile. If you must sneeze or cough, that is fine, but try to minimize the noise.

Clean clothes: Your clothes should be clean and should cover your body. For boys, clothes should cover the body at least from the navel to the knees. For girls, clothes should cover the body from the neck to the ankles, and to the wrists. The head should be covered, but the face can remain uncovered. Clothes should not be transparent. Avoid any clothing that has pictures of people, animals, or offensive writing.

Clean place: You should find a clean place to make your salāh. A prayer rug is not necessary. A prayer rug should always be clean, so it ensures a clean place while you are praying.

Direction to face: You should face *Qiblah*, which is the direction of the Ka'bah in Makkah.

Time: *Fard* (compulsory) prayers are performed at the proper time. It is preferable to perform the prayer as soon as the *Adhān* (call to prayer) is announced.

Mental preparation: We begin the prayer with full mental and physical attention. During salāh, we are worshipping and talking directly to Allāh, therefore, we must provide our total attention. Avoid any place or object that diverts your full attention.

What is a raka'ah? Each salāh can be divided into cycles of physical postures, or raka'at. Each raka'ah involves the positions of *qiyam* (standing), *ruku* (bowing), *sujud* (prostration), *jalsa* (sitting), another *sujud* (prostration), and associated recitations. The chart shows the specified number of raka'at for the five daily salāh. Some variation in the number of Sunnah prayers exists among the madhhab.

	Sunnah raka'at before Fard raka'at	Fard raka'at	Sunnah raka'at after Fard raka'at
Fajr	2	2	
Dhuhr	4	4	2
'Asr	4	4	
Maghrib		3	2
'Isha	4	4	2, then 3 (wajib)

Description for a salāh of two raka'at:

The following description of steps is for a salāh with two raka'at (for example, the Fard prayer of Fajr). At the end of this description, there are brief notes about how to perform three or four raka'at of salāh.

Step 1

(Figures above)

When you stand up for salāh, make an intention to perform the salāh for the sake of Allāh. Say to yourself (in any language) that you intend to offer this *Salāh* (*Fajr, Dhuhr, Asr, Maghrib,* or *Isha*), *Fard, Sunnat,* or *Witr,* and the number of raka'ahs (example—"I intend to offer two *raka'ah* of *Fard, Fajr* prayer for Allāh").

Position: *Qiyam*. Stand upright. Raise both hands up to the ears (palms and body facing the direction of the Ka'bah).

What to say: *"Allāhu Akbar."* (Allāh is the Greatest).

Step 2

(Figures on the right)

Position: Place your left hand over your belly, place your right hand on top of the left hand, and grip the wrist of the left hand.

What to say:

1. *"Subhanaka Allāhumma wa bihamdika, wa tabārakasmuka, wa ta'āla jadduka, wa lā ilāha ghairuka."* (This part is known as *thana*. It means "Glory be to you, O Allāh, and praise to You. Blessed be Your Name, exalted be Your Majesty and Glory. There is no god but You.")

2. *"A'ūdu billāhi mina ash-Shaytānir rajim."* (I seek the protection of Allāh against Shaitān, the condemned.)

3. *"Bismillāhir rahmānir rahīm."* (In the Name of Allāh, Most Gracious, Most Merciful.)

4. Now recite Sūrah Al-Fātihah. We must recite Sūrah Al-Fātihah during each raka'ah. A salāh is not valid if Sūrah Al-Fātihah is not recited.

"Al humdu li-llahi rabbi-l 'alamīn. Ar-rahmāni-r rahīm. Māliki yawmi-d dīn. Iyyāka na'budu wa iyyāka Nāsta'īn. Ihdina-s sirāta-l mustaqīm. Sirātal ladhīna an'amta 'alaihim, ghairil maghdūbi 'alaihim, wa la-d dāllīn. (Āmīn.)"

(The Praise belongs to Allāh, The Rabb of all the worlds; the Rahman; the Rahim. Malik of the Day of Judgment. You alone do we serve, and to You alone we seek help. Guide us on the Right Path—the path of those upon whom You have bestowed favors; not of those upon whom wrath is brought down, nor those gone astray.)

5. After reciting sūrah Fātihah, we now recite any short sūrah or a few verses from the Qur'ān. This additional recitation of part of the Qur'ān is done during the first two raka'ah only. It is always good to memorize as many sūrah as you can, so you can recite them during your salāh.

Step 3

(Figures above)

What to say: *"Allāhu Akbar."*

Position: This position is called *ruku*. Bow with your back perpendicular to your legs. Place your hands on your knees. Do not bend the knees.

What to say: *"Subhana rabbiyal 'Adhīm."* Say this three times. (Glorified is my Rabb, the Great.)

Step 4

(Figures below)

While going back to the *qiyam* (upright) position,

What to say: *"Samia Allāhu liman hamidah."* (Allāh listens to him who praises Him.)

Position: In *qiyam* position.

What to say: *"Rabbanā wa laka al hamd."* (Our Rabb, praise be for You only.)

Step 5

(Figure above)

What to say: While moving to the next position of *sujud*, say *"Allāhu Akbar."*

Position: This position is *sujud*. Place both of your knees on the floor. Try not to move the position of your feet, that is, do not move your feet away from the *qiyam* position. After placing the knees, place your two hands on the floor with palms touching the floor. Do not glide your hands on the floor. Your elbow is not on the floor. Your hands should be sufficiently apart to leave room for your head. Now place your forehead on the floor. Both your nose and forehead should touch the floor. Your hands are on the side of your head. Your stomach will not touch the floor. You should be the most humble in this position.

The most powerful part of our body is our brain, the site of our intelligence. We submit our full selves, with full understanding, to Almighty Allāh. We realize that our strength, power, wealth, and everything that we have is from Allāh. To emphasize this physical and spiritual humility, we will repeat the *sujud* position again in Step 7.

What to say: *"Subhana rabbiyal A'ala."* (Say this three times. Glory be to Allāh, the Exalted.)

Step 6

(Figures above)

The next position is *jalsa.*

What to say: While moving to the *jalsa* position, say *"Allāhu Akbar."*

Position: To move to *jalsa* position, rise from *sujud.* First you will raise your head off the floor, then you will raise your hands. Now you are sitting on the floor— this posture is called *jalsa.*

What to say: *"Rabbi-ghfir lī wa rhamnī."* (O my Rabb, forgive me and have mercy on me.)

Step 7

(Figure above)

We will repeat *sujud* again. Every *raka'ah* has two *sujud.*

What to say: While moving to the sujud position, say *"Allāhu Akbar."*

Position: *Sujud.* Place your palms on the floor and then your forehead. Both the nose and the forehead should be touching the floor.

What to say: *"Subhāna rabbiyal A'ala."* Say this three times. (Glory to Allāh, the Exalted.)

This completes one raka'ah.

Beginning of second raka'ah

Step 8

(Figures above)

Rise to the *qiyam* (standing) position. The movement should be in a systematic, graceful manner. First you will raise your forehead from the floor, next you will raise your hands and then you will raise your knees. Try not to move your feet—that is, the position of your feet should be the same as it was during the first raka'ah.

What to say: While moving to the qiyam position, say *"Allāhu Akbar."*

Position: Stand upright. Hold the left hand with the right hand on top.

What to say: Sūrah Al-Fātihah, then any short sūrah or a few verses from the Qur'ān.

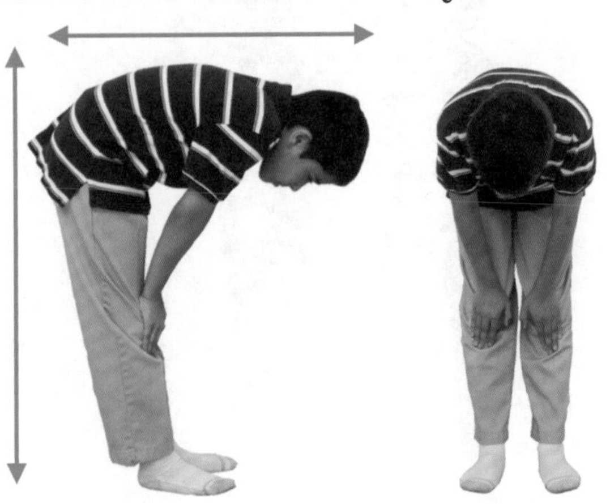

Step 9

(Figures on the previous page)

What to say: *"Allāhu Akbar."*

Position: *Ruku.* Bow with your back perpendicular to your legs. Place your hands on your knees.

What to say: *"Subhāna rabbiyal 'Adhīm."* Say this three times.

Step 10

(Figures above)

Position: While moving back to the *qiyam* (standing) position,

What to say: *"Sami'a Allāhu liman hamidah."*

Position: In *qiyam* position. You are upright.

What to say: "Rabbanā wa lakal hamd."

Step 11

(Figure below)

What to say: While moving to the sujud position, say *"Allāhu Akbar."*

Position: *Sujud.* Follow the same sequence as in Step 5.

What to say: *"Subhāna Rabbiyal A'ala."* Say this three times.

Step 12

(Figures above)

What to say: While moving to the jalsa position, say *"Allāhu Akbar."*

Position: Rise from the *sujud* position. Now you are sitting in the *jalsa* position.

What to say: *"Rabbi-ghfir lī wa rhamnī"* (O my Rabb, forgive me and have Mercy on me.)

Step 13

(Figure above)

What to say: While moving to the sujud position, say *"Allāhu Akbar."*

Position: *Sujud.* First place your hands and then your forehead on the floor.

What to say: *"Subhāna Rabbiyal A'ala."* Say this three times.

Step 14

(Figures in the next page)

What to say: While going to the jalsa position, say *"Allāhu Akbar."*

Position: Rise from the *sujud* position. Now you are sitting in the *jalsa* position.

What to say: Say *Tashahud, Durūd,* and a short prayer as follows:

"At-tahiyātu lillahi was-salawātu wattaiyibātu. Assalāmu 'alayka ayyuhan-nabiyu wa rahmat-ullāhi wa barakātuhu. Assalāmu 'alainā wa 'ala 'ibadi-llāhis-sālihīn. Ashhadu an lā ilāha illallāhu wa ashhadu anna Muhammadan 'abduhu wa rasūluhu."

(All these salutations, prayers, and nice comments are for Allāh. Peace be on you, O Prophet, and the blessings of Allāh, and His grace. Peace on us and on all the righteous servants of Allāh. I bear witness that none but Allāh is worthy of worship, and I bear witness that Muhammad is the servant and messenger of Allāh.) This is known as *Tashahud.*

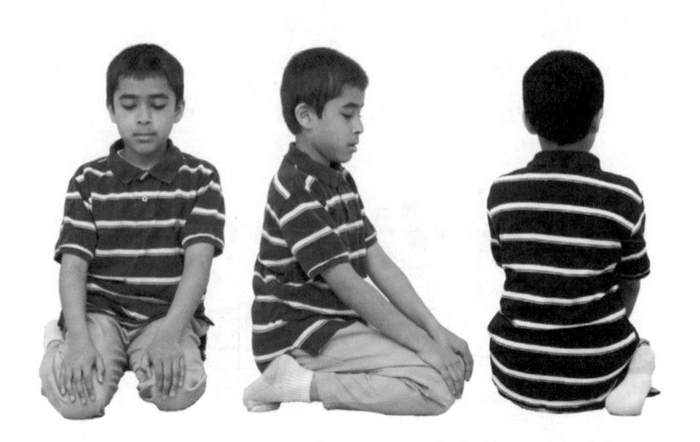

Position: Raise your right index finger, so it is pointing upward, while reciting the last part of this prayer.

Next you will recite the *Durūd.*

"Allāhumma salli 'ala Muhammadin wa 'ala āli Muhummadin, kamā sallayta 'ala Ibrāhima, wa ala āli Ibrāhima, innaka hamidun majid. Allāhumma barik 'ala Muhammadin wa 'ala āli Muhummadin, kama barakta ala Ibrāhima, wa 'ala āli Ibrahīm, innaka hamīdun majīd."

(O Allāh, send your Mercy on Muhammad and his posterity as you sent Your mercy on Ibrāhīm and his posterity. You are the Most Praised, The Most Glorious. O Allāh, send your Blessings on Muhammad and his posterity as you have blessed Ibrāhīm and his posterity. You are the Most praised, The Most Glorious.)

Now you may add a short prayer, such as:

"Rabbanā ātinā fi-d dunyā hasanatan wa fi-l ākhirati hasanatan, wa qinā 'adhāban nār."

(Our Rabb, give us the good of this world, and good in the Hereafter, and save us from the chastisement of Fire.)

Step 15

(Figure above left)

Position: Slowly turn your head and face right. This is called *salam.*

What to say: *"As-salāmu 'alaikum wa rahma-tullāh."* (Peace and mercy of Allāh be on you.)

Step 16

(Figure above right)

Position: Slowly turn your head and face left. This is called *salam.*

What to say: *"As-salāmu 'alaikum wa rahma-tullāh."*

This completes the two raka'at of salāh.

How to pray three raka'at (Maghrib)

In order to perform a three-raka'at salāh, use all the postures and prayers up to step 13.

In step 14, recite up to *"At-tahiyātu lillahi was-salawātu wattaiyibātu. Assalāmu 'alayka ayyuhan-nabiyu wa rahmatullāhi wa barakātuhu. Assalāmu 'alainā wa 'ala 'ibadi-llāhis-sālihīn. Ashhadu an lā ilāha illallāhu wa ashhadu anna Muhammadan 'abduhu wa rasūluhu."* This is known as *Tashahud.*

After saying *"Allāhu akbar,"* return to the *qiyam* position, step 8. This time recite only *Al-Fātihah* (in step 8), but do not recite any sūrah or part of the Qur'ān. All prayers and postures are the same as shown in steps 9–16.

How to pray four raka'at (Dhuhr, 'Asr, and 'Isha)

In order to perform a four-raka'at salāh, use all the postures and prayers up to step 13.

In Step 14, only the *Tashahud* prayer will be recited, and the *qiyam* position, in step 8, will be resumed.

In step 8, only *Al-Fātihah* will be recited without adding any sūrah. Steps 8–13 complete the third raka'ah. The *qiyam* position in step 8 will be resumed.

In step 8, only *Al-Fātihah* will be recited without adding any sūrah. Steps 8–16, complete the fourth raka'ah.

From the Qur'an

...keep up the salāt, as salāt controls indecent and unacceptable behaviors... *(Sūrah Al-'Ankabūt, 29:45)*

Take care to do your salāt, praying in the best way, and stand before Allāh with full devotion. *(Sūrah Al-Baqarah, 2:238)*

Outline of Curriculum – Levels 1, 2 and 3

Each year the curriculum begins with a few topics on Allāhﷻ, the Qur'ān, the Nabiﷺ, the Hadīth, or Sunnah. In the early years, emphasis is placed on the five-pillars, and each year, this emphasis increases. Every year, a history of some of the messengers is introduced in an age-appropriate manner. Several lessons are devoted to Islamic manners, values, and morals so that children grow up with a good understanding of Islamic culture. Each lesson includes a short homework assignment.

Level 1
Unit 1: Aqaid: Our Belief
Allahﷻ: Our Creator
Islam
Our Faith
Nabi Muhammadﷺ
The Qur'an
Unit 2: Knowing Allahﷻ
Allahﷻ Loves Us
Remembering Allahﷻ
Allahﷻ Rewards Us
Unit 3: Our Ibadat
Five Pillars of Islam
Shahadah: The First Pillar
Salah: The Second Pillar
Zakat: The Third Pillar
Fasting: The Fourth Pillar
Hajj: The Fifth Pillar
Unit 4: Messengers of Allah
Adam (A): The First Nabi
Nuh (A): Saved From Flood
Ibrahim (A): Never Listen to Shaitan
Musa (A): Challenging A Bad Ruler
Isa (A): A Great Nabi of Allahﷻ
Unit 5: Other Basics of Islam
Angels: They Always Work for Allahﷻ
Shaitan: Our Enemy
Makkah and Madinah
Eid: Two Festivals
Unit 6: Akhlaq and Adab in Islam
Good Manners
Kindness and Sharing
Respect
Forgiveness
Thanking Allahﷻ

Level 2
Unit 1: The Creator–His Message
Allāhﷻ: Our Creator
How Does Allāhﷻ Create?
Allāhﷻ: What Does He Do?
What Does Allāhﷻ Not Do
The Qur'ān
Hadīth and Sunnah
Unit 2: Our Ibadat
Shahadah: The First Pillar
Salāt: The Second Pillar
Zakāt: The Third Pillar
Sawm: The Fourth Pillar
Hajj: The Fifth Pillar
Wudū: Keeping Our Bodies Clean
Unit 3: Messengers of Allah
Ibrāhīm (A): A Friend of Allah
Ya'qūb (A) and Yūsuf (A)
Mūsā (A) and Hārūn (A)
Yūnus (A)
Muhammadﷺ: Rasūlullāh
Unit 4: Learning About Islam
Obey Allāhﷻ, Obey Rasūlﷺ
Day of Judgment and the Hereafter
Our Masjid
Common Islamic Phrases
Food that We May Eat
Unit 5: Akhlaq and Adab in Islam
Truthfulness
Kindness
Respect
Responsibility
Obedience
Cleanliness
Honesty

Level 3
Unit 1: Knowing About Allah
Who is Allāhﷻ?
What Allāhﷻ Is and Is Not
Allāhﷻ: The Most-Merciful
Allāhﷻ: The Best Judge
What Does Allāhﷻ Want Us to Do?
Unit 2: Teachings of Islam
We Are Muslims: We Have 'Imān
Belief in the Qur'ān
Belief in the Messengers
Hadīth and Sunnah
Jinn
Muslims in North America
The Straight Path: The Right Path
Unit 3: Life of Nabi Muhammadﷺ
Kindness of Rasūlullāhhﷺ
How Rasūlullāhﷺ Treated Others
Our Relationship with Rasūlullāhﷺ
Unit 4: Messengers of Allah
Ismā'īl (A) and Ishāq (A)
Shua'ib (A): A Nabi of Allāhﷻ
Dāwūd (A): A Nabi of Allāhﷻ
'Isā (A): A Nabi of Allāh ﷻ
Unit 5: Learning About Islam
Ka'bah
Masjid Nabawi
Bilāl ibn Rabāh
Zaid ibh Harithah
Unit 6: Akhlaq and Adab in Islam
Ways To Be a Good Person
Kindness: A Virtue of the Believers
Forgiveness: A Good Quality
Good Deeds: A Duty of the Believers
Perseverance: Never Give Up
Punctuality: Doing Things on Time

Outline of Curriculum – Levels 4, 5 and 6

By Level 5, students have learned the biography of the Nabi Muhammadﷺ, including a summary of the events that shaped his life and early Islam. By Level 6, students will have read the biographies of most of the prominent messengers. At this stage, students will have learned all the fundamental principles and key concepts of Islam. Even if students do not attend weekend schools after Level 6, they have already gained significant knowledge about Islam.

Level 4
Unit 1: Knowing the Creator
Rewards of Allāhﷻ: Everybody Receives Them
Discipline of Allāhﷻ
Names of Allāhﷻ
Books of Allāhﷻ
Unit 2: How Islam Changed Arabia
Pre-Islamic Arabia
The Year of the Elephant
Early Life of Muhammadﷺ
Life Before Becoming a Nabi
First Revelation
Makkah Period
Hijrat to Madīnah
Madīnah Period
Unit 3: The Rightly Guided Khalīfah
Abū Bakr: The First Khalifah
'Umar ibn al-Khattāb
'Uthmān ibn 'Affān
'Ali ibn Abū Tālib
Unit 4: The Messengers of Allāh
Hūd (A): Struggle to Guide People
Sālih (A): To Guide the Misguided
Mūsā (A): His Life and Actions
Sulaimān (A): A Humble King
Unit 5: Fiqh of Salāt
Preparation for Salāt
Requirements of Salāt
Mubtilāt us-Salāt
How to Pray Behind an Imām
Unit 6: General Islamic Topics
Compilers of Hadīth
Shaitān's Mode of Operation
Day of Judgment
Eid: Its Significance
Truthfulness: A Quality of Muslim
Perseverance: Keep on Trying

Level 5
Unit 1: The Creator, His Message
Tawhīd, Kāfir, Kufr, Shirk, Nifāq
Why Should We Worship Allāhﷻ?
Revelation of the Qur'ān
Characteristics of the Messengers
Unit 2: The Battles, Developments
Pledges of 'Aqabah
The Battle of Badr
The Battle of Uhud
The Battle of the Trench
The Treaty of Hudaibiyah
Liberation of Makkah
Unit 3: The Messengers of Allāh
Adam (A): The Creation of Mankind
Ibrāhīm (A) Debate with Polytheists
Ibrāhīm (A): Plan Against Idols
Luqmān (A): A Wise Man's Lifelong Teachings
Yūsuf (A): His Childhood
Yūsuf (A): His Righteousness
Yūsuf (A): Dream Comes True
Ayyūb (A): Patience, Perseverance
Zakariyyāh (A), Yahyā (A)
Unit 4: Islam in the World
Major Masājid in the World
Unit 5: Islamic Values, Teachings
Upholding Truth: A Duty for All Believers
Responsibility and Punctuality
My Mind My Body
Kindness and Forgiveness
The Middle Path: Ways to Avoid Two Extremes
Salāt: Its Significance
Sawm: Its Significance
Zakāt and Sadaqah: Similarities and Differences

Level 6
Unit 1: The Creator
Attributes of Allāhﷻ
The Promise of Allāhﷻ
Unit 2: The Qur'ān and Hadith
Objectives of the Qur'ān?
Compilation of the Qur'ān
Previous Scriptures and the Qur'ān
Compilation of Hadīth
Unit 3: Fundamentals in Deen
Importance of Shahādah
Khushū in Salāt
Taqwā
Unit 4: Messengers of Allāh
Nūh (A)
Tālūt, Jālūt, and Dāwūd (A)
Dāwūd (A) and Sulaimān (A)
Mūsā (A) and Fir'awn
Mūsā (A) and Khidir
'Isā (A) and Maryam (ra)
Unit 5: Some Prominent Muslimahs
Khadījah (ra)
'A'ishah (ra)
Fātimah (ra)
Some Prominent Muslimahs
Unit 6: Knowledge Enrichment
Al-Qiyamah
Rūh and Nafs
The Angels and Jinn
Shaitān: The Invisible Enemy
Unit 7: Current Societies
My Friend Is Muslim Now
Friendship: How to Choose?
Muslims Around the World
People of Other Faiths
Unit 8: Islamic Values
Greed and Dishonesty
Avoiding Extravagance

Outline of Curriculum – Levels 7, 8 and 9

In these levels, the application of knowledge is increasingly emphasized by offering carefully selected topics. Specific details about some of the messengers are introduced to highlight the abiding morals in their lives. In Level 8, early Muslim struggles are discussed in detail. Increased depth and informaiton in the lessons require focused attention from students. Age-appropriate moral lessons are also covered including gossip, friendship, peer pressure, dating, indecency, encouraging good and forbidding evil.

Level 7
Unit 1: The Creator
Why Islam? what is Islam?
Belief in Allāhﷻ
The Qur'ān: Its Qualitative Names
Istighfar: Seeking Forgiveness of Allāhﷻ
Allāhﷻ: Angry or Kind
Unit 2: Stories of the Messengers
Ādam (A): Trial of the Messenger
Life of Ibrāhīm (A)
Sacrifice of Ibrāhīm (A)
Lūt (A): Message for Modern Societies
Yūsuf (A)—The Will to Overcome Temptation
Unit 3: Stories from the Qur'ān
Companions of the Cave
Dhul Qurnain: Journey of a King
Effective Debate and Negotiation Styles in the Qur'ān
Unit 4: Two Companions
Abū Sufyān
Khālid Ibn Walīd (R)
Unit 5: Knowledge Enrichment
The Character of the Messengers
Rasūlullāh's ﷺ Marriages
Lailatul Qadr
Fasting During Ramadan
My Family is Muslim Now
Science in the Qur'ān
Lessons from Past Civilizations
Unit 6: Teachings of the Qur'ān
Amr Bil Ma'rūf
Guard Your Tongue
Islamic Greetings
How to Achieve Success
Permitted and Prohibited
Types of Behavior Allāhﷻ Loves

Level 8
Unit 1: Knowing the Creator
Divine Names
Sunan of Allāhﷻ
Objectives of the Qur'ān
Sūrah Hujurāt: Its Teachings
True Piety: Analysis of Ayāh 2:177
Ayātul Qudsi
Unit 2: The Messenger of Allāh
The Person Muhammadﷺ
Farewell Pilgrimage
Finality of Prophethood
Hadīth: Collection, Classification
Unit 3: Challenges in Madīnah
Hypocrites
Banu Qaynuka
Banu Nadir
Banu Qurayzah
Mission to Tabūk
Unit 4: Islamic Ethical Framework
Friends and Friendship
Friendship With Non-Muslims
Dating in Islam
Hold Firmly The Rope of Allāhﷻ
Elements of a Bad Life
Unit 5: Islamic Values, Teachings
Duties Toward Parents
Hope, Hopefulness, Hopelessness
Trials in Life
Permitted and Prohibited Food
Performance of Hajj
Parables in the Qur'ān
Unit 6: Islam After the Rasūlﷺ
Origin and History of Shī'ah
Ummayad Dynasty
Abbasid Dynasty

Level 9
Unit 1: A Reflection on the Divine
Signs of Allāhﷻ in nature
Pondering the Qur'ān
Preservation and Compilation of the Qur'ān
Ibadat—Easy Ways to Do It
Unit 2: An Islamic Perspective
Why Human Beings Are Superior
Is Islam a Violent Religion?
Shariah
Justice in Islam
Unit 3: Ethical Standard in Islam
Peer Pressure
Choices We Make
Islamic Perspective on Dating
Indecency
Alcohol and Gambling
Permitted and Prohibited Food
Food of the People of the Book
Family Values
Unit 4: Essays on Rasulullahﷺ
Khadījah (ra)
Rasūlullāh'sﷺ Multiple Marriages
Marriage to Zainab (ra)
The Prophet: A Great Army General
Prophecy of Muhammadﷺ in the Bible
Allegations Against Rasūlullāhﷺ
Unit 5: A Reflection on Islam
God's Chosen People
Mūsā's Personality
Essentials of Salah
Life Cycle of Truth
How Ramadan Makes Us Better
Muslims in North America

Outline of Curriculum – Levels 10, 11–12

In Level 10 and 11–12, Islamic topics increasingly prepare youths to fine-tune their spiritual and social lives. Significant issues that have real-life implications are introduced. The application of knowledge continues to be emphasized. The lessons in the Level 11–12 book strongly promote the application of Islamic knowledge. This is achieved through carefully selected topics. All lessons teach core Islamic beliefs and understandings based on the Qur'ān and authentic Hadith.

Level 10
Unit 1: Knowing the Creator
Understanding the Word "Allāh"
Al-Fātihah: An Analysis of its Message
Al-Fātihah vs The Lord's Prayer
Muhkam and Mutashābihat Āyāt
Al-'Asr: The Formula of Success
Qur'ānic Calligraphy
Unit 2: Interfaith Studies
The Bible and the Qur'ān
The Ten Commandments and Islam
Our Faiths: Key Differences
Unit 3: Marriage and Family in Islam
The Status of Women in Islam
Marriage to Non-Muslims
Marrying Four Women
Difficult Questions on Marriage
A Muslim Family
Unit 4: General Islamic Topics
Who are the Khalīfah on Earth?
False Piety
Superstition
Do Not Transgress Limits
Secular and Religious Duties
Islamic Views on Racism
Unit 5: Principles of Finance in Islam
Public Finance in Early Islam
Wealth in The Qur'an
Islamic Investment
Language of Investment
Faith-Based Wealth Building
Managing Earning and spending
Leading an Interest Free Life
Unit 6: Islam and the World
Islamic Architecture
Islam in Spain and Portugal

Level 11–12
Unit 1: Understanding Our Belief
Islam
Muslim
Shahādah
Belief in Allāh
Belief in the Angels
Belief in the Revealed Books
Belief in the Messengers
Belief in the Hereafter
Unit 2: The "Driver" Within Us
Life's Ultimate Purpose
Wealth Is The "Driver"
The "Driver" Within Us
Unit 3: A Heart for Allāh ﷻ
When Allāh ﷻ Seems Distant
Tawakkul: Trust in Allāh ﷻ
Du'ā: How Does Allāh ﷻ Respond?
A Heart for Allāh ﷻ
Unit 4: Controlling Our Thoughts
Controlling Your Thoughts
Maintaining a Relationship
The Power of Forgiveness
Reading the Qur'ān
Afraid to Think, Forbidden to Ask
Unit 5: A Review of Key Concepts
Lower Your Gaze
'Ā'ishah (ra): The Child Bride
"Strike" in Sūrah An-Nisā'
The Myth About the Satanic Verse
How Jesus Became Christ
Rūh and Nafs
Unit 6: Faith-Based Wealth Building
Taking financial control early
Fundamental of Finance
Islamic Investment

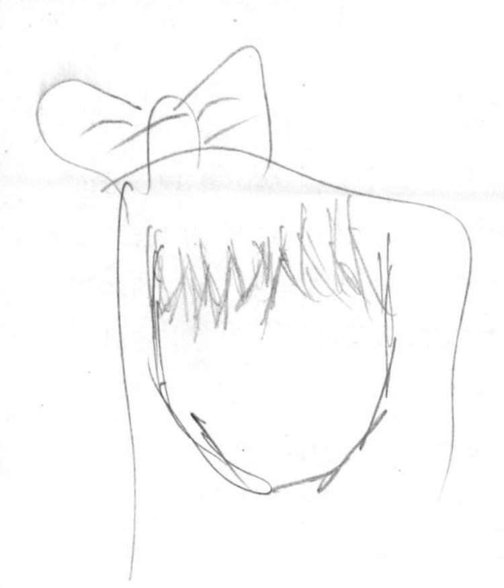

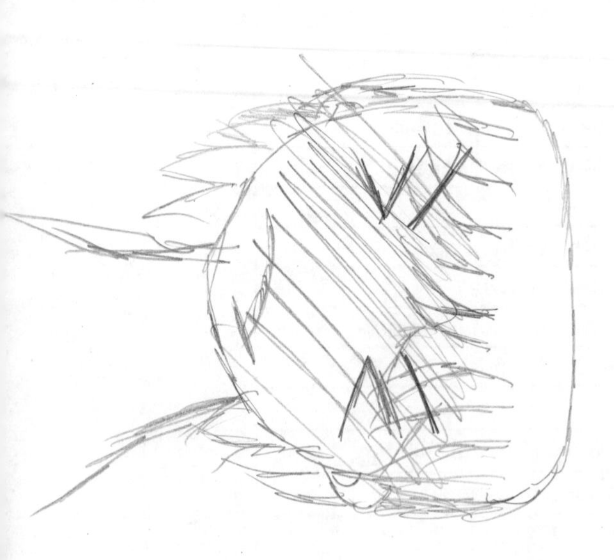